Metadata
in Practice

Diane I. Hillmann **Elaine L. Westbrooks**

American Library Association **Chicago 2004**

Composition and design by ALA Editions in Sabon and Optima, using QuarkXPress 5.0 on a PC platform

Printed on 50-pound white offset, a pH-neutral stock, and bound in 10-point coated cover stock by Data Reproductions

The paper used in this publication meets the minimum requirements of American National Standard for Information Sciences—Permanence of Paper for Printed Library Materials, ANSI Z39.48-1992.∞

Library of Congress Cataloging-in-Publication Data

Metadata in practice / Diane I. Hillmann, editor, Elaine L. Westbrooks, editor.
    p. cm.
  Includes bibliographical references and index.
  ISBN 0-8389-0882-9
  1. Information organization. 2. Metadata. 3. Database management. I. Hillmann, Diane I. (Diane Ileana), 1948- II. Westbrooks, Elaine L. III. American Library Association.
Z666.5.M48 2004
025.3—dc22   2004003428

Printed in the United States of America

08 07 06 05 04   5 4 3 2 1

During the production of this book, the coeditors lost a valued colleague. Tom Turner, metadata librarian at the Mann Library from 1997 to 2003, died in March 2003. He is much missed by friends and colleagues, particularly the coeditors, for whom he is, in a sense, the "missing link." It is to him that this book is dedicated.

CONTENTS

v

Part II   The Future of Metadata Development and Practice

FIGURES

TABLES

ACKNOWLEDGMENTS

THIS BOOK HAS been a group effort from the beginning, with much support offered to the coeditors every step of the way. Diane would like to thank in particular her colleagues at Cornell Information Science, whose assistance when she broke her arm in February 2003 was above and beyond the call of duty. Even when Diane was again possessed of two working arms, her colleagues' support for this project was generous and unconditional. Elaine would like to express her gratitude to her colleagues at Cornell University's Albert R. Mann Library, particularly Janet McCue and William Kara. A special thanks should be extended to Brian Lowe for his editing and formatting contributions.

INTRODUCTION

IT IS BOTH an exciting and frustrating time to be working in the world of metadata. Exciting because so many new communities are discovering the usefulness of metadata at the same time as librarians seriously consider the limitations of our traditional notions of the functions of libraries. New metadata formats seem to erupt like dandelions on a spring lawn, each seeking to bring together new communities with genuine needs to organize their important information.

For librarians or project managers who attempt to understand this world enough to plan a project implementation with a metadata component, the frustrations are also considerable. Although a library or cataloging background can be an asset when approaching metadata issues, to a traditional librarian the current metadata environment seems like the Wild West as seen from the point of view of a Boston Brahmin—very messy, and with armed cowboys behind every rock.

In such environments, prudent librarians review the literature. Unfortunately, information on the metadata context of relevant projects is sometimes difficult to find; and when relevant information is found, it rarely contains the detail that a planner desires. In addition, most of the research literature about digital libraries is not published in journals familiar to librarians; rather, it is scattered in digital library and computer science conference proceedings or journals. Consequently, taking advantage of the experience of others can be daunting. Those planners looking for the latest ideas in important areas of implementation have an even more difficult time. Developments are constantly in flux, and without active participation, it is a challenge to discover what is still relevant among the existing documentation.

Planning for metadata implementation is even more confusing, of course, for those without the benefit of a traditional cataloging background.

Determining what the options are for a new project, how to ensure the "interoperability" everyone seems to desire, and attempting to choose options with some promise of stability seem impossible. None of the emerging standards seems quite stable enough, there is little documentation that seems trustworthy, and each expert has a different opinion.

Even those metadata standards with the most promise have been slow to provide guidance directly to implementers. Element names, labels, and definitions may well be available, but what is often lacking is an experienced body of implementers to provide the documentation on what belongs inside the elements. Even creating simple metadata can be more difficult than new implementers might imagine, and richer metadata brings even more complications with its promise of improved discovery.

This situation is made even more difficult by the increasing requirements for metadata sharing, particularly since the emergence of the Open Archives Initiative Protocol for Metadata Harvesting (OAI-PMH). Although OAI implementation is touted as simple, requiring very little technical background, the technical skills necessary are beyond those of any but the most technically adept librarian. Since funding agencies in particular are determined to ensure that investments in data creation and maintenance will survive beyond the next grant, the project planner is on the horns of a dilemma. What's a conscientious planner to do to ensure that their project plan includes provisions for adequate technical support over time, in the face of such information gaps?

Over the past eight years, we have spent a great deal of time working in this new world of emerging metadata standards. Diane Hillmann's work with the National Science Digital Library, and as editor of the Using Dublin Core guidelines and administrator of the new AskDCMI service, has brought many questions from implementers her way. Many who ask for help are close to panic. "Where do I start?" is a common beginning. Others have made it through some initial research and decision-making but have gone aground on the details. Sometimes it is a question of determining where to find out what other, similar projects have done, perhaps regretted, and most likely redone. Perhaps the problem is determining what the current, standard manner of doing things is, when none of the documentation available uses the same terminology. Unlike the traditional library world, where there are well-trodden paths toward acknowledged competence, this new world has few maps. Many implementers find themselves working in isolation, feeling ill-prepared for the task they have taken on. This book was conceived to assist these wanderers in the wilderness, to provide both background and signposts for the journey ahead. This book is not a guide to the options available to implementers; it does not provide definitions or advise on choices of metadata format, and not every metadata standard in use today is covered. For such a survey, Priscilla Caplan's *Metadata Fundamentals for All Librarians* is surely the best source.

Metadata in Practice is divided into two parts. Part 1, "Project-Based Implementations," brings together the work of a number of significant projects. Because so much of the interesting work being done in metadata implementations is focused in specialized communities, we have attempted to cover a broad range of communities and metadata formats in this book. But aside from orienting our contributors to their target audience, perhaps the most important question we have asked them is: "What would you have done differently, knowing what you know now?" Their answers provide much food for thought.

Two early projects begin part 1. Stuart Sutton describes the work of Gateway to Educational Materials, one of the first and still one of the most influential projects gathering educational materials for teachers. Another early project, Heritage Colorado, described by Liz Bishoff and Elizabeth Meagher, is particularly significant for its statewide collaboration between libraries and museums. Museums and archives have been major players in the metadata movement, with many issues quite distinct from libraries. Angela Spinazzè describes some of these issues and the efforts of the museum community.

Three projects centered on gathering materials together on specific campuses follow. First, Robin Wendler describes Harvard University's campuswide image database and the issues inherent in bringing together image descriptions from many sources. Moving westward to the University of Minnesota, Charles Thomas discusses a project with a similar campus focus dealing with more heterogeneous data. Karen Coyle, a recent retiree from the California Digital Library, describes a project to bring vendor-supplied journal article information into the University of California's library catalog.

Clearly, metadata is an international issue, involving researchers and practitioners from many countries. Norm Friesen's chapter on CanCore, a Canadian educational project using the IEEE Learning Object Metadata, highlights the importance of integrating project implementation with standards efforts. Continuing with our survey of specialized communities and metadata formats, we examine two very different projects focused on geographic data: the Alexandria Digital Library (ADL) at the University of California-Santa Barbara and the Cornell University Geospatial Information Repository (CUGIR). Linda Hill and Greg Janée describe the groundbreaking work of the ADL, in particular their efforts to make georeferenced data more generally available in general digital library applications. The CUGIR project, presented by coeditor Elaine Westbrooks, focuses on distributing specialized geographic data through preexisting general channels in an automated fashion.

Part 1 ends with two chapters on the special problems of aggregation and sharing in the new world of metadata. The team of Rachael Bower, David Sleasman, and Edward Almasy, all of the well-respected Internet Scout Project, talk about the development of Scout as both an aggregator and disseminator of information on Internet resources. Their work has led to the creation of tools to assist others: the Scout Portal Toolkit and the Collection Workflow Information System. Last in this section is an excellent summation of the problems inherent in metadata aggregation by Timothy Cole and Sarah Shreeves, who discuss the Illinois Open Archives Initiative Metadata Harvesting Project.

A few lessons have emerged consistently from these metadata projects. They can perhaps be grouped into three major themes. The first is the most important: change happens, and it happens constantly. Get used to it, accept it, and plan for it. Waiting for emerging standards to settle down is a futile exercise; it will probably not happen in our lifetimes.

A second theme is more concrete: stick to standards as much as possible, but if and when you diverge, document what has been done and why it was done. Someone will be managing your project or using your data after your tenure, and will need to understand the context of your decisions. A third theme arises from the second: try to anticipate future uses of your data. This is, of course, why we have standards in the first place, but it cannot be too strongly emphasized.

Part 2 of this book, "The Future of Metadata Development and Practice," moves beyond the lessons learned from the recent past and looks to the future of metadata. Clearly, if change is to be a constant in our lives, we must cultivate the ability to anticipate the trends that will soon wash over us. We begin with two chapters describing how two communities are organizing the development and maintenance of metadata standards. Harriette Hemmasi describes the work being done to define the needs and options open to the music community as it attempts to come to consensus on community-specific rules, logic, labels, and vocabularies. Steven Bird and Gary Simons describe the Open Language Archives Community and the model that group has developed to manage metadata standards and aggregation, as well as the creation of tools to support reuse.

Caroline and William Arms collaborate to convey their knowledge and experience regarding searching functionality and the relation of metadata to the provision of search and browse services, particularly in large, heterogeneous projects. As metadata is shared, questions of quality and reusability become more pressing. Thomas Bruce and Diane Hillmann begin to take the quality discussion beyond the traditional boundaries defined in library experience toward one more useful in a world of harvesting, reuse, and repurposing. Rachel Heery extends the discussion to the Semantic Web and the issues of identification that underlie the promise of future interoperable metadata. Understanding these issues at the planning stages will make the future much less messy than the present.

The contributions of knowledge and experience from these pioneers in the metadata Wild West will go a long way toward disarming the cowboys behind the rocks. Project managers and planners will find much to learn from their successes, failures, and restarts, and will gain their own experience and knowledge. We ask these new pioneers to follow the lead of the contributors to this book, consider those coming behind them, and pass on their knowledge freely, for the betterment of us all.

1

Building an Education Digital Library: GEM and Early Metadata Standards Adoption

Stuart A. Sutton

BEGINNING IN 1996, the U.S. Department of Education's Gateway to Educational Materials (GEM) project framed its commitment to build a metadata repository of distributed resources on the World Wide Web around the adoption of emerging metadata standards. At that time, Dublin Core (DC), both as an initiative and as a metadata standard, was in its infancy, and many of the principles that would shape it as a metadata framework for cross-domain discovery and retrieval were yet to be articulated. Standards efforts such as the IMS Global Learning Consortium that would coalesce into the Institute of Electrical and Electronics Engineers (IEEE) Learning Technology Standards Committee's Learning Object Metadata (LOM) were in their formative stages.[1] This chapter will chronicle the issues of early standards adoption in production environments, including the creation and evolution of metadata generation tools (and the resulting instance metadata), harvesting mechanisms, and the discovery and retrieval applications needed to support a specific digital library of distributed educational resources—GEM. Some emphasis will be placed on the consequences of decisions made when metadata frameworks and their accompanying principles were unclear and evolving. This chapter will also examine how the contemporary principles of metadata extensibility, modularity, and refinement have been accomplished in an environment intent on serving the global digital resource needs of teachers

1

and learners. Forays into discussions of tools and system architectures are unavoidable.

While it is tempting to protect our egos by painting a portrait of a metadata initiative free of imperfections, we will avoid doing so in this chapter. As in many other real-world projects on the crest of the wave of evolving technologies, some mistakes were made. These mistakes are informative, so we will expose our flawed assumptions and imperfect attempts to predict where technologies and the open environment of the Web were taking us. We will also show how we tried to correct our course when we were able to admit that we had gone astray.

FIRST-GENERATION GEM

Enhanced access to educational materials on the Internet for the nation's teachers and students was one of President Bill Clinton's second-term goals. To help reach that goal, the National Library of Education (NLE) Advisory Task Force identified collections of educational materials that were then already available on various federal, state, university, nonprofit, and commercial Internet sites. The U.S. Department of Education (DOE) and the NLE charged the ERIC Clearinghouse on Information and Technology at Syracuse University with the task of spearheading a project to develop an operational framework to provide the nation's teachers with "one-stop/any-stop" access to this vast pool of educational materials. These valuable resources were difficult for most teachers, students, and parents to find in an efficient, effective manner. The initial, and still primary, goal of the GEM project was to alleviate this resource discovery problem through development and deployment of a metadata element set, accompanying procedures for its use, and tools necessary to automate the creation, harvesting, and use of metadata.

A stakeholders' meeting was held at Syracuse University in November 1996, with representatives including frontline teachers, content providers (largely public sector organizations at that time), and individuals with expertise in specific subject areas. While the initial impetus behind the mandate of the DOE was to focus on lesson plans for K–12 educators, the results of the stakeholders' meeting was a broadening of focus to include the full practice domain of teaching, training, and learning from cradle to grave; and the full range of educational resources, from lesson plans to learning objects of every sort and at all levels of granularity.

In the months following the stakeholders' meeting, a small group refined the work begun at Syracuse. The plan was to develop the foundation for GEM through the first phase of the project. In its second phase, the constituency was enlarged, forming the GEM Consortium. The full-scale deployment of the GEM metadata element set through its application to educational materials across the Internet has been the primary function of the Consortium and the GEM Directorate.

As the project evolved, the moniker "GEM" became associated with each of the following relatively distinct notions:

1. A specific repository of metadata describing educational resources on the Web (i.e., the "Gateway")
2. An organization that guides GEM activities in the form of a consortium of members, a Governance Board, and a Directorate
3. An application profile consisting of the set of schemas and schemes from various namespaces (including a GEM namespace)
4. Best practice and training materials on the generation of domain-specific metadata
5. Tools and other resources necessary for the generation, harvesting, and the search and display of metadata records

To keep these various notions clear in this chapter, we will refer to GEM the organization as the "Consortium"; GEM the metadata repository as the "Gateway"; GEM the element set as the "GEM application profile"; and the metadata tools as the "GEM tools." When the notion addressed encompasses all of these various meanings, the terms "GEM project," "project," and "GEM" are used interchangeably.

As an application profile, GEM combines metadata elements defined in both the GEM and Dublin Core Metadata Initiative (DCMI) namespaces. The profile has gone through two versions—each matching one of the GEM generations outlined in this chapter. Thus, when we say "GEM 1.0," we are actually referring to GEM application profile 1.0. In like fashion, "GEM 2.0" refers to GEM application profile 2.0. The major distinction between the two profiles is the alignment in GEM 2.0 of GEM metadata with the Dublin Core Metadata Element Set (DCMES) element refinements given recommended status by the DCMI in July 2000. While the original elements and element refinements in the GEM namespace observed the extension and refinement mechanisms defined by the Canberra Qualifiers, the original fifteen DCMES had yet to be formally "refined" in 1997, meaning that certain choices made by GEM needed to be modified to keep the GEM elements and their associated semantics aligned with Dublin Core when refinements to the DCMES were approved in 2000.[2]

While the development of the GEM project has a number of facets that evolved as the project matured, the initial thrust was to develop the Gateway. Thus, much of the early focus was on technical architecture and the development and deployment of various GEM tools. The four major technical tasks addressed by the Consortium in the first phases of the project were to:

1. Define a semantically rich metadata application profile and domain-specific controlled vocabularies necessary to the description of educational materials on the Internet.
2. Develop a concrete syntax and well-specified practices for its application following HTML specifications in use at the time by Internet browsers.
3. Design and implement a set of harvesting tools for retrieving the metadata stored as HTML metatags either in the header of the resources being described or as separate HTML files that explicitly reference the resources being described.
4. Encourage the design of a number of prototype interfaces to GEM metadata by GEM Consortium members.

The initial decisions made with regard to these tasks were guided by several core Consortium assumptions that have proved over time to be questionable in part. Since shifts in several of these assumptions have played significant roles in the subsequent evolution of the GEM project, we will state them here as simple assertions followed by brief explanations.

Assumption 1. Creating relatively useful metadata can be done by individuals without training as indexers or catalogers. A basic premise of Dublin Core is that the simple metadata statements envisioned in unqualified DC can be created by authors and publishers with casual or no understanding of metadata in terms of its nature or subsequent uses. It has been our experience that this assumption holds only in very constrained contexts, limited both in complexity and collection size. Once substantial element and value space refinements come into play with the increased cognitive load placed on the cataloger/indexer caused by the more complex semantics of the refinements, or by the growth of the repository, increased levels of expertise are needed to produce minimally useful metadata.

Assumption 2. The function of metadata creation will be readily assumed by collection holders. The Gateway to Educational Materials was conceived as a simple metadata repository without resource holdings of its own. All resources would reside in Consortium member collections distributed across the Web. In like fashion, metadata describing those resources would also be distributed—generated by the collection holders and harvested for the central repository. While the GEM Directorate is funded to provide limited metadata generation services for new Consortium members, the burden of extensive metadata generation was not considered one of its central roles. With the exceptions of metadata generation derived from existing metadata stores (e.g., GEM metadata mapped out of databases of existing metadata based on some other schema) and select Consortium members that contributed originally-generated GEM metadata, the vast majority of the metadata generation has in fact been handled centrally by the Directorate. The growing awareness of collection holders of the return-on-investment of metadata generation may yet affirm the original premise; however, to date, it has not proved to be a particularly valid assumption.

Assumption 3. Given access to a repository of quality metadata describing their own educational resources as well as those of others, Consortium members will develop access mechanisms to the repository as part of their own web presences. The GEM metadata repository presence on the Web—the Gateway—was originally conceived to be (1) a proof of concept, and (2) the backup window into the repository where the Department provided the guaranteed means for unlimited access to the full collection. The Gateway presence was never intended to be the most sophisticated window into the repository. Instead, it was assumed that the significant value-added applications working on the metadata in the repository would be provided by Consortium members. Under such a scenario, GEM would function primarily as a metadata utility. In the main, the metadata utility scenario has not happened. To date, the Gateway remains the primary window into the metadata repository. However, the maturation of the technologies underlying the GEM architecture may yet enable Consortium members to achieve the original goal of providing sophisticated value-added services through the metadata.

As the following narrative touches on these initial core assumptions, we will point out the changes that have occurred. Thus, in the eight years since its beginning, the project has evolved along three major dimensions:

1. the complexity of its technical architecture;
2. the scope of resources being described; and
3. the scope of the project's beneficiaries.

In the following subsections, we will explore the major drivers of this evolution.

GEM Element Set

From the outset, the Consortium wanted to develop the various technical aspects of GEM around emerging standards for networked information discovery and retrieval. The Consortium decided that GEM would assume the DCMES and its emerging principles as its base referent due to the nascent but growing recognition, acceptance, and support for the DCMES both in the United States and internationally.

Since it was clear to the Consortium that the fifteen base elements of the DCMES lacked the specificity to serve particularly well its domain-specific purposes, the Consortium decided to rely heavily on the Dublin Core principle of extensibility and use the two extension mechanisms defined as the "Canberra Qualifiers": (1) additional elements would be added to meet the needs of the education and training domain, and (2) the original fifteen DCMES would be enriched through the use of a broad range of element refinements and value space schemes (i.e., controlled vocabularies and encoding standards). Lacking an abstract model of the sort under development in the DCMI at the time of this writing, there was little guidance beyond broad definitional statements as to how to use the Canberra Qualifiers in a principled way. Only through sometimes painful trial and error has the DCMI community been led to such guiding principles.

The use of the DCMES as base referent meant that the GEM metadata architecture was conceived around what would later be called an *application profile* (AP).[3] The AP in 1996 was made up of the DCMES namespace consisting of fifteen elements and a GEM namespace consisting of the following eight elements: audience, catalogingAgency, duration, essentialResources, educationalLevel, pedagogy, qualityAssessment (deprecated in 2000), and educationalStandards (i.e., formally promulgated learning goals). Since the adoption of the elements and element refinements of the GEM namespace by the Consortium in early 1997 as version 1.0, the "audience" element has been adopted with equivalent semantics as the sixteenth element in DCMES, thus shifting from a GEM to the

DCMI namespace. In addition, the DCMI adopted "educationLevel" as a refinement of the DCMES "audience" element. Thus, counting the deprecation of "qualityAssessment" by GEM and the migration of "audience" and "educationLevel" to the DCMI namespace, the GEM version 2.0 namespace contains only five of the original eight version 1.0 elements.

GEM, as an application profile wedding terms from multiple namespaces (always including GEM and DCMI namespaces), has gone through two versions (GEM 1.0 and GEM 2.0)—each matching one of the GEM generations outlined in this chapter. The major distinction between the two profiles is the alignment in GEM 2.0 of GEM metadata with the DCMES element refinements given recommended status by DCMI in July 2000.

In addition to the small element set in the GEM namespace, a number of GEM controlled vocabularies were defined and encoding schemes adopted in early 1997.[4]

Sutton and Oh describe the relationship between the elements in the DCMES and GEM namespaces in the following terms:

> The general goals of GEM and DC are similar; however, in many ways, they are not congruent. Dublin Core is designed to serve NIDR [networked information discovery and retrieval] through a fielded surrogate supposedly simple enough to be applied to resources by authors and Internet providers untrained in the complexities of cataloging necessary to the creation of more richly structured surrogates (e.g., the MARC record). While its simplicity serves coarse-grained NIDR across a broad range of networked information, DC is ill equipped for more fine-grained NIDR of resources necessary to particular discourse or practice communities such as the nation's teachers. GEM is intended to serve NIDR needs of this constituency along a continuum that begins with what is achievable with a simple, unqualified, fielded surrogate as set out by the DC "minimalists" to a surrogate coming closer to (but never reaching) the richly structured surrogate. In addition, GEM assumes that the profile will be applied by a range of organizations with a higher level of commitment and expertise than that assumed by DC.[5]

First Generation: GEM Technical Architecture

In order to provide enhanced networked information discovery and retrieval of educational materials, the Consortium developed the conceptual framework for what is known as the GEM Union—a "union catalog" of resources located across the Internet. As conceived, the Union was intended to provide access to the collections of a Consortium of "high integrity" repositories of web-based educational materials. The rationale for the GEM Union can be found in the following observation of Lagoze, Lynch, and Daniel in their exploration of issues surrounding the Dublin Core:

> [T]he use of the Dublin Core in a limited context might produce very positive results. For example, assume a set of "high-integrity sites." Administrators at such sites might tag their documents . . . with Dublin Core metadata elements using a set of well-specified practices that include relatively controlled vocabularies and regular syntax. Retrieval effectiveness across these high-integrity sites would probably be significantly better (assuming harvesting and retrieval tools that make use of the metadata) than the unstructured searches available now through Lycos and Alta Vista.[6]

As it has evolved, the GEM Consortium collection holders represent just such a set of "high-integrity sites." In addition to the GEM application profile with its controlled vocabularies and regular syntactic bindings, the Consortium has developed an appropriate set of harvesting and retrieval tools for use by Consortium members to support building the Union.

SECOND-GENERATION GEM

In early 2000, the Consortium decided to develop a new generation of GEM tools that would capitalize both on the new DCMI element refinement recommendations as embodied in GEM 2.0 and on technical lessons learned over the course of the first generation. Principal among those technical lessons was the need for a flexible version of the GEMCat metadata-generation tool that could be configured by means of network-accessible application profiles and value space schemes. This need for flexibility stemmed from demands among the Consortium for the ability to create both simple and complex metadata wedding elements and element refinements from multiple schemas (including local schemas), and to use any machine-accessible controlled vocabularies that individual collection holders deemed necessary to the description of their resources. In addition to the lessons learned by the Consortium, work was under way in 2000 on the Resource Description Framework (RDF) at W3C, the Open Archives Initiative Protocol for Metadata Harvesting (OAI-PMH), and schema registries at the United Kingdom Office of Library Networking (UKOLN) and elsewhere. These initiatives fueled considerable discussion within the Dublin Core community and would inform the development of the second-generation GEM architecture.

Second Generation: Networked Environment

The new GEM metadata-generation tool was thus planned as an open-source, freely available, RDF-based implementation that, out-of-the-box, was functionally an empty shell whose attributes and values could be configured by means of malleable application profiles accessing various schemas and schemes maintained in one or more network-accessible registries. Figure 1-1 illustrates the relationships among the networked components for the GEMCat4 metadata generation tool and its associated schema/scheme registries.

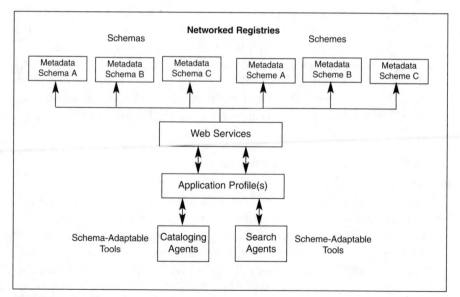

FIGURE 1-1   Registries and schema-adaptable tools

At the bottom of the figure, we see GEMCat4 (as well as other potential configurable agents) accessing 1-to-n registries containing various metadata schemas and value space schemes, situated at the top of the figure. The Gateway for Educational Materials currently maintains its own network-accessible registry of GEM schemas and vocabularies as well as a select set of controlled vocabularies from other namespaces (e.g., Thesaurus of ERIC Descriptors) as part of a registry proof of concept. We assume that others using the GEMCat4 tool will rely on schemas and schemes from any number of other registries as they become available. For a more complete explanation of the principles underlying the design of the GEMCat4 RDF metadata generator, see Sutton.[7]

Which schemas, parts of schemas, and schemes as well as how they are to be used in a particular instance of GEMCat4 are defined by the tool's configuring application profile. In the figure, the mechanism for discovering the location of registry services as well as the means for interacting with them is managed through web services. This is not to suggest that other mechanisms such as richly defined communication protocols might not also be appropriate.

The challenge of developing such an architecture in early 2000 was the paucity of knowledge and standard, agreed-upon means for implementing schema/scheme registries; and of standard communication protocols for disparate agents to discover and interact with such registries. At the time of this writing, many questions regarding these issues remain largely unanswered. However, web services such as Web Service Description Language (WSDL) and Universal Description, Discovery and Integration (UDDI) are providing one possible framework for addressing a number of these issues, as is the work on registry interoperability under way at the DCMI and UKOLN.[8]

Second Generation: GEM 2.0 Metadata

While the primary purpose of the GEM 2.0 application profile was to closely align GEM metadata with the DCMI element refinement recommendations issued in 2000, a second goal was to more closely align the GEM work with the "one-to-one" rule which plays a fundamental role in the Dublin Core abstract model as it is now emerging. The rule basically holds that a Dublin Core resource description describes one and only one entity. According to the rule, while the description of a book, article, or work of art has a creator element with its value being the creator, the e-mail address of that creator is not an attribute of the work being described but rather an attribute of the creator. Thus, to include the e-mail address of the creator in a metadata description of the resource is to conflate attributes of two entities—the resource and its creator—into one description. The GEM 1.0 application profile included element refinements in a GEM namespace for all of the DCMES agents (creator, contributor, and publisher) that violated this fundamental DCMI principle. The GEM 2.0 profile deprecated all such element refinements. Instead, GEMCat4 has the capacity to provide references to external descriptions of agents in network-addressable name authority file(s) (NAV). We will have more to say regarding such NAVs (or the lack thereof in the web environment) in the conclusion to this chapter.

Second Generation: System Architecture

In the years covering GEM's first generation, the technologies shaping the Web and the expression of metadata statements in that context advanced significantly. The original GEM technical specifications predated XML, RDF, OAI, and web services. Like all other projects of its kind—i.e., projects implementing as these technologies emerged—GEM struggled with expressing increasingly complex metadata statements (i.e., from unqualified to qualified Dublin Core) within the limited framework of HTML 2.0 and 4.0. The solutions were never elegant. Throughout this same period, the DCMI fitfully clarified underlying principles, and a body of growing practice paved the way for the now emerging, mature DCMES abstract model—a model that appears best expressed fully in RDF. However, in terms of web time, the maturation of RDF has been slow. Even slower has been the emergence of search mechanisms robust and fast enough to satisfy large information retrieval system demands and yet take advantage of the expressive power of RDF.

As this book goes to press, second-generation GEM RDF metadata will be available in the Gateway. Legacy GEM metadata based on the 1.0 application profile have been transformed and integrated into the RDF repository.

ONGOING AND FUTURE WORK

In the preceding sections, we chronicled the evolution of the metadata schemas in use in the GEM project. In this section we will note a number of matters that have influenced (or will influence) GEM that are part of the general world of metadata for the education and training domain. Attention to these matters over the course of the chronicle has been compelling, since each plays a role for metadata interoperability.

DC-Education Application Profile

Early in GEM's history, it became obvious to the GEM Directorate that metadata interoperability outside the relatively tight federation of the Consortium was going to be difficult. In other words, while guidance provided to the GEM federation of collections in the generation of metadata resulted in relatively compatible metadata within the GEM system, there was no guarantee, for example, that GEM metadata could be ingested and used by sister initiatives such as Education Network Australia (EdNA), whose metadata was also rooted in Dublin Core.[9] It was simply not enough that both GEM and EdNA used the DCMES and its underlying principles as their base referent. Problems lurked in the generality of the DCMI mechanisms of extension and refinement. In embracing the Canberra Qualifiers, GEM elected to pursue a course of minimal creation of domain-specific elements and a relatively expansive use of element refinements for elements existing in both the DCMI and GEM namespaces. On the other hand, EdNA chose to develop its domain-specific schema by creating a relatively expansive set of elements while holding the refinements of those elements to a minimum. Thus, even though both initiatives pursued generally parallel paths in the kinds of domain-specific metadata statements needing to be made (i.e., relatively congruent semantics), the two schemas were markedly different as a result of the choices made—choices that fell squarely (in most cases) within the ambit of the Canberra Qualifiers.

In late 1999, the DCMI Directorate created the DC-Education Working Group (the Group) to address this sort of problem within the education and training domain for initiatives that had chosen the DCMES as the framework for their metadata schemas. The goal of the Working Group was to explore and propose possible domain-specific additions of elements and element refinements to the DCMI namespace. The work of this Group has resulted so far in the addition of the element and element refinements noted earlier. One goal that has not been addressed is a DC-Education application profile that can provide guidance in project-specific extensions and refinements and in the use of those new elements and refinements in the DCMI namespace. This work could easily be as extensive as the work done by the DC-Libraries Working Group. Such an application profile is sorely needed, since there is little available (published or otherwise) regarding best practice in the creation of metadata for education and training.

DCMI and IEEE LOM

The late 1990s witnessed the somewhat simultaneous emergence of a number of initiatives worldwide addressing the need for standardized metadata in the education and training domain. Two strands of those initiatives sought consensus internationally—the DCMI DC-Education Working Group and the IEEE Learning Technology Standards Committee's Learning Object Metadata Working Group (IEEE LOM). There was (and remains to date) considerable confusion among the members of the community of practice regarding choices they perceive must be made between seemingly competing metadata schemas. Efforts to dispel this confusion began in August 2001 with the issuance of the Ottawa Communiqué, which was signed by representatives from the DCMI, the IMS Global Learning Consortium, IEEE LOM, and several large metadata projects, including GEM.[10] The Communiqué outlined five broad areas of cooperation:

1. Develop and promote a set of fundamental principles for the development and application of modular interoperable metadata for dissemination to the global education and training communities.
2. Develop a set of examples that illustrate how metadata should be generated in a given application profile involving both DCMI and LOM metadata.
3. Develop a set of guidelines and principles for the creation of application profiles involving both LOM and DCMI metadata.
4. Develop an example of an application profile in the form of a machine-readable compound schema.
5. Other issues identified for potential collaboration include (a) the development and maintenance of registries; and (b) an assessment of the degree of semantic drift that may have developed in the LOM interpretation of DCMI terms.

To date, only the first of these areas of cooperation has borne fruit in the form of the jointly authored *D-Lib* article "Metadata Principles and Practicalities."[11] Renewed efforts to build cooperation among the signatories of the Ottawa Communiqué were begun at the DC-2003 International Metadata Conference in Seattle, where the IEEE Learning Technology Standards Committee and the DCMI co-located meetings with the express intention to further the work begun in Ottawa, begin the evaluation of the current state of affairs in metadata for education and training, and build a cooperative path forward.

Deficiencies in a Digital Library Global Architecture

As projects such as GEM mature, they confront substantial deficiencies in the global architecture of digital libraries on the Internet. Principal among those deficiencies are generally accepted solutions to authority control of every form, including name authority. We noted earlier the GEM work on registries and a new generation of metadata tools that rely on network-accessible authority control schemes. While there are isolated efforts to address some of the issues of generally accepted protocols and schemas for managing networked communication among agents and registries containing authority control schemes (witness the Alexandria Digital Library's Thesaurus Protocol), the area remains largely unaddressed through standardization.[12] While Dublin Core-based tools such as GEMCat4 are poised to generate metadata records that reference name authority files, no such files or file architectures exist for general deployment on the Web. As a result of these deficiencies, the vast experience of the library community in the use of authority control is not being brought to bear in the generation of metadata in ways that will prove interoperable across a global network of systems in either the short or long term.[13] As a result, individual projects such as GEM are compelled to develop their own local solutions to federated systems' interoperability. The piper will have to be paid when such federations seek to network resources—something many will surely wish to do.

The GEM project was a very early adopter of the DCMES. As a result, many of its growing pains closely parallel those of the DCMI and the evolving DCMES. An abstract model for the DCMES is only now emerging through the Dublin Core community experience. The protracted discussions out of which the abstract model is emerging have taken place over the course of the evolution of the GEM project. As noted in our introduction, building a production system within such an evolving context sometimes required decisions based on community notions that were only half-baked. However, being on the bleeding edge as an early adopter has its rewards when the work done contributes to our growing body of understanding.

NOTES

1. IMS Global Learning Consortium (home page), http://www.imsglobal.org (accessed 5 November 2003); Institute of Electrical and Electronics Engineers (LOM home page), http://ltsc.ieee.org/wg12/par1484-12-1.html (accessed 5 November 2003).
2. For an explanation of the Canberra Qualifiers, see Stuart Weibel, Renato Iannella, and Warwick Cathro, "The 4th Dublin Core Metadata Workshop Report," *D-Lib Magazine*, June 1997, http://www.dlib.org/dlib/june97/metadata/06weibel.html (accessed 5 November 2003).
3. R. M. Heery and M. Patel, "Application Profiles: Mixing and Matching Metadata Schemas," *Ariadne* 25 (2000), http://www.ariadne.ac.uk/issue25/app-profiles/ (accessed 5 November 2003).
4. "GEM Controlled Vocabularies," http://www.geminfo.org/Workbench/Workbench_vocabularies.html (accessed 5 November 2003).
5. Stuart Sutton and Sam Oh, "GEM: Using Metadata to Enhance Internet Retrieval of Educational Materials by K-12 Teachers," *Bulletin of the American Society for Information Science* 24, no. 1 (1997): 21–24.
6. Carl Lagoze, Clifford Lynch, and Ron Daniel Jr., "The Warwick Framework: A Container Architecture for Aggregating Sets of Metadata," TR96-1593, http://www.nlc-bnc.ca/ifla/documents/libraries/cataloging/metadata/tr961593.pdf (accessed 5 November 2003).
7. Stuart Sutton, "Principled Design of Metadata-Generation Tools for Educational Resources," in *Developing Digital Libraries for K-12 Education*, ed. Marcia A. Mardis (Syracuse, N.Y.: ERIC Clearinghouse on Information and Technology, 2003).
8. World Wide Web Consortium (WSDL home page), http://www.w3.org/TR/wsdl (accessed 5 November 2003); Organization for the Advancement of Structured Information Standards (UDDI home page), http://www.uddi.org/ (accessed 5 November 2003).
9. Education Network Australia (EdNA Online home page), http://www.edna.edu.au/edna/page1.html (accessed 5 November 2003).
10. "Ottawa Communiqué," 2001, http://wbww.ischool.washington.edu/sasutton/dc-ed/Ottawa-Communique.rtf (accessed 5 November 2003).
11. Erik Duval, Wayne Hodgins, Stuart Sutton, and Stuart L. Weibel, "Metadata Principles and Practicalities," *D-Lib Magazine*, April 2002, http://www.dlib.org/dlib/april02/weibel/04weibel.html (accessed 5 November 2003).

12. Greg Janée, Satoshi Ikeda, and Linda Hill, "ADL Thesaurus Protocol," Alexandria Digital Library Project, 2003, http://www.alexandria.ucsb.edu/thesaurus/protocol/ (accessed 5 November 2003).
13. See, however, "What Can the Library Community Offer in Support of Semantic Interoperability?" http://lcweb.loc.gov/catdir/bibcontrol/tdg5.html (accessed 5 November 2003).

2 Building Heritage Colorado: The Colorado Digitization Experience

Liz Bishoff and Elizabeth S. Meagher

PROVIDING THE PEOPLE of Colorado with "access to the written and visual record of Colorado's history, culture, government, and industry in full text and graphic content" is the vision of the Colorado Digitization Program (CDP). The program constitutes a federation of cultural heritage institutions, i.e., archives, historical societies, libraries, and museums working together for the common purpose of making their digital collections more accessible. Digital resources are created by institutions throughout the state that run the gamut from top academic research libraries with large comprehensive cataloging departments to museums and historical societies, some open but a few hours a week and run by volunteers. What each institution has in common is its desire to make unique primary resource materials digitally available via the Internet.

The CDP began in fall 1998 with a Colorado State Library, Library Services Technology Act (LSTA) grant.[1] The LSTA grant's purpose was to develop a collaborative environment that would encourage the state's cultural heritage community to increase access to the unique resources and special collections of the cultural heritage institutions through digitization. To accomplish this goal, the CDP, working with representatives from the cultural heritage community, developed guidelines and best practices. The CDP also provided training and consultation that would enable the institutions to undertake digitization initiatives. Guidance is provided on copyright and intellectual property issues, digital asset management, collection development policy, website design, and program planning. Colorado Digitization Program staff created a toolbox of forms, macros, and templates to enhance the practitioner's ability to create quality collections and associated metadata.[2]

To minimize the cost of creating digital content and to assist the smaller institutions, the CDP established regionally based digital scanning centers. These centers allowed libraries and museums to produce quality images of photographs, photonegatives, small maps, letters, slides, and other materials that can be reproduced on average scanners. The CDP also seeded digitization projects with financial support in the form of small grants funded by the Institute of Museums and Library Services, the Colorado State Library, the Colorado Historical Society, and the Colorado Regional Library Systems. Since inception, the program has awarded more than $300,000 in grants to libraries, archives, historical societies, and museums.

To access the digital collections, the CDP developed Heritage Colorado: Digital Treasures of the West. Underpinning this effort is a metadata database that provides a single online location for users to locate the digital collections provided by Colorado's cultural heritage institutions.[3] Introduced in summer 2001, Heritage Colorado provided URLs from the metadata records to associated digital resources numbering more than 150,000.

BACKGROUND

Prior to the inception of the CDP, several Colorado libraries and museums, most notably the Denver Public Library and the Boulder Public Library, had begun digitizing their collections. By 1998 a total of fifteen Colorado libraries and museums had digitized small portions of their collections and were providing access through web-based exhibitions or databases. A variety of metadata standards and controlled vocabularies were employed and a number of different systems were used to manage these collections. Libraries used the Machine Readable Cataloging (MARC) format, the Anglo-American Cataloguing Rules (AACR2) standard, and Library of Congress Subject Headings. While most museums did not follow any consistent descriptive cataloging system, a few used Chenhall, locally defined vocabularies, or other subject thesauri for vocabulary control.[4] Libraries tended to manage their collections through integrated library management systems, while archives, smaller museums, and historical societies were more likely to store information in Microsoft Access or comparable databases. Some larger museums employed museum collections management systems, such as the ARGUS Collections Management System by Questor Systems.[5] Metadata standards such as Dublin Core (DC) and VRA Core Categories were emerging in 1998, but were still developing and no commercial software existed to support them.[6] Many of the targeted photograph collections were not organized with finding aids, and some of the projects opted to catalog these items using other standards such as MARC. Non-photographic collections, such as sound recording or three-dimensional artifact collections, might be cataloged using DC, MARC, or another standard. In addition to the diversity of metadata standards and systems for managing the metadata, the CDP was also faced with a wide diversity of materials to integrate for the participating projects. The digital surrogates in these collections were created from primary resource materials as varied as the institutions themselves. Table 2-1 illustrates the types of initial materials for which digital objects were developed for the CDP project.

METADATA WORKING GROUP RECOMMENDATIONS

The challenge for the Colorado Digitization Program was to work together with institutions to integrate separate collections using a common set of

TABLE 2-1   Digital materials available for initial projects

Institution	Resources
Libraries	Photographs (photonegatives, photos, glass plate negatives), diaries, notebooks, letters, manuscripts, posters, and music scores
Museums	Fossils, plant specimens, pottery, other artifacts, archival papers, letters, and photographs
Archives	Material culture collections, text, diaries, letters, and photographs
Historical Societies	Photographs, artifacts, diaries, and material culture collections

metadata standards while retaining the unique character of each collection. In fall 1998, the CDP's Metadata Working Group was formed to review the options for the description of digital resources and to develop guidelines for metadata to be used by project participants. The group was composed of representatives from libraries, archives, and museums.[7]

As the Working Group proceeded with its review, it became clear that many potential project participants had existing cataloging, collection management, or inventory control records for their original works or objects. In order to realize the goal of providing functional web-based access to the descriptions and digital surrogates from multiple institutions, the Metadata Working Group developed a matrix that looked at common elements across the standards that were available at that time. The study group document illustrated in table 2-2 provided an analysis that compared the elements of all the available standards.

TABLE 2-2   Title and author sample from matrix of common standards

	MARC	CDWA[*]	DC[†]	FGDC[‡]	GILS[**]	REACH[††]	VRA[‡‡]
Title; Object Name Title	245 la	Titles or Names-Text	Title	Title [8.4]	Title	Object name; Title [#4]	Title [W2]
Author; Creator; Originator; Maker	1xx, 7xx, + 1xxe, 7xxe	Creation; Creator; Identity; Names[*]; Role	Author; Creator; Other Contributors	Originator [8.1]; Dataset Credit [1.11]	Originator; Contributor	Creator; Maker [#10]	Creator [W6], [W7]

* J. Paul Getty Trust and College Art Association, "Categories for the Description of Works of Art," 2000, http://www.getty.edu/research/conducting_research/standards/cdwa/ (accessed 11 December 2003).

† Dublin Core Metadata Initiative (home page).

‡ Federal Geographic Data Committee, "Geospatial Metadata Standards," 2002, http://www.fgdc.gov/metadata/meta_stand.html (accessed 11 December 2003).

** Global Information Locator Service (home page), http://www.gils.net/ (accessed 11 December 2002).

†† RLG, "Research Libraries Group Reach Metadata Element Set for Shared Description of Museum Objects," 1998, http://www.rlg/reach.elements.html (accessed 11 December 2002).

‡‡ Visual Resources Association Data Standards Committee, "VRA Core Categories."

The Metadata Working Group also looked at a similar comparison of elements found in the Getty Research Institute's publication, *Introduction to Metadata: Pathways to Digital Information*.[8] These early comparisons indicated that Dublin Core provided a common set of data elements across the cultural heritage community that would support a resource discovery objective. The proposed database would not have an authority control component, so variant forms of personal and corporate name headings as well as a variety of controlled and uncontrolled subject terms would be tolerated. Through the database, which was the resource discovery tool, the CDP provided users with basic identification and URLs to the digital surrogates for objects residing in closed stacks and warehouses, with limited hours of access. The users saw the images and information about the object, including who owned the object. The digitization initiatives and the Heritage Colorado database increased access to important collections while the "official" catalog of record for the original objects remained the local institution's catalog, collection management system, or inventory control system.

To facilitate the integration of the various collections into a common database, the Metadata Working Group recommended the development of procedures that allowed for the reuse of existing metadata and cataloging to the maximum extent possible. The Working Group was sensitive to the fact that staff resources were limited at many institutions and the ability to create new metadata records for digital versions of the objects was unlikely to become a priority. In many cases, adding the URL and some information regarding the digital version allowed the institution to minimize its investment and still participate in the digitization initiatives.

DUBLIN CORE AS THE CDP STANDARD

In addition to its recommendation to reuse existing data, the Working Group recommended qualified Dublin Core as the standard for CDP records, with the addition of local extensions. The CDP adopted a mandatory subset of Dublin Core metadata elements to facilitate the building of the union catalog or database, and to assure interoperability among the databases from the participating institutions. The original mandatory elements were revised from the CDP's 1999 General Guidelines for Descriptive Metadata Creation and Entry in 2003 as part of the effort by the Western States Digital Standards Group to reflect the changes in the

Dublin Core standard.[9] One additional local element and an additional element refinement were designated as mandatory in the Western States best practices. "Date: original" was considered of primary importance, particularly for primary source materials. "Rights management" was designated as mandatory to assist with the use of these resources. The Western States Group believed that users would want to know, for instance, if they could reproduce the image.

The Western States Digital Standards Group also recommended the incorporation of more technical and administrative metadata. Since Dublin Core's "one-to-one" rule separated the description of an original resource from its digital surrogate, CDP in its 1999 Metadata Guidelines document established the "Format: creation" refinement, reflecting the work then under way in Metadata Encoding and Transmission Standard (METS).[10] The 2003 Western States documentation significantly expanded this refinement, as illustrated in table 2-3.

Other modifications to the DC standard introduced in July 2000 were also incorporated into the revision. The Metadata Working Group recognized that additional elements might be required for particular formats, so a "full" record that utilized all elements was specified. The recommendations of the Group for the mandatory elements (core) and mandatory (full) plus optional elements for DC records are shown in table 2-4.

Each Dublin Core element was accompanied by full guidelines articulated in the Western States Dublin Core Metadata Best Practices document.[11] Guidelines for each element included the Label, DC Definition, and Description, as well as whether the element was mandatory and/or repeatable, and what refinements and schemes were authorized. A list of established recommended encoding schemes as recommended by the Dublin Core Metadata Initiative (DCMI) was also provided for practitioners.

THE COLORADO DIGITIZATION
PROGRAM'S DUBLIN CORE

In addition to establishing the mandatory and desirable elements, two major and several minor local additions were made to the original Dublin Core elements for use in the CDP collaborative environment. These modifications facilitated the use of DC with digital surrogates of primary source materials and were necessitated by the decision not to separate the

TABLE 2-3   Colorado Digitization Program "Format: creation" element guidelines

File Size	The number of bytes as provided by the computer system. Best practice is to record the file size as bytes (i.e., 3,000,000 bytes) and not as kilobytes (Kb), megabytes (Mb), etc.
Quality	For visual resources, characteristics such as bit depth, resolution (not spatial resolution); for multimedia resources, other indicators of quality, such as 16-bit audio file
Extent	Pixel dimensions, pagination, spatial resolution, playtime, or other measurements of the physical or temporal extent of the digital object
Compression	Electronic format or compression scheme used for optimized storage and delivery of digital object. This information often supplements the "Format: use" element.
Checksum Value	A numeric value used to detect errors in file recording or file transfer, checksum helps ensure the integrity of digital files against loss of data
Preferred Presentation	Designation of the device, application, medium, or environment recommended for optimal presentation of the digital object
Object Producer	Name of scanning technician, digitization vendor, or other entity responsible for the digital object's creation. Distinguishable from the descriptive "Creator" element, this element is mainly useful when different persons generated multiple versions of the object's content.
Operating System	Computer operating system used on the computer with which the digital object was created. (Examples: Windows, Mac, UNIX, Linux.) Also include version of operating system.
Creation Hardware	If a hardware device was used to create, derive, or generate the digital object, indicate from a controlled list of terms the particular hardware device. (Examples: flatbed reflective scanner, digital camera, etc.) Include manufacturer, model name, and model number.
Creation Software	Name and version number of the software used to create the digital object
Creation Methodology	If creation process used a standard series of steps, derivations, or techniques, either state or refer to a URL describing the creation process

TABLE 2-4   Mandatory and optional elements for CDP Dublin
Core records

Mandatory Elements	Optional Elements
Title	Contributor
Creator (if available)	Publisher
Subject	Relation
Description	Type
Date: original (if applicable)	Source
Date: digital	Language
Format: creation	Coverage
Format: use	
Identifier	
Rights Management	

description of originals and digital surrogates. The two major modifications were the "Date" element and the "Format" element.

The "Date" element was the subject of much discussion among the
members of the Metadata Working Group. Many of the resources in the
project were nontextual, including photographs and museum objects.
Several members in the group believed that a user would want to qualify
a search by the date of the original object, i.e., a photograph of a town
from 1890 or the date of the event depicted in the photograph, i.e., an
automobile from 1935. Because of the "one-to-one" rule, Dublin Core
guidelines instructed users to place information about the original photograph in the "Source" element, which was not indexed as a date by the
CDP. The CDP, wishing to use a refinement of the "Date" element, considered using "original," until Rebecca Guenther of the Library of
Congress indicated that this was considered and discarded by the DCMI
Libraries Working Group.[12] The solution chosen was to create a new local
element refinement, "Date: original." To allow the unrefined "DC: date"
to function as the date for the surrogate, it was relabeled in the CDP application profile to "DC: Date: digital." This allowed the CDP to map either
local refinement unambiguously if future developments required it. If the
item was "born digital" then only the "Date: digital" refinement was used.

Other element refinements that the CDP developed for internal use were "Format: creation" and "Format: use." The "Format: creation" refinement was established to supply administrative metadata about how the digital object was created and stored, for which DC has made little provision. Information in this element could include the hardware and software used to create the resource, image resolution, and information on the digitization process. The Western States Digital Standards Group further developed "Format: creation" by adding specific categories of details, primarily to support the migration of the digital object over time and to control the quality of the digital object. Development and implementation of the Metadata Encoding and Transmission Standard may obviate the need for this element in the future, as METS supports robust functional and administrative metadata. The refinement "Format: use" utilized the existing DCMI definition for the "Format" element.

In addition to these major extensions, several smaller extensions were made. The CDP created local elements to record system requirements such as the holding institution, since it was critical in a collaborative environment to identify the institution that owned the object. While the "Publisher" element might fulfill such roles, in many of the collaborative projects, it became clear that contributing parties could play multiple roles. The museums held the original object, the library created the metadata, and an Internet service provider, a third party, made the digital object available online. For the CDP the holdings information also served an administrative function, linking authorization and access to DCBuilder, the data entry and maintenance system. (See figure 2-1.) A recent addition to the administrative information is a "Project" element, to allow institutions with multiple projects to indicate which project was applicable to a particular record. The current system already accommodated other administrative elements such as date and time stamps for record creation and record modification, as well as a unique identifier for each record.

DATABASE OF IMAGES

As part of its recommendations, the Working Group suggested that the CDP should create a Dublin Core-based software application in order to include a form-based data entry tool for online record creation for those cultural heritage institutions lacking access to information management

Navigation	Edit Record

■ Search
■ Add Record
  (Short Form)
■ Add Record
  (Long Form)
■ Results
■ Previous Record
■ Next Record
■ Delete record …
 	
■ Logout	

CDPID: 0009193
Owner: University of Denver
Created: 09:45 AM on 19-Sep-01
Modified: 02:17 PM on 20-Jul-03

Term Tools
■ Colorado Terms

[Add/Edit] **Titles:** 1. United States Army jacket

° Prospector Search
(name as author)

[Add/Edit] **Creators:**

° Prospector Search
(name as subject)

[Add/Edit] **Subjects:** 1. Military uniforms. [LCSH]
2. United States. Army -- Uniforms. [LCSH]
3. United States. Army -- Reserves. [LCSH]
4. United States. Army. 6th Army Group -- Insignia.
5. United States. Army. 6th Army Group -- Medals, badges, decorations, etc.
6. United States. Army. 6th Army Group -- Non-commissioned officers -- Costume.
7. United States. Army. 6th Army Group -- Uniforms.
8. Military decorations -- United States. [LCSH]
9. Good conduct medal.

CDP Links
■ CDP Website

Resources
■ Metadata
  Best Practices
  & Input Guide
  (PDF)
■ Controlled
  Vocabularies
■ CDP Metadata
  Resources
■ DC Builder
  Handbook (PDF)

[Add/Edit] **Descriptions:** 1. Digital image of a World War II U.S. Army olive drab green wool "Ike" jacket, that belonged to Phillip Hornbein Jr.According to his insignia, Hornbein was a Sergeant First Class/Platoon Sergeant with a ranking of E7. The insignia on the shoulder indicates that he was a member of the 6th Army Group. The bar style pinned ribbons above the left pocket are from top to bottom and left to right: the Good Conduct Medal, the European/African/Middle Eastern Campaign Medal, the Reserve Component Achievement Medal and the American Campaign Medal; the stars on the ribbons are service stars and represent participation in a particular campaign or multiple awards of that particular medal. Hornbein was a U.S. Army Reservist who was called to active duty during WWII; the bird-in-flight patch over the right pocket was either awarded for specialty skills or for participation in a specialty unit.

[Add/Edit] **Identifiers:** 1.
http://www.penlib.du.edu/specoll/beck/tx181full.htm
[Access] [URI]
2. tx181

[Add/Edit] **Contributors:**

[Add/Edit] **Publishers:** 1. University of Denver, Penrose Library

FIGURE 2-1   Example of record in DCBuilder

systems. Because of this need, the Colorado Digitization Program began to investigate extant systems that could support a union catalog of metadata. After studying the various software packages, the CDP initially decided to use OCLC's SiteSearch and its Record Builder software, which supported both MARC and DC.[13] Unfortunately, Record Builder proved to have limited capacity for simultaneous multiple-institution data entry, and could not accommodate the crosswalking or mapping of MARC records to DC. Abandoning this approach, the CDP developed its own DC-based application, DCBuilder, using MySQL and Macromedia's ColdFusion.[14]

DCBuilder supported the conversion of metadata from a variety of systems and formats to Dublin Core, as well as the direct entry of metadata into a DC form-based application. Once the local records were imported to DCBuilder, institutions could further modify the resulting DC record using the capabilities of DCBuilder. Table 2-5 shows the CDP crosswalk that maps MARC to DC and DC to MARC.

In order to assist institutions with the consistent use of geographic and topical headings specific to Colorado, the CDP created Colorado Terms, a list that included a "Colorado Names Search" and a "Colorado Subject Search."[15] Both are extracted from Prospector, the Colorado Alliance of Research Libraries' union catalog.[16] Since libraries participating in Prospector followed the MARC authority format in their individual subject headings, only limited editing was required to remove duplicate headings and correct errors. There are currently more than 46,000 headings in the subject file alone, but because the CDP only extracted name lists, they do not include cross-references.

SUCCESSES

The Colorado Digitization Program capitalized on the desire of Colorado's cultural heritage institutions to share their unique resources. The CDP has been successful in accomplishing two tasks. The first task was educating practitioners in the application of Dublin Core to a wide range of reformatted digital resources. The second task was offering metadata workshops and providing web-accessible metadata guidelines. In addition, the CDP demonstrated that individual institutions can continue to use existing standards and best practices, while repurposing their legacy

TABLE 2-5 Customized MARC-to-Dublin Core crosswalk

DC Element	MARC	MARC Subfield	DC Modifier	DC Scheme
Title	245	a		
	246	a	Alternative	
Creator	100			
	110			
Subjects	600		Personal Name	
	610		Corporate Name	
	650			LCSH
	651			LCSH
	655			
Description	520			
Identifier	856	u	Access	URI
Contributor	700		Personal Name	
	710		Corporate Name	
Publisher	533	c		
Original Date	260	c	Created	
Digital Date	533	d	Created	W3C-DTF
Relation	440		Is Part of	DCMI Type Vocabulary
Type	856	q		
Creation Format	533	aeh		
	856	s		
Use Format	533	n		
Source	300			
	246	ia		
	260	abc		
	500			
Language	1			
Rights	540			
DDC	O82			

cataloging records as a basis for digital resource records for the CDP projects. Through the adoption of Dublin Core and the use of crosswalks, a single database could be developed that provided access to the rich resources of these institutions with a minimum investment by the institutions. Heritage Colorado: Digital Treasures of the West, the union catalog of metadata linking to images, was one of the first Dublin Core databases to be created from a variety of formats, MARC and non-MARC.

The CDP successfully extended standard Dublin Core to meet its collaborative and digital resources needs while retaining the ability to map records to the Dublin Core standards. As the CDP worked with the University of Illinois, Urbana-Champaign staff on the Mellon Foundation's Open Archives Initiative project, this premise was tested. The University of Illinois staff decided to map the "Date: original" element into the "Date" element with the refinement "Created." They also successfully mapped the "Holding Institution" information into the "Publisher" element.

The CDP established a collaborative program that continues to build on the strengths of the individual participating institutions, leveraging their capabilities in a strategic partnership. One of the most successful initiatives was partnering with libraries to make their metadata and cataloging knowledge available to assist historical societies and museums. Museums provided the research and information content while libraries translated that data into the Dublin Core elements, a win-win situation for each institution. Most importantly, information seekers gained access to subject-rich materials previously unavailable to them online.

Museums and libraries further shared new approaches to information dissemination through the use of the web exhibition, the traditional model of museums. Based on the results of a study entitled "A Comparison of Web-Based Library Catalogs and Museum Exhibits and Their Impacts on Actual Visits: A Focus Group Evaluation for the Colorado Digitization Project," many users prefer the web exhibition as their initial introduction to a topic, with use of the database for in-depth research.[17]

Applying traditional library concepts, the CDP added new dimensions to accessing images through its union catalog. The program established pre-coordinated searches and browsing capabilities that greatly facilitated searching and information retrieval. In addition, pre-coordinated searches partially solved the problem of specialized subject terminology. The pre-coordinated search is illustrated in figure 2-2.

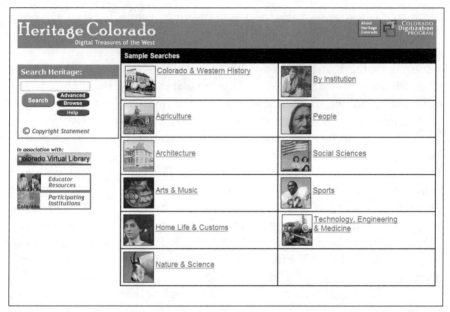

FIGURE 2-2   Heritage Colorado pre-coordinated search

For example, Heritage Colorado houses records for 6,000 fossils, of which table 2-6 is one example. A fossil museum generally uses genus and species to describe the fossils, while a small museum with few fossils may use the terms "plant fossil" or "animal fossil." In order for the user to retrieve a full range of specimens, the search for fossils was pre-coordinated for the general taxonomy, thus including a highly specialized collection with specialized headings where general subject headings are not used.

CHALLENGES

One of the major but unexpected challenges of the Colorado Digitization Program was the lack of cataloging expertise, a problem for all types and sizes of institutions, not just the small libraries and historical societies. The cataloger or metadata creator often did not know how to treat items within a collection, or when it was best to create a metadata record for the individual item rather than add a URL to a collection-level record. For example, the cataloger could create a separate metadata record for a col-

TABLE 2-6   Example of a museum record for a fossil

Title	Acer florissanti
Creator	
Contributor	
Link	http://planning.nps.gov/flfo/tax3_Detail.cfm?ID=13484004 [Access] [URI]
Publisher	Florissant Fossil Beds National Monument 2. National Park Service
Description	Plant (Angiosperm, Dicotyledon) Family: Aceraceae
Date Digital	2000
Subject(s)	Aceraceae - Colorado
	Angiosperms, Fossil - Colorado
	Dicotyledons, Fossil - Colorado
	Florissant (Colo.)
Type	1. image [DCMI Type Vocabulary]
	2. text [DCMI Type Vocabulary]
Source	National Museum of Natural History, Smithsonian Institution
	USNM-333761
Languages	eng [ISO 639-2]
Relation	MacGinitie, D.D., Fossil Plants of the Florissant Beds, Colorado, Carnegie
Format Use	1. image/jpeg [IMT] [medium]
	2. text/html [IMT] [medium]
Rights	National Museum of Natural History, Smithsonian Institution
Project	Florissant Fossil Beds National Monument

lection of photographs, and then create a "Relation" element title for each photograph within the collection. This approach became cumbersome for large collections, even when the individual items were linked via a collection title in the "Relation" element rather than a URL. The other option was a finding aids approach, but finding aids were not available for many of these collections and can be expensive to create. A similar granularity issue was encountered with photograph albums. Should the institution create a single metadata record for the album with no access to the unique photographs within the album, or should it provide item-level cataloging for the individual photographs in the album and consider the album a collection?

Few catalogers had experience analyzing and describing digital objects. Many had cataloged websites and electronic resources, but translating that knowledge to digital surrogates provided more of a challenge than initially anticipated. While the CDP strongly recommended providing separate metadata for the digital object, catalogers were struggling with whether they were really cataloging the original object or its digital surrogate, and whether it was best to have two records or one.

Traditional print catalogers were faced with objects that did not come with title pages, and they had to rely on outside research that could help describe objects. As a consequence, the quality of the metadata for these types of objects was totally dependent on the quality of the research conducted on the object. Consulting with curators, archivists, and sometimes volunteers working with the collections was frequently necessary to create the metadata, which significantly increased the time and the costs to create it. As a result, the majority of the Heritage Colorado records are based on legacy records that describe the original resource, with a URL that links to the digital resource. Even when creating new metadata, many institutions still opted to catalog the original object and merely add a few relevant elements describing the digital object, rather than create both a record for the digital object and the physical object, particularly when they had never cataloged the original item. In working with the museum and historical society community and their three-dimensional artifact collections, the CDP faced a challenge with the required "Title" element, because many three-dimensional artifacts do not have titles. While library cataloging rules provide directions to create a title where none exists, the museum community had no similar practice. When the CDP Metadata Working Group established the title as a mandatory element to enable a title keyword search, museums and historical societies struggled with the concept of creating descriptive titles for their objects. Museums with numbered fossil collections had to give serious consideration to what constituted the title. Was it the scientific name of the fossil along with the accession number, or just the accession number, which might be in their inventory control system? Was the title the term that was in the object name field in the collection management system?

Developing subject-rich descriptions to support keyword access was an additional challenge encountered by the CDP. Practitioners often lacked sufficient information about the digital resource, particularly photographs and three-dimensional artifacts. Experience showed that archives and museums often had more information on their collections than libraries, and therefore were able to create richer descriptions. In some cases, the descriptions were so detailed that they would include reference to the smallest bit of information in the photograph; for example, only a small portion of a car (a part of a front fender) would be visible in the photograph, but the metadata would include reference to the automobile. A search on "automobile" would retrieve that photograph, leaving the user with a potentially large number of marginally relevant results. The descriptions created by marketing staff frequently contained hyperbole and opinion rather than verified factual information. For instance, a man in a photograph was a "prominent businessman" with no detail on why he was prominent.

Because the CDP was an early adopter of Dublin Core, there was also a need for extensive training on the application of DC for digital objects. More surprisingly, there were training needs for MARC catalogers as well, since few libraries at that time had experience cataloging digital formats. Practitioners needed examples, particularly for the technical metadata, whether they were working in MARC or in Dublin Core. Some libraries produced multiple MARC 500 tagged notes, mixing the description of the digital object and the original object, creating problems for mapping.

As the CDP began crosswalking collections' records into DCBuilder, it became apparent that each institution's MARC records were also unique. Because the CDP was working in the early days of digital object description, technical information sometimes appeared in a local MARC field and sometimes in standard MARC fields. Libraries grappled with the problem of using MARC tags in an environment where the description of both originals and surrogates was accomplished on the same record. The project supported customization, so in theory any record could map to DC, but each institution had to complete its own crosswalk template, which required consultation with the CDP staff. Granularity was an issue in the "Format: creation" element, where technical metadata was stored. The individual components of the technical metadata were not parsed, so there was no way to distinguish between equipment and the characteristics of a file without developing an additional local set of refinements.

In order to accommodate Dublin Core, the CDP built its own data entry system and database, modifying and enhancing it over time. Commercial systems are now available, but are costly. In addition, most commercial systems are not optimized for collaborations between multiple cultural heritage institutions.

Interoperability remains a major issue for the future, since many individual institutions still do not consider issues of interoperability when making local decisions. If an institution established a note field (500 tag) that indicated, "Everything below this line pertains to the digital image," such a note caused problems for mapping, and thus interoperability. Another issue for interoperability was the handling of dates. Date ranges presented problems when transferring from Heritage Colorado to other systems because the representation and indexing of date ranges is notoriously difficult.

COMPROMISES

The Colorado Digitization Program is one of many statewide collaborative projects today. To achieve the goal of increasing access to the resources of Colorado's cultural heritage institutions, it was necessary to make some compromises in the area of metadata. The CDP began with the concept that through the process of creating Heritage Colorado, the CDP would be integrating metadata from institutions that used different standards and records which vary in quality, depth of description, and extensibility of description. Because the content of the records differed greatly from institution to institution, the challenges for the CDP were to minimize the differences in the standards among several institutions, develop tools for normalizing data as part of the preprocessing of data, and enrich the DC records with additional controlled vocabulary.

Issues of inclusion and exclusion of particular data elements pushed the CDP to compromise in order to ensure the fullest institutional participation. For example, concerns among museums, archives, and historical societies about the security of collections were a major and legitimate issue, particularly in the early years of the project. As a result of these concerns, the CDP recommended that donor, provenance, and physical location information be omitted from records in Heritage Colorado.

Heritage Colorado is a resource discovery tool, not a library catalog. To some the distinction may be subtle, but the differences are very real. Although some functions of a library catalog can not be supported by Heritage Colorado, in the end, the program created a greater "discovery" resource than had previously existed, a significant improvement over what was then available online. In the process, the CDP paved the way for many other projects featuring collaboration between libraries and cultural institutions.

LESSONS LEARNED

Given a similar collaborative environment today, the Colorado Digitization Program would change very little of its program and recommendations. There is still no compelling reason to require all institutions to use the same standard or the same software, or to create new records when legacy records exist, in order to meet discovery goals. Economic reality requires this level of flexibility.

Today the CDP would not have to create its own DCBuilder software, since there are commercial systems available that support the creation of Dublin Core records. However, the CDP probably would still be writing many of its own customized crosswalks, since no one crosswalk fits all files created by museums and libraries. One enhancement the CDP would consider is the establishment of a more formal mentoring program that would enhance quality and provide for education opportunities and an editorial review system for new projects. This additional step in the training process could have a positive impact on the quality of the database. In future, as the CDP migrates to a new database management system, it will also explore other avenues for improving quality control, perhaps using authority control systems and record validation techniques.

NOTES

1. Colorado Digitization Program, "Project Description," 1999, http://www
.cdpheritage.org/about/project_description.html (accessed 15 November 2003).
The first year the CDP operated under an LSTA grant from the Colorado State
Library. The purpose of the project was to create a cultural heritage collaborative
and to develop best practices for metadata, scanning, and legal issues. The project
was to obtain funding for subsequent years and also undertake a pilot project.
2. Colorado Digitization Program, "Project Toolbox," 1999, http://www.
cdpheritage.org/resource/toolbox/index.html (accessed 10 November 2003).
3. Heritage Colorado: Digital Treasures of the West (home page of Heritage
Colorado, the Colorado Digitization Program), http://www.cdpheritage.org/
heritage/index.html (accessed 15 November 2003).
4. American Library Association, *Anglo-American Cataloguing Rules,* 2d ed., 2002
revision (Chicago: Canadian Library Association; Chartered Institute of Library
and Information Professionals; American Library Association, 2002); Library of
Congress Cataloging Policy and Support Office, *Library of Congress Subject
Headings,* 25th ed. (Washington, D.C.: Cataloging Distribution Service, Library
of Congress, 2002); James R. Blackaby, *The Revised Nomenclature for Museum
Cataloging: A Revised and Expanded Version of Robert G. Chenhall's System
for Classifying Man-Made Objects* (Walnut Creek, Calif.: AltaMira, 1995).
5. Questor Systems, ARGUS Collections Management System, "Introduction to
ARGUS," 1999, http://www.questorsys.com/argusintro.htm (accessed 16
November 2003).

6. Dublin Core Metadata Initiative (home page), http://dublincore.org/ (accessed 16 November 2003); Visual Resources Association Data Standards Committee, "VRA Core Categories," version 3.0, http://www.vraweb.org/vracore3.htm (accessed 16 November 2003).

7. Colorado Digitization Program, Metadata Working Group, 1999, http://www .cdpheritage.org/about/committee/metadata/index.html (accessed 16 November 2003).

8. Tony Gill, Ann Gilliland-Swetland, and Murtha Baca, *Introduction to Metadata: Pathways to Digital Information* (Los Angeles: Getty Research Institute, 1998), also available at http://www.getty.edu/research/conducting_research/ standards/intrometadata (accessed 16 November 2003).

9. Colorado Digitization Program Metadata Working Group, "General Guidelines for Descriptive Metadata Creation and Entry," 1999, http://www.cdpheritage .org/resource/metadata/documents/CDP_Metadata_Guidelines_Elements.pdf (accessed 26 November 2003).

10. METS: Metadata Encoding and Transmission Standard (home page), http:// www.loc.gov/standards/mets/ (accessed 17 November 2003).

11. Colorado Digitization Program, "Western States Dublin Core Metadata Best Practices," version 1.2, January 2003, http://www.cdpheritage.org/ westerntrails/wt_bpmetadata.html (accessed 16 November 2003).

12. Rebecca Guenther, e-mail correspondence with the Colorado Digitization Project concerning the "date original" discussion by the DCMI Libraries Working Group, 21 August 2000.

13. The Colorado State Library held a license to OCLC's SiteSearch software, so the Colorado Digitization Project used it to support a union catalog of metadata.

14. Dublin Core Builder (DCBuilder) is a DC form-based application that the CDP developed in 2000. It uses MySQL, an open-source relational database, as well as Macromedia's ColdFusion. See MySQL, "About MySQL AB," 2003, http://www.mysql.com/company/index.html (accessed 17 November 2003); Macromedia (home page), http://www.macromedia.com/ (accessed 17 November 2003).

15. Colorado Alliance of Research Libraries, "Colorado Terms," 2000, http:// babu.coalliance.org:10101/ (accessed 16 November 2003).

16. Colorado Alliance of Research Libraries, "Prospector: The Colorado Unified Catalog," 2003, http://prospector.coalliance.org/ (accessed 16 November 2003).

17. Thomas K. Fry et al., "A Comparison of Web-Based Library Catalogs and Museum Exhibits and Their Impacts on Actual Visits: A Focus Group Evaluation for the Colorado Digitization Project," 2001, http://www .cdpheritage.org/resource/reports/cdp_report_lrs.pdf (accessed 17 November 2003).

3 Museums and Metadata: A Shifting Paradigm

Angela Spinazzè

FOR DECADES, DIGITAL solutions have been used in museums to mimic centuries-old paper-based practices designed to document and manage institutional information and memory. Metadata has played a key role in both the analog predecessors and the current digital instantiations of these systems. The original systems, which frequently relied on beautifully bound ledgers and exacting penmanship, focused on questions that are at the heart of collections management, such as who made or discovered it? For whom was it made? What was it used for? Where did it come from? Where is it now? Why was it made? When was it discovered? When was it created? How did it get here? Collecting and organizing information in this way allowed the keeper of the collections to ask basic questions and to find answers quickly.

Today the frame of reference is different. Metadata is no longer taken for granted as a benign characteristic of collections documentation and management activities. Instead, it has been elevated to center stage as an important tool touching all aspects of museum practice. Museums use metadata to describe collections and individual artifacts, to assist teachers with their use of collections for educational purposes, to conserve and preserve digital assets, to provide online experiences, and much more. One of the most discernible effects of this elevated status is the museum paradigm shift from inward-gazing institutions that focused almost exclusively on scholarly research and preservation to outward-projecting organizations that serve a wide range of specialized audiences. Museums are communicating with more audiences than ever before, and metadata is helping to support this effort.

Metadata in practice helps museums do the following:

create a sense of community

demonstrate the importance of documentation

expose the complex nature of museum activities such as collection, curatorial, educational, service, and support activities

raise standards for professional practice and encourage higher levels of performance

broaden the scope of professionals in the field

open doors to diversity of perspective and opportunities for educational experiences outside of the traditional exhibition/publication paradigm

challenge traditional roles and responsibilities within the museum

occupy a different space in society, i.e., become more important elements of everyday life

In this chapter we will explore the shifting paradigm between museums and their use of metadata in three ways. First, we will take a step back to look at some of the initial uses of metadata in museums. Second, we will explore how those initial practices were codified through standards development and community collaboration. Finally, we will examine where we are today and what that means for the future.

A NASCENT PRACTICE: DOCUMENTATION AND PROCESS

The introduction of information technology into museums was the result of collections managers and registrars looking for ways to improve paper-based systems, bring together disparate data components as information, and streamline procedures for managing museum collections. Some of the first fruitful forays into metadata "best practice" in museums focused on documentation and procedural standards. In a brochure first printed by the Getty Art History Information Program (AHIP) in 1993, and now available through the CIDOC website, four main types of standards are described: information system, data, procedural, and information interchange. The definitions of these standard types, included here, provide insight into the priorities for professionals working, for the first time, with information systems rather than ledger books or catalog cards.[1]

1. *Information system standards* define the functional components of the information system as a whole. For a museum, these might be the requirements for separate facilities in cataloging and collections management, membership, administration, finance, and publishing.

2. *Data standards* define the structure, content, and values comprised in collections information. *Data structure* concerns what constitutes a record, such as the different fields used to record information and their relationships. *Data content* relates to the rules and conventions governing how data are entered into fields, including cataloging rules and syntax conventions. *Data value* has to do with the vocabulary used in the various fields and the specifications for individual character sets.

3. *Procedural standards* define the scope of the documentation procedures needed to manage operations effectively. Examples include rules for logging on and off an electronic mail system, or policies governing an institution's acquisition or loan procedures.

4. *Information interchange* standards define the technical framework for exchanging information, whether between systems in a single institution or among systems in multiple institutions. Examples of interchange formats include ISO 8879, Standard Generalized Markup Language (SGML); ISO 2709, originally developed to support the exchange of bibliographic information; and ISO 9735, Electronic Data Interchange for Administration, Commerce, and Transport (EDIFACT), all developed by the International Organization for Standardization (ISO).

The emphasis on system, data, process, and interchange reflects the concerns of those early adopters as well as their practical needs. These definitions were the start of community-wide efforts toward standardization that are still being forged today. Data structure and procedural and information interchange standards have been codified through several initiatives over the past ten years. Three of them are described here.

In 1991 the mda, a British organization devoted to supporting the management and use of museum collections, began work on the first version of SPECTRUM, its documentation standard.[2] The standard was the result of contributions by more than 100 practitioners working in a variety of cultural settings. In addition, SPECTRUM was designed to articulate the common functions across museums as well as to document the process and information needs associated with those functions. By documenting the workflow and metadata elements commonly used by museum professionals, a standardization of approach would eventually lead to coordinated efforts to share like information. SPECTRUM describes twenty museum procedures associated with collections management, ranging from acquiring and deaccessing collections to procedures associated with loans, insurance, and audits. The units of information are organized around the procedures and reflect the lowest common denominator in terms of data and metadata requirements, an approach designed to make information interchange less arduous. The SPECTRUM standard became a benchmark, first in the United Kingdom and then internationally, against which automated versions of collection management systems were initially tested. The second version of the standard came out in 1997. Today it exists in both book and interactive digital formats, and the third version is currently in the works.

From 1992 through 1996, CIDOC Working Groups published a flurry of documents focused on metadata issues in museums.[3] Among them were descriptive data standards for fine art objects, archaeological artifacts, sites and monuments, ethnology and ethnography, a relational data model, and a directory of thesauri for object names. These documents reflected the community's need to understand and agree on how to describe objects and artifacts and the geographic locations they come from or were found in, as well as how to structure that information in a way that would allow it to be electronically exchanged with one or more institutions. An initial articulation of metadata basics currently known as the cornerstones of metadata practice, structure, syntax, and semantics, was a by-product of this effort.

During this same time, the Consortium for the Computer Interchange of Museum Information (CIMI) Standards Framework sought to articulate a technical framework for the electronic exchange of museum information.[4] The framework was conceived of as a road map to bring together the use, or purpose, of an information exchange with its technical and content requirements. The result provided a means through which individual museums could benefit from existing technical standards based on their specific information interchange needs. The document addressed the needs of museums engaged in the planning, acquisition, and implementation of information systems; of application developers and network service providers engaged in the design and development of systems and services; and of museum professionals engaged in professional development and collaborative information exchange activities.

The emphasis on standardization of approach and the realities of meeting needs with practical solutions meant that metadata was a key component of successful documentation and electronic information exchange from the start. Museums went through the same process as libraries, with automated systems replacing their catalog card and ledger book predecessors. The growth of task-oriented metadata was a natural outcome of a focus on practical requirements and basic procedural improvements.

THE GAZE SHIFTS FROM INSIDE TO OUT

As more and more museums implemented first-generation collections management software applications, new opportunities for metadata emerged. The gaze began to shift outward, away from the day-to-day activities of the registrar and collection manager's offices to other areas of the museum. Museum websites with online exhibitions and collection highlights started to emerge as a new communications mechanism connecting museums with new audiences. Curatorial departments were called on to begin using internal systems for collection cataloging to feed the websites. And in-house digitization projects began in earnest so that objects highlighted on the website could be accompanied by both a textual description and an image. Online exhibitions also spawned new collaborative projects bringing together objects from different departments within a single institution or from several museums. This shifting gaze, and the projects that followed, resulted in a practical demonstration of return on investment for those initial information systems, and also exposed new metadata requirements.

In 1995 CIMI embarked on a demonstration project it called CHIO, Cultural Heritage Information Online.[5] CHIO had two goals. The first goal was to build a useful multidisciplinary information resource and make it available on the Web. The second goal was to demonstrate the feasibility of a standards-based approach to searching and retrieving the information held in the online resource. The third, unstated, goal of the project was to demonstrate that museums, libraries, and archives could join together in offering access to their collection information.

The data model was designed from the point of view of the online resource's user. This approach reflected the museum community's comfort in addressing visitor needs in the galleries, as well as the cross-disciplinary approach of the project, with the participation of librarians and archivists in addition to museum professionals. Working with approximately 1,500 questions that visitors ask of museums, culled from two independent projects, the data model was the result of an analysis of the content of the questions as well as the likely responses to those questions. A set of commonly occurring data groups emerged from the content analysis that represent the most commonly requested attributes of the objects held in the collections.[6] The analysis also revealed that while visitors most often requested a single data group in their questions (People, for example), some common pairings of more specific details—such as the role the person played, Creator, with the name given to identify the object created, Title—were also common occurrences.[7]

One quickly realizes that these data groups, derived from questions asked by visitors to physical museums, reveal a bias toward a fine art view of objects. There is an absence, for example, of data groups based on archaeological or ethnographic investigations into use (what was it used for?) and cultural identity (who used it?). Regardless of this fine art focus, the project proved to be a test case for the use of two highly popular technologies of the time, SGML and Z39.50, across disciplinary lines. In addition, the access points served as a test case for the reuse of descriptive content traditionally presented in a gallery setting. The results demonstrated that a database of heterogeneous object records, organized around a metadata schema derived from visitor requirements, could successfully be presented online to provide an alternative visitor experience. This was an important project in many respects. First, the data model marked a turning point in its approach to presenting museum information. For the first time, the visitor was part of the equation. Second, the same descriptive metadata routinely captured and cataloged by curators for use in museum galleries found an additional use in the online environment. And third, technologies already proven to be successful in the library community could be incorporated into museums.

The collaborative nature of a library network is similarly reflected in the collaboration of museum collection managers and registrars to organize large traveling exhibitions. It takes a distributed group of professionals working together to coordinate the exhibition and manage all of its

components. There is a natural fit here for a distributed information network reliant on process-based metadata. The technological approach to Project CHIO might have set the stage for this type of network; however, several factors prevented a move toward the implementation of Z39.50 and SGML on a broad scale. While many large museums might have been in a position to afford the introduction of this technology at the time, the technology was not well understood, and museums did not have the technical staff to support it.

As the focus shifted outward to the presentation of scholarly information to a World Wide Web audience, other museum stakeholders were welcomed into the information technology equation, but not in a way that decreased workload or made work easier. The efficiencies of scale worked in the opposite direction in this case. The traditional home for cataloging and scholarship activities resides in the curatorial departments of museums. At issue was not that these staff members were being included in the process of using and creating metadata, but that the systems they were being asked to use were not designed or based on curatorial practice. These systems did not reflect curatorial working methods or vocabulary, and were based on an assumption that the metadata being created for curatorial purposes would be automatically transferable to an online audience. To these curators, the idea of exposing information maintained for a select set of eyes to the world was unthinkable. This reaction reflects a core value of the role of the museum as interpreter of artifacts, as well as the recognition that one interpretation does not serve all audiences.

A dilemma was revealed: on the one hand, new technologies offered advantages to streamlining internal management activities; on the other hand, implementing these technologies meant more and different work for staff involved with interpretation activities and content development. Metadata was at the center of the discussion. Who would create the metadata? Who would maintain the metadata? What about vocabulary? How would creation and dissemination be coordinated when these activities were handled with different processes and procedures? Fortunately, the vocabulary standards developed by groups like CIDOC and the Getty AHIP were already available for use, and led to the early adoption of controlled vocabularies such as the Art and Architecture Thesaurus and the Categories for the Description of Works of Art (CDWA). Data models and application profiles were being developed as well, and the Standards Framework was a means through which to understand how to apply and use them. The biggest remaining challenge is the internal change from legacy to new methods for capturing, organizing, and sharing metadata. As a result, for the average museum visitor, in-person or online, the volume of information offered at any given time remains small compared to what remains hidden in file cabinets, storage vaults, and the knowledge banks of the museum specialists.

METADATA IN OVERDRIVE

The surge in importance of metadata to museums and museum professionals has been deeply felt in recent years as collaborative projects have brought museums and their sister cultural organizations together toward common goals. Metadata element sets, the schemas used to express them, and meta-centers grew quickly throughout the museum community from approximately 1997 to 2000.

National initiatives, such as those undertaken by the Canadian Heritage Information Network (CHIN) in 1998 and Australian Museums and Galleries On-Line (AMOL) in 1999, provided museums with a new method for including their collections information in a collaborative service that offered Internet visitors a single point of access to distributed resources.[8] Neimanis and Geber, the designers of the CHIN initiative, described this as a "meta-center":

> Theoretically, an information Meta-Center is the integrated state of the accessible or available information. It is not a centralized collection of information but a series of relationships established among multiple information resources. It involves managing the process of communication or relationships among the components and constantly re-building the network of connections. It is intimately linked to a group of resources, in close and continuous communication, and it classifies the similarities and differences among them. Thus, through a cumulative process of experience, the Meta-Center has the potential to build up a more complete knowledge of the information environment, acting as a specialized gateway or access agent.[9]

The CHIN initiative attempted to integrate heterogeneous data sets and was among the first of the national websites to do so. It has evolved into the present-day Virtual Museum of Canada, a gateway to distributed resources held in museums across Canada that includes virtual exhibits, an image gallery, a teachers' center, a listing of museum events, an online store, and a "make your own" virtual museum experience. The AMOL initiative also had the integration of heterogeneous data sets among its original goals. From the start, what set the AMOL initiative apart was its focus on the professionals working in museums, their contributions to the process of content creation, and their importance to the success of the network. In essence, the AMOL portal fostered a virtual community and spawned a new means for collaboration among professionals.[10]

Both of these organizations contributed metadata from their national initiatives to an international metadata project, the CIMI Dublin Core Test Bed.[11] With the Dublin Core Metadata Element Set in the throes of being defined, CIMI members spent two years working with the developing standard, participated on its committees, and built a database of Dublin Core (DC) records that came from existing museum databases and represented art, cultural/historical, and natural science collections. In addition, the group made a crosswalk between the DC element and a variety of existing museum element sets used for much more detailed cataloging activities. This crosswalk exercise was important for two key reasons. First, it demonstrated how the DC element set could be used as a metaset, acting as a layer between the free-form Internet search and the detailed, fielded search provided by museums as the entry point into online, structured content hidden from those search engines. Second, the crosswalk made a subset of information that could be derived from existing information visible. In other words, it clarified that metadata could be derived from existing content and used to provide new ways of accessing more complex content. Other Test Bed results included a Guide to Best Practice that included interpretations of the elements and the working definitions from the perspective of museum professionals using examples taken from existing museum records, and a workshop about the DC and its potential for use by museums.[12]

The Test Bed not only proved useful in articulating how schemas can be combined to produce more complex methods for search and retrieval, but also made very clear the complexity of museum metadata requirements. In an effort to diagram the landscape of these increasingly complex requirements and relationships, the CIDOC Documentation Standards Working Group decided to reinterpret its data model. In 1999 a special interest group was formed to update the model originally published in 1994. Referred to now as the CIDOC Conceptual Reference Model (CRM), the CIDOC CRM provides definitions and a formal structure for describing concepts and relationships used in the broadest range of museum documentation activities. The model was derived through a process that examined the majority of extant metadata schemas currently in use in museums and the associated concepts, entity relationships, and metadata requirements defined by them. The model has been tested by an independent research group to determine its ability to enable interoperability between communities and is currently an International Organization for Standardization Committee Draft.[13]

In this second phase of the museum and metadata paradigm, several key advances have been made. First, the conceptual framework has been defined and serves to expose the complex nature of museum activities and their associated metadata needs. Second, the scope of museum professionals involved in metadata creation and management has expanded. Museums are now participating in metadata efforts related to education, collection-level descriptions, rights and reproductions, digitization of photographic assets and their born-digital counterparts, learning objects, biodiversity, preservation, conservation, distributed search and retrieval, ontological issues, virtual environment reconstructions, and much more. Third, the importance of documentation has been underscored. And last, but by no means least, some of the traditional roles and responsibilities of museums with regard to the communities and audiences they serve are starting to be challenged.

METADATA COMES OF AGE

As the twenty-first century unfolds, the metadata and museum paradigm is beginning to come of age. The focus now is on skills and professional development, with an increased openness to more broadly based cultural heritage conversations and intradisciplinary projects. There is also a feeling of coming full circle, as many of the standards first agreed to in the 1980s and 1990s are being revisited, rewritten, and reengineered. Four examples are included here.

The European Museum's Information Institute (EMII) is a virtual network of cultural organizations across Europe that began working together in 1999.[14] In March 2002, EMII began work on its Distributed Content Framework. A reflection of CIMI's Standards Framework can be found in this effort "to promote the exchange of best practice and the effective use of standards in information management."[15] What makes this initiative unique is its investigations into both the technical and legal standards associated with online environments and museum content.

The meta-centers of old still exist, but priorities for national standards organizations have shifted from outreach and new audiences to training for museum professionals. The CHIN website, for example, now focuses on professional development. The Virtual Museum of Canada is still there, but it is now secondary to the website's use as a resource for museum professionals in Canada. Intradisciplinary projects are now focused on ways to provide access to important museum content without imposing additional burdens on institutions working with decreased budgets and staff resources. BioCASE, A Biodiversity Collection Access Service for Europe, aims to enhance the overall value of biological collections through the cooperative development of collection-level descriptions, thesauri, and information flow between European natural history organizations.[16] Through the use of a common approach to collection-level description metadata, this network of institutions hopes to make it easier to identify collections that contain similar materials, as well as to provide access to those larger data sets for more focused research on taxonomy, geography, and timeline issues as they pertain to the natural sciences.

Old user models and application profiles continue to be rewritten. Members of CIMI, in concert with the mda, have authored an XML Schema based on the SPECTRUM documentation standard and have made it available for use by museums and other interested organizations.[17] The goal was to explore use of the schema as a bridge to other applications, as the documentation standard undergoes an update.

Today's museums are increasingly under pressure to cut costs as endowments, private contributions, and public funds decrease. Despite this decrease in funds, expectations of service continue to rise. Metadata has become even more important to the work of museum professionals, but there are not enough professionals with the necessary skills to produce all of the content, interpret it for all audiences, and preserve it for the future.

WHERE EXACTLY DO WE STAND?

Despite all of the progress we have made, several key stumbling blocks remain on the road of progress. The skills gap for museum professionals continues to widen, and one of several significant side effects is the misuse of standards. One example of this is Dublin Core. This standard seemed to possess much potential as an initial access point into the mass quantities of metadata held by museums. It serves as the second step in information access, the one that comes after a generic search engine search, leading the visitor on to a more complex resource cataloged using discipline-specific standards. However, Dublin Core lacks the capacity to adequately handle museum-specific standard data, and continues to be misused as a sole element set by many institutions, resulting in page upon page of undifferentiated inventory-style records being made available online.

It is also clear that the virtual environments, three-dimensional images, and digital sounds and simulations used to explain, dissect, and transform are all at risk of being trapped within the technologies used to create them. Without metadata capture occurring at each critical juncture along the creative pathway, the work we have done to date will not matter in the future because it may well be lost. This is already happening with metadata stored in software applications that no longer exist or are no longer compatible with newer hardware devices.

In addition to the substantial preservation issues we face, there are other obstacles that need to be overcome. For example, flexible (meaning personalized and customizable) access to collections information continues to elude most cultural institutions, including museums. This is due, in large part, to the need for more and different content than that which is currently available. Content creation still requires human interaction with the artifact, object, or specimen, and from experience we have learned that content created in one context is not automatically applicable in another context.

One of the most difficult obstacles to overcome is that the software applications first designed for collections managers and registrars several decades ago are already past their useful lives. New approaches to automated content capture, creation, and reuse cannot be fully realized, in large part, because the systems designed to house the information are not adaptable to new methods. Despite the cost of change, the time has come to reflect on lessons learned and redesign these tools.

We also need to approach metadata use in a more informed way, based on user needs rather than ease of reuse. The museum and metadata paradigm continues to shift, but unless we revisit some of our initial assumptions, bring the user back into the equation, and contribute to changes in our methods and tools, we will continue on the metadata treadmill.

NOTES

1. The Getty Art History Information Program was an initiative on the part of the J. Paul Getty Trust to use information technology to improve access to art and humanities information for research and education. In 1996 it was renamed the Getty Information Institute, and it has since been subsumed into the Getty Research Institute. Information on it is available at http://www.getty.edu/research/ (accessed 25 November 2003). Publications of the International Committee for Documentation of the International Council of Museums (ICOM-CIDOC) are available at http://www.willpowerinfo.myby.co.uk/cidoc/pub1.htm (accessed 2 December 2003). See also International Committee for Documentation of the International Council of Museums (ICOM-CIDOC), "Museum Information Standards," http://www.willpowerinfo.myby.co.uk/cidoc/stand0.htm (accessed 2 December 2003).
2. mda, "SPECTRUM Interactive," http://www.mda.org.uk/specint.htm (accessed 2 December 2003).
3. International Committee for Documentation of the International Council of Museums (ICOM-CIDOC) Working Groups, http://www.willpowerinfo.myby.co.uk/cidoc/wg1.htm (accessed 2 December 2003).
4. Consortium for the Computer Interchange of Museum Information, *Standards Framework for the Computer Interchange of Museum Information,* 1st ed. (Ottawa, Ont.: Museum Computer Network, 1993), also available at http://www.cni.org/pub/CIMI/framework.html (accessed 25 November 2003).
5. Consortium for the Computer Interchange of Museum Information Profile Development Working Group, "The CIMI Profile: Z39.50 Application Profile Specifications for Use in Project CHIO," draft version 3, 1996, http://www.loc.gov/z3950/agency/profiles/cimi2.html (accessed 25 November 2003).
6. The Project CHIO logical data groups, also called access points, were identified as Style and Movement, Time-Span, Material, Method (process and technique), Mark, Award, Event, History of Ownership, People (person, group), Role, Occupation, Place (location, address, geopolitical), Opus (form of expression), Object, Collection, Resource, Classification, Concept, Subject, and Bibliography.
7. Project CHIO's most commonly requested element pairs were Creator/Title, Subject/Date, Classification/Date, Material/Object/Style, Subject/Place, Object/Place, and Classification/Style.
8. Canadian Heritage Information Network (home page), http://www.chin.gc.ca/ (accessed 25 November 2003); Australian Museums and Galleries On-line (home page), http://www.amol.org.au/ (accessed 25 November 2003).
9. K. Neimanis and E. Geber, "'Come and Get It' to 'Seek and You Shall Find': Transition from a Central Resource to Information Meta-Center," in *Museums*

and the Web Proceedings, ed. D. Bearman and J. Trant (Archives and Museum Informatics, 1998), CD-ROM.

10. S. Kenderdine, "Inside the Meta-Center: A Cabinet of Wonder," in *Museums and the Web Proceedings,* ed. D. Bearman and J. Trant (Archives and Museum Informatics, 1999), CD-ROM.

11. A. Spinazzè, "Finding Museum Information in the Internet Commons: A Report on the CIMI Dublin Core Metadata Testbed Project," in *International Cultural Heritage Informatics Meeting Proceedings,* ed. D. Bearman and J. Trant (Archives and Museum Informatics, 1999).

12. A. Spinazzè, "Collaboration, Consensus and Community: CIMI, Museums and the Dublin Core," *Cultivate Interactive* 1 (3 July 2000), http://www.cultivate-int.org/issue1/cimi/; International Council of Museums, "CIDOC Conceptual Reference Model," http://cidoc.ics.forth.gr/index.html (accessed 25 November 2003).

13. Cultural Heritage Interchange Ontology Standardization (CHIOS), the expanded name of the CIDOC Conceptual Reference Model, is currently being elaborated by the International Organization for Standardization as Committee Draft ISO/CD 21127, http://cidoc.ics.forth.gr/chios_iso.html (accessed 25 November 2003).

14. Members of the European Museums' Information Institute (EMII) network include the Royal Museum of Fine Arts in Belgium, National Cultural Heritage Agency in Denmark, National Board of Antiquities in Finland, Direction of Museums of France, Institute of Museum Studies in Germany, Hellenic Ministry of Culture in Greece, National Museum of Iceland, Portuguese Institute of Museums, Swedish National Council for Cultural Affairs, and the mda in the United Kingdom. Information on the EMII is available at http://www.emii.org/ (accessed 25 November 2003).

15. The EMII Distributed Content Framework Project (EMII-DCF) was funded by the European Commission's Information Society Technologies program of work and was coordinated by the mda based in the United Kingdom. The project ran from March 2002 to November 2003. Information on it is available at http://www .emii.org/dcf.htm (accessed 25 November 2003).

16. BioCASE: A Biodiversity Collection Access Service for Europe (home page), http://www.biocase.org/default.shtml (accessed 5 November 2003).

17. Consortium for the Computer Interchange of Museum Information, XML SPECTRUM Schema Working Group (home page), http://www.cimi.org/wg/ xml_spectrum/index.html (accessed 25 November 2003).

4   The Eye of the Beholder: Challenges of Image Description and Access at Harvard

Robin Wendler

IMAGES PRESENT A different descriptive challenge than mass-produced published works such as books and serials. Many, if not most, images are unpublished and unique. They almost always lack the intrinsic metadata on which mainstream cataloging codes rely, e.g., title pages, other "chief sources" of information, or imprints. In consequence, the description of images is inherently subjective. How they are described is determined by the context in which they are held and the qualities of the image which are valuable in that context. A theology department might describe a given painting in terms of Saint Anthony, while an agricultural museum might describe the same painting in terms of Saint Anthony's pig.

While traditional library collections, largely driven by the desire to share catalog records, have greatly benefited from decades of national and international metadata standards development, visual resources collections have not. In most visual collections, the needs to be met by cataloging were deemed to be local, and the application of cataloging standards was viewed as an intrusion on local autonomy, a burden with no compensating benefits. No infrastructure such as the OCLC or RLIN bibliographic utilities grew up to support cross-institutional cooperation. Typically, each visual resource collection has stood alone.[1]

THE BIRTH OF VISUAL IMAGE ACCESS

Within Harvard University, visual resources reside in dozens of independent organizations with a range of missions that represent varying philosophies of selection, organization, and research methodology. Visual resources are held in museums, mainstream library collections, dedicated slide and photograph libraries, archives and special collections, academic departments and laboratories, administrative units such as real estate and buildings and grounds, and in public relations and news offices. Historically, these organizations have had little or no contact with each other and have described their collections according to local dictates. Most use locally defined data structures, data elements, classification schemes, and vocabularies—some of which represent the accumulation of more than a century's worth of politics and curatorial personalities.

After a University Library Council-sponsored survey of image collections at Harvard in 1997 identified between eight and ten million images in units across the university, creating a public union catalog for a meaningful set of these materials became a priority.[2] Several factors contributed to this decision:

> At that time, none of the units provided public online access to their catalogs of images and few had the technological resources to do so. A centrally supported system was their best hope for sharing their information beyond their own walls. Central support was not likely to be offered to create separate systems tailored to different collections.
>
> A union catalog, rather than a system in which many separate collections had individual catalogs, was seen as making image discovery easier in a highly decentralized environment.
>
> Fostering interdisciplinary scholarship had become a university priority, and teaching with images was on the rise beyond the traditional bastions of art and architecture. Providing integrated access to images across disciplines would support such teaching and research.

The University Library Council created a suite of working groups, drawn not only from libraries but also from archives, museums, and other types of repositories, to coordinate with the Harvard University Library Office for Information Systems on the development of the union catalog. For the initial project, the groups selected departments that already had part of their metadata in digital form and were eager to participate. The Fine Arts Library and the Harvard Design School Library were already collaborating on a staff-only system for tracking their image collections. The Harvard University Art Museums had metadata in a collection management system, as did the Peabody Museum of Archaeology and Anthropology. This core group of art, architecture, and anthropology collections was joined by the Schlesinger Library on the History of Women in America, which had cataloged thousands of photographs from its archival collections into a local database. The inclusion of the Schlesinger archival images was central to determining the scope of what would become the new Visual Image Access (VIA) catalog.[3]

There were a number of givens in this project. First, Harvard is a microcosm of the larger community in the sense that no person or body can dictate practice throughout Harvard, nor can participation in any initiative be coerced. Every cooperative effort within the institution is the result of consensus building and compromise. Second, the metadata to be presented in the shared catalog would, for the near future, be drawn from so-called legacy metadata, that is, metadata already in existence. Therefore, compatibility could not be achieved by constructing metadata explicitly for this purpose according to a common set of rules. Third, the catalog would not be limited to those visual resources for which digital images were available. In fact, the majority of resources will not have digital images for the foreseeable future. This sets VIA apart from many otherwise comparable projects and determines to some extent the way the interface is designed. Finally, VIA was to be a catalog only, that is, there would be no online input component. Metadata creation and maintenance happen in other systems, which feed into VIA.

Within these constraints there were still details to work out, many of which required us to weigh differences between equally valid perspectives. These perspectives were born of divergent descriptive traditions far more than of any actual differences in the material being described. The most significant discrepancies were in data structure, data elements, and how data content was formulated.

Critical requirements in phase 1 of VIA included the following:

> to make the metadata from different repositories physically compatible;
>
> to represent the metadata accurately and effectively; and
>
> to provide an environment in which participants can see how their metadata interact, and then subsequently work toward greater agreement on the form and content of the metadata.

Descriptive Approaches

One of the first questions when designing a new catalog for a collection is: what is the unit of description? In other words, what is being cataloged? The answer, in the absence of community rules, depends on how the materials are expected to be used. For one collection of nineteenth-century watercolors of taxonomic specimens, there are several possible units of description:

> the piece of paper, which could contain one or more watercolors of one or more specimens;
>
> a specimen, which might be represented by multiple watercolors on one or more pieces of paper; or
>
> an individual watercolor, one of several on a sheet.

There is no objectively correct choice. The decision will be based on local and community expectations and norms. In designing a union catalog, the question becomes whether multiple approaches can be accommodated, and which ones. Metadata from the initial VIA contributors reflected three fundamentally different descriptive techniques.

Until the proliferation of electronic materials, libraries using the Anglo-American Cataloguing Rules (AACR2) knew what they were describing: they cataloged the item in hand. For a photograph, this means that the photographer, the date the photograph was taken, the photographic technique, and so on are primary characteristics.[4] The content of the photograph would be represented in subject headings, as in figure 4-1.[5]

While some image collections are focused on the item in hand, in many contexts photographs simply stand in for objects of study that are physically remote or otherwise unavailable to be viewed directly. In these cases, the characteristics of the photograph itself—such as who took it and when—are of decidedly secondary importance. The central unit of description in these collections is not the physical photograph or slide, but the object or place it illustrates. Figure 4-2 is an example of this.

In contrast, archives often describe a conceptual unit rather than a physical one, for example, a folder of material on a specific topic or one generated as the result of a particular event, with only minimal information about each component piece. (See figures 4-3A and 4-3B.) While the unit of description varies, all of these examples use textual metadata in comparable elements such as title, work type, creator, date, materials/techniques, and topic.

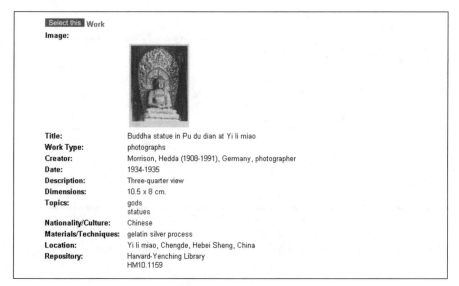

Select this **Work**
Image:

Title:	Buddha statue in Pu du dian at Yi li miao
Work Type:	photographs
Creator:	Morrison, Hedda (1908-1991), Germany, photographer
Date:	1934-1935
Description:	Three-quarter view
Dimensions:	10.5 x 8 cm.
Topics:	gods
	statues
Nationality/Culture:	Chinese
Materials/Techniques:	gelatin silver process
Location:	Yi li miao, Chengde, Hebei Sheng, China
Repository:	Harvard-Yenching Library
	HM10.1159

FIGURE 4-1   Metadata describing a photograph

Select this **Work**
Image:

Title:	Standing Buddha with Hands Clasped
Work Type:	Sculpture
Production:	China
Date:	mid 6th century
Dimensions:	84.0 cm x 27.0 cm x 12.0 cm
	sight
Style:	Eastern Wei (534-550) to Northern Qi (550-577) dynasty
Nationality/Culture:	Chinese
Materials/Techniques:	Stone with traces of polychromy; from Tianlongshan(?), Shanxi province
Notes:	Bequest of Grenville L. Winthrop
Repository:	Arthur M. Sackler Museum, Harvard University Art Museums
	1943.53.33

FIGURE 4-2   Metadata describing an object

Select this Group

Title:	Eleven views of Japanese sculpture, temples, and gardens taken during Esther Peterson's visit to Japan.
Work Type:	non-projected color photograph
Production:	Japan, Asia
Date:	1981 Nov
Description:	11 non-projected color photographs
Topics:	Voyages and travels
	Art
	Sculpture
	Buddhist art and symbolism
	Temples, Buddhist
	Decoration and ornament, Architectural
	Gardens
	Statues
	Shinto shrines
Materials/Techniques:	Chromogenic color prints
Item ID:	HOLLIS collection-level record: ADA0046
Repository:	Schlesinger Library on the History of Women in America, Radcliffe Institute
Related Work:	Is part of the Esther Peterson Papers, 1884-1998 (inclusive), 1929-1998 (bulk). Folder: 1981-94: Correspondence. Alphabetical file: Japan, 1981: Photographs of EP, granddaughter, and others..

FIGURE 4-3A   Aggregate metadata for a group of photographs taken in a particular context

Select this Work 2

Image:

Creator:	unknown
Dimensions:	3.375x3.5 inches
Repository:	Schlesinger Library on the History of Women in America, Radcliffe Institute
	Photonumber: MC450-2098-36
Copyright:	http://www.radcliffe.edu/schles/libcolls/Photo/viacpyrt.htm

FIGURE 4-3B   Brief metadata for a single photograph from the group

A Word about Surrogates

The bulk of VIA's content comes from museums and study collections of art and architecture images. A single object or site may be represented by many images. Think of the *Mona Lisa* itself and imagine a set of images of the *Mona Lisa:* a full image, details of her nose, her smile, an infrared image, an X-ray. Such images are often referred to as surrogates. The descriptions of each surrogate must be associated with a description of the original object itself. (See figure 4-4.) At Harvard, the ability to group multiple surrogates under a single common description was deemed critical for a visual resource union catalog.

Select this Work
Title: Standing Buddha
Work Type: sculpture
Date: N. Ch'i
Description: Excavated in October, 1996.
Dimensions: H: 115 cm
Personal name: Buddha (n.d.), India, subject
Style: Northern Qi
Nationality/Culture: Chinese
Materials/Techniques: limestone
                       color
                       gilding
Location: find spot; Ruins of Lung-hsing Temple, Ch'ing-chou, Shan-tung, China
Classification: Harvard Fine Arts Library, Visual Collections - Slides and Digital Images; 1302Z1881 L95 Fu05 221(m)
Repository: Municipal Museum, Ch'ing-chou, Shan-tung, China

Select this Surrogate
Image:

Title: Front view
Work Type: color slide
Classification: 1302Z1881 L95 Fu05 221(m)
Repository: Harvard Fine Arts Library, Visual Collections - Slides and Digital Images
                       2002.22077

Select this Surrogate
Image:

Title: Rubbing taken from the front of the statue
Work Type: color slide
Classification: 1302Z1881 L95 Fu05 221(m)
Repository: Harvard Fine Arts Library, Visual Collections - Slides and Digital Images
                       2002.22078

Select this Surrogate
Image:

Title: Det: Buddha's left side
Work Type: color slide
Classification: 1302Z1881 L95 Fu05 221(m)
Repository: Harvard Fine Arts Library, Visual Collections - Slides and Digital Images
                       2002.22079

FIGURE 4-4   Metadata for a work and multiple surrogates

To complicate matters, however, an image originally created as a surrogate may come to be valued as a work itself over time. Perhaps the photographer becomes famous, the image becomes recognized for aesthetic qualities, or the form of photography becomes exotic. Conversely, an original artwork may be viewed in a particular context as a surrogate. For example, an etching by Piranesi would usually be cataloged as a work, but in an architecture collection it might be described as a surrogate, subordinate to the building it depicts.

In designing VIA, it was necessary to accommodate all of these descriptive approaches in a way that made it easier for a searcher to find related materials, regardless of the approach taken in cataloging any single image. This was accomplished through the choice of data structure and data elements.

DATA STRUCTURE

Having determined the kinds of description destined for VIA, we had to develop a data structure that would support the entire range of contributed metadata. We needed a model that would support legacy metadata from dozens of collections.

We examined several existing data standards, in the hope that by adopting a standard we could leverage existing software and improve the portability and interoperability of our metadata. The key library standard, MARC 21, is a flat record and does not model hierarchical relationships well.[6] At the time VIA was being developed, the Visual Resources Association (VRA) Core Categories was in version 2.0. The VRA Core had a work segment and one or more segments for visual documents of the work, with different elements at those two levels. This was a useful foundation, but it was not a perfect fit. Archival description, we found, did not match the VRA model, since archives usually do not create work-level descriptions. They describe instead groups of items (e.g., folders) within a collection; groups based on topics, time periods, participants, or other criteria. Virtually all of the metadata that supports retrieval resides at this group description level, although specific characteristics such as dimensions, caption, and so on may be provided for some items. However, not every aspect of the group description applies to every item in the group, so the metadata cannot accurately be replicated for each item. For this reason, our conceptual model augments the VRA Core Categories structure with one additional layer of hierarchy: the group.

Our proposed three-tier hierarchy of Group, Work, and Surrogate could be implemented in several ways, each with benefits and drawbacks:

> encapsulate all three levels (when present) in a container;
>
> create separate modules for each Group, Work, and Surrogate with pointers expressing the relationships between them; or
>
> create stand-alone modules with required contextual information from higher levels replicated in each module.

Replicating data inherited from higher levels would be inaccurate due to the archival practices described above, so that was unacceptable. Separate modules with relationship pointers would be the most flexible and theoretically pure approach. It would also allow individual modules to function in more than one hierarchy. However, this approach splits access information that might need to be retrieved together across modules, and it also requires software to intelligently follow links in order to build meaningful result displays. As such, it would have required a truly huge amount of analysis and programming, and even then there were no guarantees that response time would be acceptable, considering all the data-crunching involved. As philosophically appealing as this option appeared, it simply was not practical given our development environment and timeline. Therefore, we adopted a container model, where all modules and relationships would be expressed in what was effectively a single large record. In this model, works that are part of more than one group, or surrogates related to multiple works, would appear in more than one container. Contributing repositories would convert their metadata into a common SGML format for loading into VIA.[7]

DATA ELEMENT LIST

Visual Image Access was not meant to be the last word on visual resources, but a way for users to discover what resources exist at Harvard and where they can be found. In the interests of creating a usable union catalog, we agreed to generalize data elements and access points where possible rather than to proliferate fields tailored to particular types of material. For example, a textiles database may have special fields for weave or thread count, which in VIA are mapped into a Physical Description field that serves all kinds of materials. The group reviewed several standards and proto-standards, including the Categories for the Description of Works of Art (CDWA), VRA Core Categories, Dublin Core (DC), the Art Museum Image Consortium (AMICO) data dictionary, and MARC 21, in search of a good fit.

None of these schemes matched our requirements, although each of them contributed to our understanding. Categories for the Description of Works of Art is best suited for the creation of new metadata for artworks.[8] It is less applicable to images other than art or as a target element list for preexisting metadata. The AMICO data dictionary, based in part on CDWA, is extremely specific, with, for example, separate subject subelements for pre-iconographic description, iconography, and index terms.[9] Contributors to VIA would not be able to characterize their metadata that finely. MARC 21 was too elaborate and not detailed enough to support material culture image cataloging. For example, MARC does not provide distinct elements for style and culture, which are mainstays of this kind of image description. Today, using Extensible Markup Language (XML) schemas, we would be able to make more use of Dublin Core than we could in 1998.[10] However, when VIA was being developed, DC would have imposed unacceptable constraints. For example, we needed the ability to associate dates, nationalities, and roles with creators, which Dublin Core did not permit. We had to be free to develop a data dictionary that would support collaboration among diverse units within the university; adding complexity imposed from outside was simply too much. Throughout the project, staff have been mindful of how our choices would affect the ability to map to metadata standards such as DC in the future.

In the end, we hewed most closely to the VRA Core. The initial VIA data dictionary contained twenty-six descriptive elements, many of which included subelements.[11] This is more than simple Dublin Core's fifteen elements and far fewer than the hundreds of elements found in MARC 21. In addition to adding a "group" level to the "work-visual document" hierarchy of the VRA Core Categories 2.0, we reconciled the elements from both VRA levels into a single data element list to be used as a repeatable module at every level of the hierarchy. After all, groups may have titles, works may have titles, and surrogates may have titles. Using the same elements at each level was a concrete recognition that the different descriptive models contributed to VIA would result in like metadata falling in different levels of the hierarchy from record to record. Subsequently, the VRA Core 3.0 adopted our use of the same elements for both work and image description.[12] Virtually all VIA elements are repeatable within a module.

There are a few key discrepancies between the VIA data dictionary and VRA 3.0 today. The VRA Core does not provide a place to put non-creator names such as donors, former owners, and publishers. It also separates the repeatable "identifier" element from the repeatable "repository" element (which is a type of "location" in the VRA Core) so that it is not possible to maintain the association between multiple former repositories and their respective identifiers for an object. The VRA Core also separates Material from Technique, a distinction not all of our contributors have made. This demonstrates the difference between an element set developed to guide prospective metadata creation and one designed to accept diverse legacy metadata. The latter tends to develop broader element definitions.

The wide range of participants' needs was accommodated through the liberal application of a "type" subelement in such fields as notes and titles. For example, rather than proliferating such fields as accession number, catalog number, and former repository number, or enumerating a fixed list of identification number types, a single, repeatable Item ID field was defined, along with a free-text "type" subelement which is used as a label. For example:

```
<itemid>
    <type>Accession number:</type>
    <value>97-1234A</value>
</itemid>
```

There was no functional advantage in enumerating and controlling title types, note types, and so on. In our catalog, they function purely as display labels. By using a free-text "type" subelement, contributors can supply what best fits their material, and no central authority has to enforce conformity.

The concept that was most difficult to express was "place" or "location." A location could be a place of creation or publication; a place where an object was found, to which an object was moved, or where it currently resides; the subject of a work; and so on. Establishing data elements for these concepts was complicated by the different approaches to research that each repository envisioned. For example, the Schlesinger Library on the History of Women in America primarily supports social science research. In its view, a photograph taken in Buffalo, New York, is in fact "about" Buffalo on some level, and therefore the library does not distinguish in its metadata between the place a photograph is taken and a place being depicted. However, another researcher might want to distinguish between photographs of Buffalo and portrait photographs taken in a studio in Buffalo.

For the time being, we chose to retain the distinctions between different meanings of location in the metadata and defined three distinct location fields: production, subject, and other location, with other locations having a "type" qualifier which is used in displays. There is a separate field for Repository, which is conceptually something of a cross between a location and an institution. The vast majority of the Schlesinger Library's place-names actually described the place of production, and that is how they were mapped. VIA indexes all places together in a Place index, as well as indexing places as subjects in the Subject index.

Agreeing on a master list of data elements was time-consuming but not truly controversial. However, the repositories did find it difficult to come to consensus on *required* data elements, which are important for formulating brief search results screens. In the end, a "title" element in the top segment of the hierarchy was required (e.g., group or work), along with at least one "repository" element somewhere in the container.

Five years after its development, the VIA data dictionary has held up better than anyone anticipated. Changes planned to the data dictionary when VIA is reimplemented at the end of 2003 are few, with most changes driven by new functional requirements:

> In order to support greater integration with geospatial services, VIA will need to accept bounding coordinates expressed as decimal degrees. It will also accept textual location data with more subfielding (e.g., country, region) where contributors can supply it, in order to facilitate gazetteer lookups.

> To improve the ability to repurpose VIA data for harvesters, in web publications, and in virtual collections, we expect to add a repeatable complex element for the name of a subset in which an image has been included and topical terms associated with this image in that subset.

To facilitate the retrieval of authored works as subjects, e.g., a Canova sculpture shown in a daguerreotype, VIA may accept "creator," "title," and other subelements within the "subject" element.

The fundamental principle that emerged as we developed a local data dictionary for a union database was "do not create obstacles for yourself or others." In practice, this played out as follows:

> Let fields be repeatable unless there is a superb reason not to. It is impossible to anticipate every case.
>
> Do not require an element unless it is truly necessary. Always ask: should records absolutely be excluded if this element cannot be supplied?
>
> Do not invest in semantic specificity unless it is necessary for display, indexing, or other functionality. It is bound to create a problem for some contributor.
>
> Conversely, make sure the specificity is there to support the functional requirements.

This leads to the final principle: be disciplined about defining what you are trying to accomplish, and everything else follows. Mapping data elements from one scheme to another can be done well or poorly, depending on how compatible the schemes are to begin with. Once the analysis is complete, however, the actual processing tends to be easy.

DATA CONTENT

It was difficult even to discuss how each repository formulated the content of its data elements until the first phase of VIA was in place. Until the participants could actually see how their data looked when pooled together, they had to rely on manual comparison of a few records, which was time-consuming and not very effective. It is only now, when the union catalog is in place, that the work of building consensus on best descriptive practices can really begin to take place.

Specificity

A general problem affecting many fields is determining the appropriate level of specificity or granularity. For example, in a mixed material collection, "photograph" is a useful Work Type. However, in a photography collection, it is not much help; a term such as "crystalotype" is more effective. Unfortunately, the generalist searching for photographs would never find it. Units without the necessary specialist expertise cannot be expected to provide highly specific terms, but the VIA best practice recommends that specialized units supply broader terms in addition to their narrower terms where possible.

Context

A related problem comes from the loss of context when local metadata is placed in a broader environment. We call this the "on a horse" problem, in honor of a local Teddy Roosevelt database in which all subject headings are presumed to be about the great man. If you encounter the subject "on a horse" in this context, you can safely assume that the Bull Moose himself is riding. Remove this record from its context, however, and it becomes completely baffling. In another example, initially none of the photographs described by the Schlesinger Library on the History of Women in America could be retrieved by searching the term "women," although photographs about "men" could be found. Within Schlesinger, the fact that the photographs were in some way about "women" was assumed, but when the records were shared outside their institution the context was lost. Solving this problem requires contributors to become aware of how their assumptions play out in their metadata. Once they become sensitized to the problem, they can generally address it without too much upheaval in their local environments.

Form

Conflicts in the form of content arise for nearly every metadata element. In VIA, the use of keyword rather than string searching can mitigate some conflicts. However, even simple discrepancies such as the use of mixed singular and plural forms, or adjectival versus nominal forms, can foil inexperienced searchers. Variant forms of personal and corporate names, decisions on whether (and how) to translate names and titles, whether to use current or historical jurisdictions—all of these have a profound impact on the comprehensiveness of retrieval.

Dates for cultural materials are often complex, and may even take the form of a short essay explaining when a work was commissioned, built, damaged, renovated, or destroyed. To accommodate this, dates are represented two ways in VIA: in a free-text field that is displayed in the catalog, and in formatted start and end dates used only for retrieval. Contributors supply both.

Place names raise a different question about data content: should place names be formulated hierarchically, with qualifiers, or in some other fashion? This is the difference between "United States. District of Columbia. Washington. Georgetown" and "Georgetown (Washington, D.C.)," a big difference if you are browsing ordered results. Should United States locales be qualified with postal abbreviations, traditional abbreviations, or state names spelled out in full? This decision has tremendous implications, both for data entry and for retrieval.

Obviously, these cases demonstrate the value of syndetic structures, which help users to move between related, broader, or narrower terms with relative ease. However, there are obstacles to implementing such structures in our heterogeneous environment. Although the Art and Architecture Thesaurus (AAT) and the Union List of Artist Names (ULAN) are becoming more widely used at Harvard, they are by no means sufficient or appropriate vocabularies for all VIA contributors.[13] The ULAN is notoriously inadequate for non-western European artists, and both the AAT and ULAN face competition from the Library of Congress subject and name authority files in library and archive-based repositories. Dedicated image departments, even within a library, may well be best served by a specialized vocabulary such as the AAT. However, archival and special collections within libraries face a painful choice: to coordinate terminology with other image collections or with other departments within the library.

Given the legitimately diverse sources of vocabulary coming into VIA, using one or more thesauri either to add functionality to the VIA system or to preprocess incoming metadata into standard forms would be difficult and only partially successful. It would also require a greater commitment in systems development than the libraries are willing to support. An interim approach is for VIA to accept authority records from all contributors on a "see also from" basis—that is, references that tell users that they will find something useful under the following alternate term. This approach does not resolve discrepancies between contributors, but it does provide the opportunity to direct users to another term that is used in the database. Meanwhile, sixteen VIA contributors create their cataloging in a staff-only union database called OLIVIA. Within that environment, standards have been established for each element, and authority records and controlled vocabulary terms are shared. The VIA Data Standards Subcommittee continues to work toward greater compatibility of metadata from the four contributing systems: OLIVIA, the Harvard University Art Museums' EmbARK database, the Peabody Museum's EmbARK database, and Schlesinger's FileMaker Pro database.

SCOPE

While the initial phases of VIA deliberately included a wide range of material culture images, the question of where to set the boundaries of VIA's topical scope has never been far below the surface. Early on the question turned from "What collections are in scope?" to "What would cause a collection to be deemed out of scope?" Ultimately, the criteria were these: to be included in VIA, the metadata for a collection must be able to be meaningfully searched with other VIA records, and no specialized functionality must be necessary to discover or use the materials. The Harvard College Observatory collection of glass plate negatives illustrates both criteria. These 400,000 plates were created in sky surveys over a period of almost 100 years. In their discovery and use, they are quite unlike the materials in VIA.

Incompatible Metadata

The rationale for creating a union catalog was to make resource discovery simpler for users and to bring to their attention relevant materials they might miss by searching within a single collection. The effectiveness of pooling metadata from different sources depends on several factors. The most significant is the definition of the data elements. Where the elements differ, they can often be mapped to a common, broader element. There are times, however, when such homogenizing is not possible. While descriptive metadata from most of our image collections is textual, the glass plate negatives at the Harvard Observatory are briefly described in numeric terms, as shown in table 4-1.

   If part of the rationale for creating a union catalog is to provide the opportunity for the serendipitous discovery across repositories or across

TABLE 4-1 Harvard College Observatory Plate Stack Catalog metadata example

Plate Number	17359
Right Ascension	13.02
Declination	+82.5
Exposure	10
Date	1921-03-30
Julian Date	2422779.771 g
Comment	susp. var.

disciplines, there is little here to work with. Date is the only common element between this set of metadata and that routinely created for images in the humanities. Clearly this is an extreme case, but it demonstrates why the idea, so attractive at first, of having a single place to find all the images at Harvard is neither practical nor useful.

Incongruent Functional Requirements

A researcher would approach the observatory's collection with astronomical coordinates or the name of an object such as a star. A researcher would need an easily understood way to enter his search. The catalog would then need to look up the name in a gazetteer to acquire coordinates before performing a search. Once a relevant plate was identified, the user would retrieve not the entire image, but an extract of the image centered on the astronomical object for which he searched. These specific requirements, both for searching and delivery, made these images a poor fit for this union catalog.

Using these criteria, the scope of VIA has continued to be limited to images and objects in the area of material culture and social history. Scientific and medical images were excluded because their metadata and access needs were different and needed to be evaluated separately. This division has been reexamined periodically and has held up surprisingly well. Even five years later, the scientific collections largely prefer to maintain discipline-specific systems for ants, plants, stars, and so on. Separate catalogs have been established for biomedical images and taxonomic specimens. Images have been added to VIA from science libraries such as the Arnold Arboretum and, soon, the Kummel Geological Library, but these have been described from a humanist perspective and lack dedicated scientific metadata elements. Respectively, these collections document collecting expeditions and their encounters with local culture and the historical geomorphology of landscapes later claimed by urban sprawl. We have found that these materials complement others in art, architecture, anthropology, and history.

CONCLUSION

Since its debut in May 1999, VIA has grown to include over twenty repositories. As of June 2003, there were 189,225 records in VIA—each of which could represent hundreds of images. Of those records, 58,696 linked to one or more digital images. Pulling content together, not only from libraries but from image repositories anywhere at the university, has made a powerful statement, and recognizes the fact that to Harvard users, the administrative oversight of a resource is unimportant. Clinging to the narrow boundaries of organizational units would have perpetuated barriers to access that make no sense in a digital environment.

Bringing metadata to light from so many diverse collections has led to an interesting form of discontent. Faculty and students want more: metadata for more images, more images in digital form, a more visually oriented interface, greater integration with course management tools, library support for personal image management tools, and more services from visual resources units. In response, large-scale retrospective conversion of both metadata and images is under way. In addition, an upgraded database and catalog interface are in development, linking to a map service is planned, and close ties with local courseware developers have been established. VIA has been enhanced to allow users to export their saved records, with image links, in XML for import into online slide carousels or other software. Several visual resource units are providing support for digital teaching, including scan-on-demand and associated cataloging. As usual, the reward for work accomplished is more work, and we hope that the catalog, its capabilities, and the user community continue to grow and evolve.

NOTES

1. OCLC, the Online Computer Library Center, and RLIN, the Research Libraries Information Network, are commercial providers of library cataloging records as well as many other types of services.
2. "Visual Resources at Harvard University: Task Group Report, May 30, 1997," http://www.peabody.harvard.edu/VRTG/report.html (accessed 21 September 2003).
3. Harvard University Library, "Visual Image Access," http://nrs.harvard.edu/urn-3:hul.eresource:viaxxxxx (accessed 21 September 2003).
4. American Library Association, *Anglo-American Cataloguing Rules*, 2d ed., 2002 revision (Chicago: Canadian Library Association; Chartered Institute of Library and Information Professionals; American Library Association, 2002).
5. All illustrations copyright President and Fellows of Harvard College.

6. Library of Congress, Network Standards and MARC Development Office, "MARC Standards," http://lcweb.loc.gov/marc/ (accessed 9 September 2003).

7. Harvard University Library Office for Information Systems, "Metadata in VIA," http://hul.harvard.edu/ois/systems/via/via_metadata.html (accessed 9 September 2003).

8. J. Paul Getty Trust and College Art Association, "Categories for the Description of Works of Art," http://www.getty.edu/research/institute/standards/cdwa/ (accessed 9 September 2003).

9. Art Museum Image Consortium, "AMICO Data Specification: Data Dictionary," version 1.3, http://www.amico.org/docs/dataspec.html (accessed 9 September 2003).

10. Dublin Core Metadata Initiative, "Dublin Core Metadata Element Set, Version 1.1: Reference Description," 2003, http://www.dublincore.org/documents/ 2003/02/04/dces/ (accessed 21 September 2003).

11. Harvard University Library Office for Information Systems, "VIA Overview," http://hul.harvard.edu/ois/systems/via/index.html (accessed 9 September 2003). Database documentation and metadata specifications for VIA can be accessed from this site.

12. Visual Resources Association Data Standards Committee, "VRA Core Categories," version 3.0, http://www.vraweb.org/vracore3.htm (accessed 9 September 2003).

13. Getty Research Institute, "Art and Architecture Thesaurus Online," http:// www.getty.edu/research/tools/vocabulary/aat/ (accessed 21 September 2003); Getty Research Institute, "Union List of Artist Names On Line," http://www .getty.edu/research/tools/vocabulary/ulan/ (accessed 21 September 2003).

5

Building a Metadata-Sharing Campus: The University of Minnesota IMAGES Initiatives

Charles F. Thomas

As is the case at most research institutions, faculty and departmental initiatives at the University of Minnesota are producing rich and significant digital collections. These collections of images, data, texts, and multimedia are diverse and reflect a wide range of scholarship and teaching that is usually not replicated in the formal channels of scholarly communication. The creators and owners of these collections typically have concentrated on meeting the use preferences of targeted user communities. As a consequence, wider discovery and sustainability often have been secondary considerations at best.

As is also the case at most research institutions, the degree of expertise and the capability to build and sustain online databases and digital collections varies greatly among campus units. The many barriers to entry include high costs; the need for expertise in technologies, content subject matter, and information organization; multiple, overlapping, and incomplete choices of standards; and few guarantees of success or sustainability. Faced with such obstacles, many departments choose to avoid the risks of trying to create their own online resources.

In April 2000, the University of Minnesota Libraries (the "Libraries") determined that much could be gained by working both with those already building digital collections on campus and with those who had refrained from such efforts. To some degree, the University Libraries acted in its self-interest. Even with a flourishing digital initiatives department, the quantity of new digital content that could be generated by this unit was finite, with a maximum capacity of adding 5,000–8,000 new digitized objects per year. The Libraries realized that identifying and collecting metadata about appropriate, existing digital collections already distributed on campus would quickly and dramatically expand both the scope and depth of the digital library. Furthermore, by building a framework that would encourage more campus units to build digital resources, the size and quality of a campus digital library could grow even faster.

To be successful, however, the Libraries determined that it had to identify real, pertinent problems in the current environment that would resonate with campus content owners. Furthermore, partnerships with campus units would succeed only if existing or potential content owners were able to exert significant control over their digital resources. The ideal initiative would clearly demonstrate the potential benefit for each partner.

The most significant problem that the Libraries identified, even with its own internal digital collections, was a general lack of discovery and consequent use of digital collections on campus. Many of these resources were hidden from web search engines that did not readily index metadata or the content embedded within databases. Even the Inktomi campus search engine for the University of Minnesota could not properly index such resources.[1] Additionally, nearly any search of the campus web-accessible resources generated an unmanageable number of hits, meaning that searchers could not quickly, confidently, or thoroughly discover online resources (images, text, or other) produced on campus that might be relevant to their queries.

Based on these realizations, the Libraries initiated the IMAGES (Institutional Metadata Aggregation for Enhanced Searching) project, to establish a centralized discovery point for collections existing on campus, and to provide a hosting service that would encourage other departments to create valuable digital collections for teaching and learning. IMAGES would be a suite of standards, partnerships, and technology to reaffirm the Libraries as the first place to begin looking for information, even distributed or locally created digital collections. By promoting greater discovery and use of these types of collections, the Libraries would help campus units leverage their efforts and investments to realize maximum use of their content.

Since its official launch in late 2001, IMAGES has substantially met all of its initial goals. This chapter explains how the IMAGES initiative has fostered a metadata-sharing campus. It provides visual and narrative examples of the key concepts as well as the components and reasoning behind IMAGES. The closing pages provide readers with some of the lessons learned during the past eighteen months, and point to campus needs still not fully met through IMAGES. Hopefully, this chapter will help others evaluate the value of more communication and partnerships between the library and other agencies.

A CORE CAMPUS METADATA STANDARD

The first step toward the envisioned IMAGES system and partnerships was to anticipate the scope of content and metadata that might be discoverable through a metadata aggregator. Contacts with department heads and individual faculty, relationships with key funders for campus technology initiatives, and meetings with managers of known digital collections helped the University Libraries identify a group of allies in areas such as the Art History slide library, the College of Architecture and Landscape Architecture, the Agricultural Experiment Station, campus museums, and all of the Libraries' departments with existing digital collections. Representatives from each of these units, as well as archivists and others with relevant expertise, were invited to draft a campus core metadata standard.

The campus responded enthusiastically, knowing that participation in the IMAGES partnerships would be voluntary and that the library was committed to preserving owners' control over collections. The proposed core descriptive standard had to be extensible to a variety of content, and had to balance ease of adoption against the ability to contain rich technical and preservation metadata. The primary considerations addressed by the core metadata working group were the semantic differences in how different disciplines refer to different types of information, and the need for a metadata structure robust enough to support effective searching and management tools. The final metadata structure also needed to be flexible enough to describe any existing or potential digital objects indexed by IMAGES.

A core metadata structure was proposed after three months of work. The proposed standard for the campus was a synthesis of Dublin Core, the Visual Resources Association (VRA) Core, some aspects of the archives community's Encoded Archival Description (EAD) standard, and portions of the RLG's (Research Libraries Group's) emerging recommendations for preservation metadata.[2] Additionally, selected pragmatic recommendations from the Getty Institute's Categories for the Description of Works of Art were adopted, such as providing separate metadata elements to contain both free-textual dates value for display-only purposes and regularized date elements to enable machine sorting by date.[3] The proposed standard, formally stated in an XML Document Type Definition (DTD) named "images.dtd," subsequently was approved by the University Libraries as its core standard for internal and hosted digital collections (see figure 5-1 for an example).

The DTD (available online at http://digital.lib.umn.edu/elements .html) serves as the essential crosswalking map for owners of differently structured databases on campus who wish to share metadata with the IMAGES aggregator. Early in the campaign to promote this core standard for the university, the Libraries gained a key ally, a campus committee charged with redistributing student technology fees to support worthwhile technology initiatives. Since 2001 this committee has explicitly recommended the IMAGES metadata core for all applicants seeking funding to digitize content. This endorsement produced immediate results, bringing faculty to the Libraries to inquire about using our metadata core. The IMAGES metadata core has been refined slightly since its creation, but has proven to be a flexible, extensible standard for metadata creation and sharing on campus.

At the present time, the unit owning a digital object is responsible for creating all of the metadata that goes into IMAGES. Presumably, the owner(s) have much greater subject expertise within the topic of their content. While some units would certainly be happy if the Libraries took on this responsibility, they appreciate the fact that the Libraries is hosting the metadata at no cost, and is willing to create quality descriptions of their digital content.

METADATA AGGREGATOR SYSTEM CONCEPTS

Some basic ideas have shaped IMAGES' technical infrastructure, including:

> All local digital assets of the Libraries will be managed in a common way.

> Digital content across campus should remain in the care of its creator for as long as that person or agency can or is able to sustain it.

> A core system and standards can be provided by the Libraries to host and sustain valuable digital content for those units that cannot afford it alone.

FIGURE 5-1   Metadata record created according to images.dtd specification

```
<image>
    <digitalid>ama00059</digitalid>
    <standardid>Ames Library rare books:  Quarto DS352 .E5</standardid>
    <title>A Dooraunee gentleman.</title>
    <series>
        <level1>Ames Library</level1><level2>Illustration</level2>
    </series>
    <published>In Elphinstone, Mountstuart, An Account of the Kingdom of Caubul, and
its dependencies in Persia, Tartary, and India. London: Longman, Hurst, Rees, Orme, and
Brown, 1815</published>
    <imgyear display="1815" normal="/1815"/>
    <imgperiod>19th Century</imgperiod>
    <holding>Univ. of Minnesota Libraries, Ames Library of South Asia</holding>
    <prov>Donated by Charles Leslie Ames.</prov>
    <medium>Illustration</medium>
    <dimensions>20 x 27.5 cm.</dimensions>
    <subject>Afghanistan--History</subject>
    <subject>Clothing and Dress--Afghanistan</subject>
    <subject>Kabul (Afghanistan)--History</subject>
    <userights>This image is subject to U.S. copyright laws. Do not reproduce for any
commercial purpose without written permission of the Ames Library of South Asia. Please
include attribution of the image source with any reproduction of this image.</userights>
    <thmbimg>
    <thmbpath>http://xxxx.umn.edu/thumbnail/am/ama00059.jpg</thmbpath>
    <thmbformat>image/jpeg</thmbformat>
    </thmbimg>
    <refimg>
    <refpath>http://xxx.umn.edu/reference/am/ama00059.jpg</refpath>
    <refsize>692K</refsize>
    <refres>100ppi</refres>
    </refimg>
    <archimg>
    <archsize>15.3M</archsize>
    <archres>300ppi</archres>
    <archloc>A high resolution version of this image is stored off-line. To obtain a high-
resolution copy for a fee, please contact the University of Minnesota Libraries Digital
Collections Unit (http://digital.lib.umn.edu) and identify the image by the Digital
ID.</archloc>
    </archimg>
    <relatedurx relation="IsPartOf" relationtitle="Ames Library Digital Image
Collections">http://xxx.umn.edu/am/amessearch.html</relatedurx>
</image>
```

System development will focus on features that can benefit all partners. No customization can be devoted to the functionality of just one digital collection.

An appropriate balance is achievable between the benefits of centralized content management and the power of content owners to control the presentation and use of their intellectual property.

Heavy usage maximizes returns on the investment in building digital collections.

A well-known search and discovery site promotes usage of distributed collections.

Libraries continue to be the best place to begin looking for authentic information.

Accordingly, the Libraries constructed IMAGES to serve as a metadata collector for distributed collections, and as a metadata and content management system for all Libraries collections. This same system is available to campus partners who trust the Libraries to host their collections. As figure 5-2 demonstrates, by pulling together into a central site the metadata of Libraries and hosted collections, and then using a common crosswalk to bring in metadata for distributed digital collections on campus, users searching the central metadata repository or "metabase" can know they are finding more digital content relevant to their searches, regardless of its campus location.

DISTRIBUTED CONTENT AND OWNERSHIP INFLUENCE DESIGN

Building a system to accommodate distributed content and varied ownership required more flexibility and less uniformity of presentation than is possible in a wholly centralized digital library. Distributed content implies the sacrifice of some functions that might be possible in a more tightly controlled system. For example, the ability to provide advanced features, such as progressive-zoom viewing of all digital graphics discovered within IMAGES, was disqualified as a development option, because not all of the images reside on a library server. If such features were implemented only for images on a library server, users might become confused and frustrated if the same features were not available when viewing digital objects stored elsewhere.

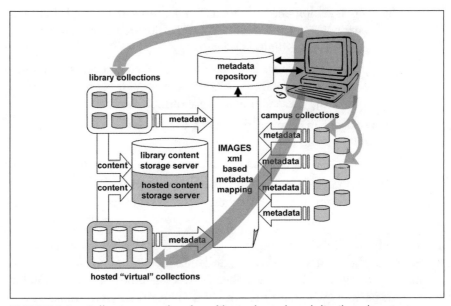

FIGURE 5-2   Collecting metadata from library, hosted, and distributed content

Furthermore, the Libraries recognized early on that the IMAGES system would succeed on a highly decentralized campus only if strong assurances were made to content owners that control and attribution of their collections would be an essential principle of the partnerships. For distributed collections, this has meant that the metadata records in IMAGES for distributed objects will always contain:

> holding statements attributing ownership to the proper campus unit;
>
> access and use conditions specific to the distributed location; and
>
> "escape" hyperlinks to quickly transport users from IMAGES to a distributed site.

Managers of the distributed sites—the permanent and real homes for such digital collections—obviously have total control over their own sites. It is worth mentioning that the home site for distributed resources often contains more project-specific metadata that is not suitable for sharing with the IMAGES metadata aggregator. For example, some technical metadata that is used exclusively by the content owner's particular delivery system might be useless or confusing for users in a centralized discovery environment.

Just as owners of distributed collections control the presentation of their content through their distributed systems, digital collections owned by the Libraries, and digital collections owned by other campus units but existing only on the Libraries' infrastructure, are able to exploit advanced technologies to provide "preferred views" of both metadata and digital objects. The screenshot in figure 5-3 shows the initial search screen presented for cross-collection searching.

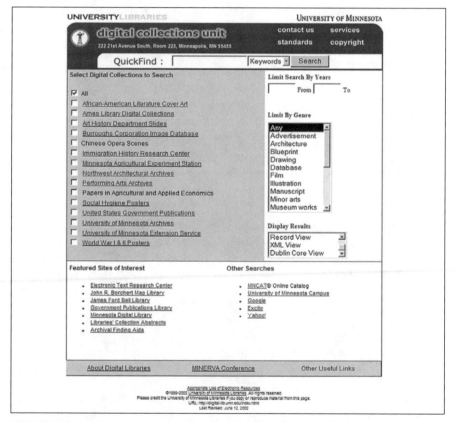

FIGURE 5-3   Initial search screen for all collections discoverable in IMAGES

Every contributed metadata record is searchable through the IMAGES home site (http://digital.lib.umn.edu). The search page for IMAGES includes options such as specific search keys (creator, title, keywords, record number, subject); the ability to search one, many, or all digital collections simultaneously; Boolean operators; phrase and fragment searching; date range searches; and limiting searches by material genres. Even within this default environment, users can choose different ways to view search results. Figures 5-4 and 5-5 show how a particular item is discovered and the metadata record is accessed in the default IMAGES view.

In the initial discovery environment, colors, graphics, organization, and even labels for result sets and item record information aesthetically identify the IMAGES union database. However, these records clearly mark the identity of the unit that created or owns the digital content, its identity as part of a specific digital collection or project, as well as access and use conditions chosen by the owning department. In these ways, the records in the default IMAGES discovery environment are identical to the records for distributed content.

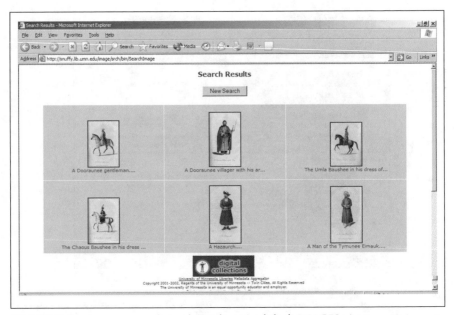

FIGURE 5-4   Appearance of search result set in default IMAGES view

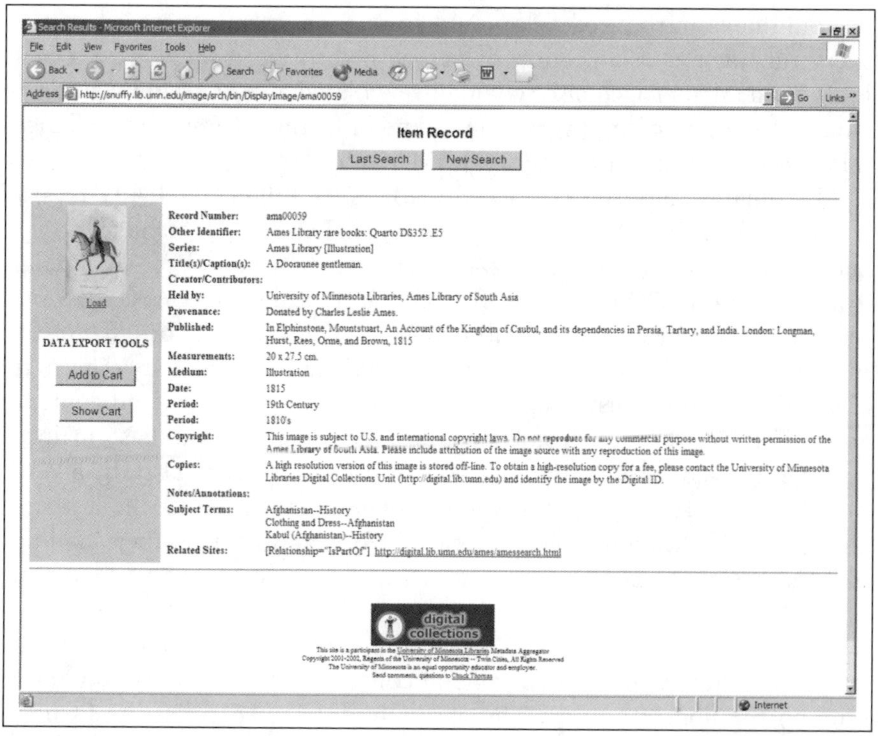

FIGURE 5-5   Appearance of item record in default IMAGES view

If the Libraries had limited these clear indications of ownership to distributed collections, only library departments and those who could afford to build and sustain their own digital collections would participate. After all, asking units with fewer resources to entirely forfeit the ability to brand, label, and present their metadata and collections probably would not have attracted many partners. The IMAGES system needed the capability to permit owners of hosted collections to provide a "preferred" presentation of all of their collection. In this manner, all of the hosted digital library item records could have "escape" hyperlinks equal to those for distributed collections.

Programming specific presentation aesthetics into the IMAGES system for each collection was impractical, however. Not only would this increase the workload and development time for the IMAGES system administrator, it would have introduced delays and frustration in all concerned parties every time a digital collection owner wished to experiment with a new look. Such an approach also would have violated a key development principle of only investing programming time in features common to *all* digital collections discoverable through IMAGES.

Fortunately, one of the core technologies underlying the IMAGES system is XML (Extensible Markup Language). The suite of standards associated with XML includes XSLT (Extensible Stylesheet Language Transformations). XSLT permits IMAGES technical staff to leave the work of defining presentation style to its owner. Owners of collections that reside only within the IMAGES system can write their own XSLT stylesheets to create one or more customized views of the same metadata and content. Separating presentation from other programming and database maintenance effectively reduces the overall workload for technical staff, invests maximum control in content owners, and permits more frequent aesthetic changes by collection owners. The IMAGES system further exploits XSLT's benefits to content owners by permitting customizable searching options.

By establishing alternate or preferred search forms, content owners create a "virtually distributed" digital collection that in reality still exists only on the library's server. This virtually distributed collection identity can then be incorporated into each IMAGES metadata record as the basis for the "escape" hyperlinks provided for distributed collections. In the same way, then, users of the union database discover that an entire digital collection of particular pertinence exists, and the users virtually escape from IMAGES to just this virtually distributed collection.

Figure 5-6 provides an example of a hosted collection's virtual presence as a separate online resource. The site's search options and presentation are customized to the owner's preferences. After searching through this interface, figures 5-7 and 5-8 present the same records and metadata that were presented in an earlier example. XSLT has enabled the owner of this digital collection to arrange, label, and present this information to the user in a significantly different manner. At the same time, all of this work was done by the collection's owner, not by IMAGES technical staff. XSLT has freed database administrators to concentrate on data management, not customization. Equally important, XSLT empowers content owners to change, test, and prototype new looks for their digital collections without worrying about the extra work it might cause for system programmers.

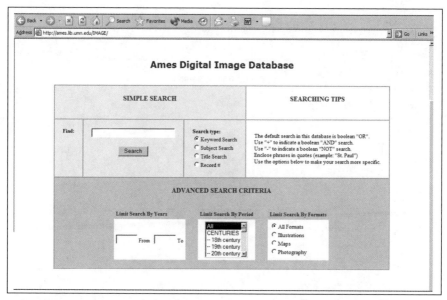

FIGURE 5-6   User-created search form limits IMAGES search to one collection

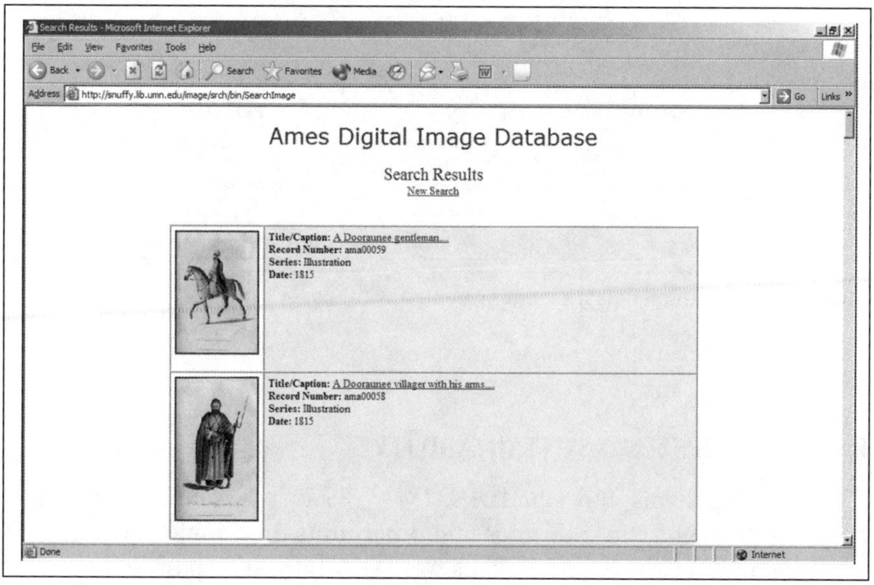

FIGURE 5-7   Search result set in preferred view set by owner

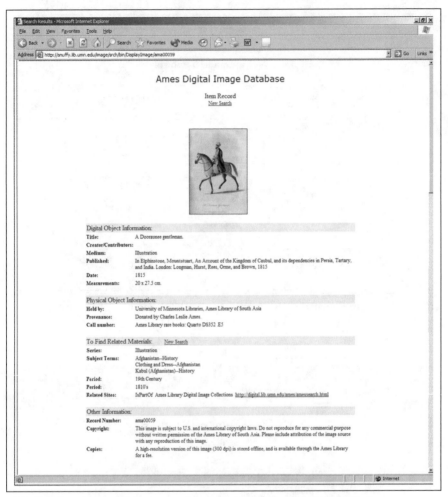

FIGURE 5-8   Item metadata record presented with owner's preferred view

PARTNERSHIPS AND SUSTAINABILITY

Along with systems and standards, IMAGES is a series of partnerships between the University Libraries and other units on campus. For the first eighteen months, these partnerships were very informal, in order to attract participants and test the concepts of metadata sharing. So far, no campus units have been charged a fee for hosting their metadata or content. As the range of service requests grows and the nature of partnerships diversifies, the Libraries gains a much better sense of the issues that should be addressed to formalize and sustain partnerships. These include the following ones:

Rights and responsibilities of both parties. The Libraries will formally state its intent to maintain robust, stable systems for around-the-clock access to all metadata and content within IMAGES. Partners providing metadata for distributed resources must maintain stability of the metadata and paths to their distributed digital objects, and inform the Libraries whenever metadata is added, changed, or deleted. A formal process and conditions for disengaging from the partnership also must be established.

What is free, and what is for-fee? As long as storing digital objects does not present a drain on Libraries resources, hosting of metadata and content likely will be a free service to individual units. If a partner wishes for the Libraries to hold significant quantities of data, content, or large files, funding sources must be found by the content's owner. Associated services such as digitization, digital archiving, and cataloging are very costly for the Libraries and must be offset by cost recovery.

Long-term funding to support growth. At the moment, IMAGES is entirely subsidized by the University Libraries. The system currently contains 25,000 records for individual digital objects. Of the fifteen participating partners, more than half are outside the Libraries. As figure 5-9 demonstrates, the total number of records being added to IMAGES is growing more quickly from external contributions than from internal digitization projects. This was expected, and even desirable. At the point when support for other campus units becomes drastically disproportionate in terms of required storage space and bandwidth, however, the issue of sustainable funding models will inevitably arise.

Metadata records alone will never create an undue drain on library resources, for they are only incremental textual additions to a database. The real source of a drain will be storing actual content objects, which at the present time is done mainly for campus units that have limited resources. A central issue that must be resolved is whether the source of funding should come from units or from a central funding source to support a "campus good." How can cash-strapped smaller departments find this money? If IMAGES is a resource for the benefit of the campus, should it not be funded from a central administrative source? These questions currently are being considered.

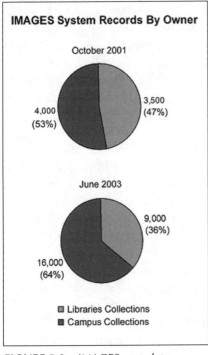

IMAGES System Records By Owner

October 2001

4,000 (53%)

3,500 (47%)

June 2003

9,000 (36%)

16,000 (64%)

☐ Libraries Collections
■ Campus Collections

FIGURE 5-9   IMAGES metadata records by owner

USEFUL LESSONS

Building and managing IMAGES has provided valuable lessons for the Libraries, and these lessons can in turn help other libraries. The following sections highlight some of the lessons learned that will help the University of Minnesota Libraries to allocate resources and extend IMAGES as a campus resource.

Establish and promote standards. One reason IMAGES has been so successful is the documentation and promotional material that was created for the core campus metadata standard. Library staff invested much time talking to database owners to learn about their information and suggest logical mappings for metadata sharing. As new projects arise, similarly extensive discussions are devoted to understanding how a partner's needs can be reconciled with the Libraries' requirements.

Deciding the right place to put information within a metadata structure is only part of the challenge. The equally important part is helping partners understand the need for controlled vocabularies, data consistency, and what is required for a particular set of metadata records to function well in a union database with other metadata.

Even automated harvesting will require substantial human annotation. One area requiring further exploration within IMAGES is the possibility of automating more of the metadata harvesting from distributed, existing digital collections. Even when a creator of metadata has been verified as trustworthy, substantial variation between groups of records is a fact of life in decentralized metadata environments. Human reconciliation and annotation is therefore likely to be a continuing necessity in metadata aggregation. Recent metadata harvesting experiences at the University of Michigan and the University of Illinois at Urbana-Champaign confirm that diverse groups of metadata being accumulated into a single database require enhancements such as global insertions of labels and entire fields, normalization of dates and other data, and clues to users about ownership and access.[4]

In a more centralized environment, one way to minimize this diversity would be to prescribe more specific content standards, controlling not only metadata content but also the selection and use of particular metadata elements. In a distributed environment this approach is not feasible, so the Libraries expects that some attention to metadata integration will always be a necessary allocation.

Shared infrastructure is badly needed. If the University of Minnesota can be seen as a "typical" large public university, then the campus response to IMAGES indicates that substantial needs exist for a centralized technical framework for publishing digital collections. By devising sustainable approaches to support this framework, and minimizing redundancy and expense on campus, the Libraries has proved that shared infrastructure will be welcomed by many even in the most decentralized organizations.

Indexing distributed content does lead to faster growth of a digital library. The IMAGES initiative so far has proved that metadata aggregation is a viable strategy for dramatically expanding the scope and depth of a campus digital library.

Participants need many options. If IMAGES existed solely as a metadata aggregator, it would be collecting only records that pointed to other preexisting resources. In this scenario, a single aesthetic for all metadata records would be satisfactory, because the system would serve exclusively as an initial discovery point to direct users elsewhere. Because IMAGES also exists to directly host content, the Libraries guessed correctly that hosted collection owners desire flexibility and a certain degree of control over their content. So far, partners have tended to ask for particular additional features repeatedly. Some of these frequent requests included more staff-side management tools, more customized sorting and display options for users, and a page-turning navigation device for multi-component digital objects. Some of these suggestions have been adopted into the plan for future IMAGES development; others were too specific to particular digital collections to be worthwhile.

Establish and enforce key development principles. Multiple constituencies with multiple missions translate into a variety of requests and needs. Faced early on with many functional needs and development requests, Libraries staff chose one primary principle to allocate development time: "No system customization or changes will be made unless they are relevant and of benefit to all contributors." This design principle has helped immensely in setting initial agreements with new partners.

Enabling digital preservation is very difficult in a distributed environment. The Libraries routinely integrates its own digital collections into a digital archiving process. The IMAGES initiative, however, involves many collections not owned by the Libraries. Though the Libraries has not assumed formal digital preservation responsibility for any of the hosted or distributed content in IMAGES, future digital preservation opportunities are always a consideration. The greatest hindrance to future digital preservation of these other collections is that many of the existing or growing digital collections do not incorporate preservation planning into the associated digitization and cataloging workflows. The need for archival file formats and preservation metadata is often ignored because current use needs take precedence. A major aspect of the IMAGES effort so far has been educating content owners about preservation issues, and even helping them to retrospectively create the metadata and formats that promote a long life for their content.

FUTURE ENHANCEMENTS

Existing and potential IMAGES partners continually provide many helpful suggestions to make the system more appealing and useful. While adhering to the basic design principles explained earlier, the following prioritized enhancements to IMAGES are planned:

>   online metadata cataloging tool
>   automated metadata harvesting tools
>   metadata annotation and export tools
>   use analysis, statistical tools
>   support for other structured information

CONCLUSION

Since IMAGES was first conceived in early 2000, many new and helpful standards have emerged for those creating digital collections. One such example is the emergence of "application profiles" within the larger

Dublin Core community that may address some of the key needs that shaped the IMAGES metadata standard.[5] Still, within a complex organization such as a large university, a few basic realities exist. These realities include widely varying skills and capabilities among university units, different constituencies and expectations for digital collections, overcrowded and frustrating searching environments for the whole organization, and the unfortunate yet true fact that many departments and individuals continue to develop similar systems at great expense and redundancy. Given this reality, IMAGES has positioned the University Libraries as a trusted center of expertise in building and supporting digital collections. The IMAGES project has succeeded because the Libraries demonstrated many benefits and few requirements of sacrifice for partners. As a result, many potential partners have approached the Libraries inquiring about service and participation options. The greatest benefits yielded from this initiative are the opportunities it has presented for the Libraries and campus units to learn more about each other's information and users, and to discuss good database design, metadata, and digital preservation.

IMAGES currently contains more than 25,000 metadata records from multiple sources. At least 80,000 more items are available on campus right now for metadata sharing. As the creators and owners of this rich and diverse content have come together, IMAGES has helped the University of Minnesota community transition to a more communicative organization. Future innovations such as campuswide content management and course management systems are now more likely to be supported, and the campus library has demonstrated its enduring value as an information broker and center of expertise.

NOTES

1. Inktomi Corp. marketed web search services and products from 1996 to 2003, until the company was acquired by Yahoo. The University of Minnesota used the Inktomi indexing engine until 2002, then switched to a Google product.
2. Information about the Dublin Core Metadata Initiative can be found at http://dublincore.org/ (accessed 25 November 2003); information about the VRA Metadata Core can be found at http://www.vraweb.org/vracore3.htm (accessed 23 August 2003); information about the EAD standard can be found at http://www.loc.gov/ead (accessed 23 August 2003). In 2001, OCLC and RLG were in the early stages of developing preservation metadata recommendations. At the time, the best available resource was OCLC/RLG Working Group on Preservation Metadata, "Preservation Metadata for Digital Objects: A Review

of the State of the Art," 2001, http://www.oclc.org/research/pmwg/presmeta_
wp.pdf (accessed 23 August 2003).

3. J. Paul Getty Trust and College Art Association, "Categories for the Description
of Works of Art," 2000, http://www.getty.edu/research/institute/standards/cdwa/
(accessed 23 August 2003).

4. In 2002 the University of Michigan and the University of Illinois at Urbana-
Champaign experimented with metadata harvesting techniques. Their final
reports and harvesting tools are available at http://oaister.umdl.umich
.edu/o/oaister/ and http://oai.grainger.uiuc.edu/ (accessed 23 August 2003). See
also Timothy W. Cole et al., "Now That We've Found the 'Hidden Web,' What
Can We Do with It?" presentation at the 2002 "Museums and the Web" conference, http://www.archimuse.com/mw2002/papers/cole/cole.html (accessed 23
August 2003).

5. More information on Dublin Core application profiles is available at
http://dublincore.org/usage/documents/profiles (accessed 23 August 2003).

6 Crosswalking Citation Metadata: The University of California's Experience

Karen Coyle

THE METADATA PROJECT: ABSTRACTING AND INDEXING DATABASES

In 1987 the Division of Library Automation (DLA) at the University of California brought up an online version of the National Library of Medicine's (NLM's) Medline database.[1] The records were received on tape from the NLM and loaded into a local mainframe system. The interface to the database was a version of the telnet system that connected users to the universities' union catalog, MELVYL. Two years later the DLA added the Institute for Scientific Information's Current Contents data to the databases available under the MELVYL brand.[2] Although some consideration was given to consistency and "look and feel," each of these databases within the MELVYL system had been developed separately, used significantly different file designs, and had few metadata elements in common even though the general structure of the data, that of journal article citations, was similar.

The experience of creating two separate and individual databases was enough to convince the developers at the DLA that if more abstracting and indexing databases were to be made available on a reasonably rapid schedule, then the work of creating and maintaining the databases would have to follow a common template. This template would serve to enforce both a common database design and a relatively uniform metadata structure.[3] This technique would not only speed up development time but would provide users of the databases with a search and display environment that was the same, or nearly the same, across multiple resources. A common database and indexing structure also would facilitate cross-database searching, a capability that was new and untested at the time but deemed worthy of experimentation by the DLA using local software and the Z39.50 information retrieval protocol.

There was never any question that the underlying metadata structure would be the MARC bibliographic record. The organization had a significant investment in the MARC format in the form of programming tools and staff expertise. This meant that the transformed records would have fields with tags, indicators, and subfields, and could be processed by the existing MELVYL development software that had been designed for library catalog records. It did not require that the records precisely follow the tagging of the MARC record. In fact, the MARC standard had some obvious gaps in its repertoire for journal citation records. Some adjustments would have to be made.

The metadata challenge was complex for the following reasons:

> Each data provider used its own proprietary record format, and none of the files were available in the MARC record format.

> Each data provider's records had some fields that were not formatted in the way that they were in MARC, i.e., there were multiple authors in a single field, or series titles were included in the string of the title field.

> Each data provider's records had some data elements that were not accommodated in the MARC format, such as fields for special indexes or local identifiers.

For most abstracting and indexing services of the late 1980s, the main product was a printed publication and the metadata was entirely oriented toward print. For example, data elements that needed to print on the same line were often combined into a single field. Some distinctions were more typographic than data-related, such as subject headings in uppercase. The machine-readable product was an afterthought, a by-product of a print-dominant era.

Metadata crosswalks were created by the DLA to accomplish the following goals:

Develop records that were as close as possible to standard MARC so that existing software and database functionality could be used.

Provide some uniform search elements across databases for cross-database searching.

Simplify user training and assure that users could transfer their skills in searching existing databases to new databases as they were introduced.

Equally support functions like interlibrary loan and downloads to bibliographic software packages from all databases.

Provide a common set of searches and displays.

Enable linking from the citation metadata to full text where available.

It is important to note that neither "common" nor "consistent" means that all data elements will be identical. The more metadata experience we have, the more it becomes clear that metadata perfection is not attainable, and anyone who attempts it will be sorely disappointed. When metadata is crosswalked between two or more unrelated sources, there will be data elements that cannot be reconciled in an ideal manner. The key to a successful metadata crosswalk is intelligent flexibility. It is essential to focus on the important goals and be willing to compromise in order to reach a practical conclusion to projects.

The fact that the article citation records were not in MARC format was the least of our challenges. Many libraries are only able to process MARC-formatted metadata, but with minimal programming skills it is relatively simple to take any data and place it in the tagged format used by MARC.[4] This gets the data into the correct structure, but it does not accomplish what really matters, and that is to format the data elements in a way that makes them equivalent for searching and display. In other words, there is less difference between these authors:

> au=Smith, John and 100 $aSmith, John

than there is between these:

> au=JM SMITH, D JONES, FB DOE and   100 $a Smith, J. M.
>
> 700 $a Jones, D.
>
> 700 $a Doe, F. B.

CHALLENGE AREAS

It sounds simple to say that we wanted to create a relatively uniform record with authors, titles, and subjects, as well as a clear statement of the citation information (journal, volume, pages). Yet nearly every data element involved in these basic bibliographic areas had some distinct challenges. Not surprising to anyone who has worked with library cataloging, author names pose particular problems. For example, some abstracting and indexing (A&I) databases include full author forenames, while others limit their entries to the forename initials; and the order of the names and use of punctuation varies between them, sometimes even within a provider's file of data. Titles can be fairly straightforward, but the inclusion of translated and transliterated titles, and in some cases series titles, complicates that field. And the key elements of the citation that allow a user to locate an article within a journal, such as volume, number, and pagination, proved to be the elements with the greatest amount of variation between the A&I vendor files that the DLA received.

Authors

Author fields come in a number of different stripes. The first issue that we faced was: what is considered an "author"? Some A&I metadata combined authors and editors in the same field; others provided separate fields. Corporate authors are not recognized as authors in some A&I systems but are placed in a separate "corporate entity" field. In other systems, there is no distinction between corporate and personal authors and both are placed in the same author field. Our original goal had been to create separate personal and corporate author fields for searching, as we had in the union catalog, but we decided that the effort to separate these programmatically would be great and there would be a degree of error. The impact of allowing both corporate and personal authors to be indexed as "author" would be low, however, since the vast majority of citations have personal authors and most users do not think of corporations as a natural author. So for the citation databases we created a single author field that mixed personal and corporate authors for some data sources.

The author field often contained additional data elements beyond the names of authors. Role indicators, such as "editor," were often incorporated into the field, e.g.:

DeVries, D. R.: Ed.

The final author name field could contain the phrase "et al" or "and others." This appeared either by itself as the last author in a sequence or as a qualifier in the last-named author's field. In the first example below, each author name is separated by a comma, so "et al" occupies the place of an author name. In the second example, the author names are separated by semicolons, and the "and others" is included as part of the third author name:

> Li LM, Nicolson GL, Fidler IJ, et al.

> Ishida, Yasuo; Chused, Thomas; Murakami, Shinya, and others

The subfielding of the author name varied from none (as in the examples above) to even more than one finds in the MARC record, as in this example:

> $a Jackson $o Frederick $s Jr. $r Ed

In some A&I databases, the distinction between the author's last name and forename was not represented by any specific coding. In the following database example, author names were presented in last name first order, but with no delimiting of forenames or initials:

> Hsieh-Ma S T

In the next examples, the comma that one usually expects to separate last names and forenames in citations is instead used to represent the division between multiple authors in a single author field:

> Qian F, Chan SJ, Gong QM, Bajkowski AS, Steiner DF, Frankfater A

To put these names into a MARC-like format, the DLA had to develop a complex algorithm that could attempt to add the comma into names after creating separate author fields from each of the authors represented in the comma-delimited list. It was necessary to take into account that corporate and personal author names could be found in the same field, and that author forenames could be complex. Using this algorithm:

> Smith J R *becomes* Smith, J R

> Smith J R Jr *becomes* Smith, J R Jr

> Smith-Jones M F T *becomes* Smith-Jones, M F T

but:

Tran Duc Hinh *stays as* Tran Duc Hinh

American Society of Enology *stays as* American Society of Enology

Ney, J. J. *stays as* Ney, J. J.

The last instruction above is necessary because, as was the case with many sets of data, coding of data elements had changed over time, and current data contained either more subfielding or different punctuation than earlier data had. In fact, one often-used routine was designed to turn bibliographic data from uppercase, as was common in the early files of some vendors, into a reasonable but not wholly accurate title case.

The distinction between main author (MARC 100 field) and added authors (MARC 700 fields) was not found in citation metadata. We attempted to preserve the journal publishing convention regarding the author order, which is that the first named author on a journal article is significant for the attribution and citation of an article. In keeping with the MARC requirement, which mandates that only one 1XX main entry field be in a record, the first listed personal author was moved to the 100 field and all others were placed in 700 fields.

Author Affiliation

Author affiliation is an important element in citation databases because it takes the place of name authority control, which is generally not used in A&I cataloging. The author affiliation distinguishes this Jane Jones as the one working at RocketDyne Laboratories in 1997 from Jane Jones who worked at State University in that same year. Author affiliation is sometimes presented as a subfield in the author field, but it was most often encountered as a separate data element that may or may not have been clearly linked with a particular author. Some systems present only the affiliation for the first-named author; others had awkward encoding to indicate to which of the authors the affiliation pertained. In this example,

200 $a Jones, Paul $a Smith, Jane $a Johnson, Harry $a White, Betty

700 $a $a $a University of California $a

the first three authors are affiliated with the University of California based on the relative subfielding of the two fields, and no affiliation information is given for the last author.

Titles

Titles are clearly important data elements in the citation not only bibliographically but because they contain relevant keywords and subject terms that are often rich in information. Fortunately, titles were usually simple data elements that contained the title of the article. They became complex in sources that indexed works in languages that use non-Latin alphabets, such as Russian. In such cases, there was a translated and transliterated title, sometimes in the same field. We also encountered a source that added series titles to the book titles in the book title field. Based on punctuation, series and book titles were moved to a different data element.

The Host Periodical Citation

The vast majority of entries in the A&I databases are for journal articles. The data elements for the journal title and the enumeration (volume, number, date) are key to finding the article in a hard-copy or digital archive of that journal. However, there are no generally accepted standards for how those key data elements are expressed. In the area of scholarly publishing, there are many different styles that are used for book and article footnotes, references, and bibliographies, and many different treatments of these key elements. As an example, volume and number may be written as "v. 5, no. 6" in one citation style, but as "5(6)" in another. Unfortunately, the lack of standardization in this area carries over to the citation styles of the A&I databases. Not only are the citation formats between A&I databases different from each other, but they also may not correspond to any of the citation style standards used in scholarship, such as those established by the Modern Language Association or the American Psychological Association.

The target data format, the MARC 773 field, brought together the entire enumeration (volume, part, and number), the date, and the pagination statement into a single subfield. Although our development was taking place before the use of the OpenURL for citation-linking services, we were using our own linking methods to locate both full-text versions of articles and library holdings for journal issues.[5] These linking methods required us to create separate subfielding for volume, number, date, and pagination. Meeting our needs for precision in this key area meant that we had to diverge from the MARC standard in our metadata crosswalk.

Journal Title

Journal title is straightforward with one exception: the use of abbreviated titles. Fortunately, the metadata records containing abbreviated titles often carry full titles as well, but not always. Some vendors provide a separate list of journal titles for customers that can be used to expand the abbreviated titles in the records.

Volume and Number

Because of the importance in identifying and locating a journal article, volume and issue number are usually present in the vendor data. When they are presented as separate data elements in the record format, they are easily dealt with. Their formats can differ, but as long as the formatting is consistent, as in this example, there is little problem:

> vo=6 or vo=v. 6

Volume and number are sometimes presented as a single element with punctuation, such as this encoding, which means "volume 6, number 12":

> (6)12

The hardest situations to deal with are those that resemble MARC records, where the volume, number, date, and pages are combined into a single string, e.g.:

> 213, no. 1/2 (2000): 43-50 (8 pages)
>
> Source: Nature, vol.408, no.6810, 16 Nov. 2000, pp.320-4.
>
> 34(1):68-78. 2001 Fall

Parsing the enumeration is important for full-text linking and linking to other resources. Parsing also provides a neutral format that can be rendered in any of the many display formats that a system might want to provide. Where possible, specific formatting was removed from the enumeration (e.g., "v. 6" became "6") so that display programs could re-create either the "v. 6" or the "(6)" at the time of display. Once parsed into separate data elements, however, there is no standard location for these in the MARC format.[6] To accommodate these data elements, we allowed ourselves to digress from the MARC standard and created nonstandard subfield codes to carry them in the 773 field.

Date

Date is another data element that is presented in A&I metadata records in a variety of formats. Although the date that is given is generally the cover date of the publication, one source we received gave only the year of publication, not a more specific date, even for journals that have cover dates for issues. In the MARC record, the date appears in both a standardized format in the fixed field (MARC 008) area and in a display format in the publisher field (MARC 260). In citation metadata there may be a standardized format, a display format, or both, e.g.:

> 1999 Fall
>
> June 26, 2003
>
> Sep 2001
>
> 08 Feb 2002

The greatest difficulties with dates are in interpreting the many ways that months, seasons, and other nonnumeric parts of dates are presented. Fortunately, most of the creators of the citation metadata rendered all of these terms in English regardless of the language of publication, so we only had to understand and interpret English terms. We had two uses for dates: the first was for display and download, the second for sorting and retrieval. For display and download we used the form "month day, year," e.g., "Sep, 2001" or "Feb 8, 2002." Where possible we normalized the names of months to a three-letter abbreviation. For the purposes of sorting we turned the dates into numbers, using "12/32" for winter and "9/32" for fall. These numeric dates could be used to limit retrieval to a date or date range, and to present the retrieved citations in date order.

Pagination

Not only can pagination be rendered differently, such as with or without captions like "pp.," but different vendors record different data for pagination. Some give beginning and ending pagination; some provide only the first page of an article; some provide the total number of pages of the article's length. Pagination, or at least the beginning page number, is a key data element for the interlibrary loan function with a human seeking the print copy, as well as for automated linking to full text. A link to a full-text database typically includes the ISSN of the journal, the volume, and the page number of the start of the article. Some links require the issue number or date, if volume alone is not sufficient. Where possible we created a "start page" data element for linking purposes, but for the purposes of display we allowed a richer pagination statement to remain in the record. Similar to our normalization of volume numbers, we removed captions like "pp." from the actual data so that display programs and bibliographic software could caption this data element according to their own sets of rules.

Publication Types and Genres

In library catalogs each record is coded for the type of publication of the item, such as "book" or "music score" or "serial." There are also genre terms, such as "bibliographies" or "dictionaries," that are facets in the subject heading fields. Publication type is commonly offered as a way to limit a search to certain materials, so that a user can indicate that they are looking for the film version of *Romeo and Juliet,* not the text of the play. Genre terms are not generally presented as limits in library catalogs but are considered part of a subject search.

The A&I database records that the DLA processed often had publication type information in their metadata as well as genre terms. In most databases there is a single list, often called "publication type" or "document type," that covers both type and genre. This means that the metadata does not distinguish between the publication characteristics, i.e., journal article, and the content of the publication, i.e., book review, and there is no guarantee that a publication type in the library metadata sense is present in the record. In some databases, we found that we could only determine the difference between monographic publications and articles by the presence or absence of certain bibliographic elements such as the journal title, volume, and number. Where ISSNs and ISBNs were reliably present, they distinguished between books and journals, but the types of monographs covered by these databases do not consistently receive an ISBN (e.g., technical reports).

It was clear that in developing the search and limit capabilities for the A&I databases, the distinction between type and genre would not be the same as it was in the library catalog. We decided to follow the conventions of the A&I databases and create a single limit that intermingled the two. The next difficulty was that each database had its own list. These lists vary from a handful of basic document types to a few dozen types and genres. As an example, BIOSIS Previews, an A&I resource for finding life sciences information, assigns only these terms to its citations: article, meeting, patent, book, meeting report. PsycINFO, which indexes psychological research, has at least twenty-eight terms with some overlap with BIOSIS (book, journal article) but many more specific genres such as bibliography, law or statute, dissertation, and others. PsycINFO also covers other formats of materials such as films and maps. ABI/Inform has about as many genres in its list as PsycINFO, yet the only overlap is the term "review." Many databases have some genres that are specific to their topic, such as "product review" in a business database, or "clinical report" in a medical database. Finding the commonality across a variety of databases is a challenge, as table 6-1 illustrates.

Where possible, we normalized the wording and indexing of the genres, so that "literature review" and "review of the literature" both became "literature review"; "handbook/manual/guide" and "student handbook" became just "handbook." The gain in consistency made up for the potential loss of specificity in choices. The DLA produced a small core list of types and genres that was fairly consistent across databases that served general searching needs; those with expanded lists retained them, although this meant that cross-database searching by publication type was best limited to the core types.

The core types were analogous to the MARC record's publication type, emphasizing the structure of the publication rather than its content. Basic types would obviously be "journal article," "book," "book chapter," with the possible addition of "report" or "technical report" to cover those mono-

TABLE 6-1   Brief table of the variety of publication types and genres

ABI/Inform	BIOSIS	INSPEC	PsycINFO
	Article	Journal paper	Journal article
	Meeting	Conference proceedings	Conference
Review Audio review Book review Product review			Review

graphs not normally known to users as books. However, the publications resulting from conferences are so essential to many scientific fields that "conference paper" and "conference proceeding" were often found in the short list of main publication types in the vendor data. In the minds of researchers, these are a publication type unto themselves, and so in databases where these designations were used we included them as primary types along with "journal article" and "book." Because the publication type makes a difference when downloading records into bibliographic software or formatting it into a standard citation display, we looked at the types recognized by those software packages for the databases we were analyzing in order to help us create the core set.

Subject Headings

There is no common controlled subject vocabulary among A&I databases, and the degree of subject specificity in the metadata varies from undifferentiated fields of keywords to highly structured hierarchies of related terms. Often there are specialized subject fields relating to the main topical area of the database, and they are well known to regular users of the indexing service. Searchers in the business database ABI/Inform can find companies quickly and accurately using the ticker symbol index. INSPEC, which covers a wide range of engineering topics, has special topical headings for chemical names and astronomical objects. BIOSIS has a number of topical fields for biological terms like diseases, chemicals, and particular methodologies. It also provides headings that are structured hierarchically to represent taxonomies.

Experienced researchers and library reference staff would be able to make good use of these specialized indexes, and in each database that the DLA converted and provided to its users an effort was made to retain some of the database-specific search capabilities. At the same time, our usage statistics showed that the most frequently used search in all databases was the general keyword search that combined terms from all topical fields, so we created a keyword index for each database. Although less precise in nature, this keyword search was useful in cross-database searching.

Character Set

The data that the DLA received used the character set options available to data processing at the time, which means that the data was either in ASCII or in one of the extensions of ASCII such as Latin-1, which includes the accented characters found in western European languages. None of them used the character set of MARC records, MARC-8, which was the character set expected by the indexing and display software that the DLA employed in its database development. The bulk of the translation of the A&I database character set to MARC-8 was quite routine, but invariably the A&I databases each had employed some characters or character combinations that were not available in MARC-8. Some of these characters have since been defined in MARC-8, such as the spacing tilde. Most, however, were characters that had particular typographical roles, such as left and right quote marks and the em-dash. These are characters that are commonly found in word-processing software and used in printing but are not defined for library metadata. They were easily translated to equivalent characters in the MARC-8 character set by replacing them with their nearest keyboard equivalent.

More complex, and harder to solve from the point of view of usability, were the ways that some database developers had stretched the ASCII character set to accommodate chemical or mathematical notation, two notoriously difficult typographical challenges. The database vendors had clearly developed conventions that marked these special characters for the printing process, where they would be rendered correctly. Subsequently, some titles in the files contained some odd character sequences, like the following examples:

> Preparation and properties of Ba and La substituted PbNb/sub 2/O/sub 6/ ceramics . . .
>
> Bases of exponentials in the spaces $L\sp p(-\pi,\pi)$

Such titles are unattractive for display and are problematic when it comes to indexing. Clearly we could not expect users of the system to imitate this entry method for a chemical formula in their query. We also could not make use of superscripts or subscripts since there was no convention for entering these at a keyboard. Instead, special routines were developed that produced searchable keywords from these chemical name designations with only the characters a-z and 0-9, for example, "cs2pbnb6cl18," and user training and documentation instructed users to input a query for H_2O as simply "h2o." Although this formula will look "incorrect" to the trained eye, we did provide a predictable way that chemical names could be searched. We were able to overcome the indexing problems, but our display retained odd notation because our own system at that time was ASCII-based and could not render the special characters.

CONCLUSION

The examples in this chapter are just that: examples. They illustrate some of the manipulation of data done in the years in which the DLA loaded A&I datasets into the MELVYL system. Each database presented unique challenges and each was a learning experience for the analysts and developers on the projects. There were times when we went to great effort to produce an index or a display that, in the end, was rarely used. We struggled along the way with our desire to respond to the complex searching needs of the most sophisticated users and the simple searching that the majority of users actually utilize. Although we did provide some precise database-specific searching, it was obvious that our real success was in taking data from different sources and in different formats and providing a common look and feel for searching and display. Our system allowed users to search across databases without having to learn new search techniques for each one.

In the year 2002 the University of California ceased the practice of locally mounting A&I databases, and it now licenses them through the vendor interfaces. The economics of this are fairly obvious: as the number of databases available for licensing grew, the feasibility for the university to provide a reasonable portion of those resources using its own technology diminished. Our work with citation metadata was not over, however, and the years that we had spent normalizing input proved valuable as we shifted the focus to citation linking and automated interlibrary loan requests. The digital library is still interacting with a wide variety of metadata formats and is still coding algorithms to interpret authors' names, variant publication date practices, and the meaning of "pages" in different bibliographic environments. What was learned during the 1990s is helping the library cope with the next decade and the next step in bibliographic automation.

The conceptually "neat" era of cataloging rules and MARC records is drawing to a close. In the future librarians will be working increasingly with motley assortments of metadata that have few elements in common.

It is also likely that they will be creating real or virtual collections out of heterogeneous records. Although these will not have the internal consistency that can be achieved with well-crafted library metadata that follows AACR2 rules, this doesn't mean that the library has to give up the idea of providing quality service to users. It does mean that there is a burden on the library to clearly define its service goals and how those goals will be manifested in the metadata work of the library. The intelligence of our metadata transformations and crosswalks will be key to the success of future services to our users.

NOTES

1. In 1997 the Division of Library Automation was absorbed into a broader University of California project, the California Digital Library.
2. Current Contents is a current awareness resource that provides access to complete bibliographic research information from articles, editorials, meeting abstracts, commentaries, letters, book reviews, and all other significant items in recently published editions of over 8,000 of the world's leading scholarly journals and more than 2,000 books. Updated weekly, it is available in seven discipline-specific editions.
3. The DLA subsequently went on to load Information Access Company's Magazine, Computer files, Newspaper indexes, PsycINFO, BIOSIS, and ABI/Inform.
4. The Library of Congress has placed a few MARC-related programs on its website, at http://www.loc.gov/marc/marctools.html (accessed 10 December 2003). There are also programs available through the Open Source Software for Libraries site available at http://www.oss4lib.org/ (accessed 10 December 2003). Using most of these requires some programming skill.
5. The OpenURL is a protocol for interoperability between an information resource and a service component that offers localized services in an open linking environment. It is in effect an actionable URL that transports metadata or keys to access metadata for the object for which the OpenURL is provided. More information is available at Ex Libris, "SFX," http://www.sfxit.com/openurl/ (accessed 2 December 2003).
6. A proposal was passed by the MARC standards body, MARBI, that creates a subfield for enumeration details in the 773 field. See "Proposal 2003-03: Definition of Data Elements for Article Level Description," http://www.loc.gov/marc/marbi/2003/2003-03.html (accessed 10 December 2003).

7 CanCore: Semantic Interoperability for Learning Object Metadata

Norm Friesen

WITH ITS RECENT approval as a standard and its subsequent submission to the International Organization for Standardization (ISO) for further development, the Learning Object Metadata (LOM) data model has achieved a level of stability and international recognition requisite to its implementation in large-scale e-learning infrastructures.[1] As is the case with the Dublin Core Metadata Element Set (DCMES), the consensus represented and codified in the Learning Object Metadata data model provides implementers and developers with a common foundation for achieving interoperability. As a part of this development and implementation process, LOM is being refined and adapted by a wide variety of consortia and projects to meet the requirements of specific communities and domains. The CanCore Learning Object Metadata Application Profile represents one such effort at adaptation that has been undertaken in Canada—but whose relevance extends beyond Canada's borders. This chapter provides an overview of the LOM data model and undertakes a comparison of CanCore to other application profiling efforts. It discusses CanCore's contribution in terms of what has been called "semantic interoperability" and describes challenges presented by what is known as "syntactic" or "technical interoperability."

CHARACTERISTICS OF THE LOM DATA MODEL

Unlike the DCMES, LOM focuses on the description of modular, reusable, and specifically *educational* resources (or "learning objects") to facilitate their use by educators, authors, learners, and managers. In further contradistinction to the DCMES, LOM undertakes this task through what has been called a "structuralist" rather than a "minimalist" approach to metadata.[2] Instead of presenting a relatively simple data model that defines a minimal number of elements, LOM identifies seventy-six data elements covering a wide variety of characteristics attributable to learning objects, and places these elements in interrelationships that are both hierarchical and iterative.

At the top of the hierarchy of LOM elements are nine broad "category" elements: General, Lifecycle, Meta-metadata, Technical, Educational, Rights, Relation, Annotation, and Classification. Each of these category elements presents its own particular characteristics and in many cases its own challenges for implementation (see table 7-1).

TABLE 7-1   The nine broad "category" elements of the LOM data model

Element Category	Characteristics/Challenges
General	Defined as applying to the "learning object as a whole," the elements in this category include many that have equivalents in the DCMES (such as title, description, and coverage). However, the precise ways that a number of these elements are defined in LOM departs significantly from the corresponding DCMES definitions. For example, the General. Title element is not repeatable (except where a title is listed in multiple languages), making it difficult to accommodate title variations, series titles, or loosely translated title values.
Lifecycle	Uses hierarchically structured "contribute" elements along with the "Electronic Business Card" data model to record the roles and identities of various contributors.* The vCard specification mandates the use of its own nonstandardized encoding format, requiring the use of multiple parsing systems for LOM records. Because vCard is a specification for "virtual business cards," it also presents challenges for indicating corporate authorship and other collective contributions.

Table 7-1   continued

Element Category	Characteristics/Challenges
Meta-metadata	Reuses the "contribute" element construction from Lifecycle in slightly modified form, allowing for the attribution of the creation and validation of the metadata record itself.
Technical	Indicates the format, size, and other "objective" characteristics of the learning object.† Also provides a "requirements" element construction that allows for the formulation of machine-readable statements about specific technical supports needed for the use of the object.
Educational	Focuses on more "subjective" characteristics of the object, indicating audience attributes such as age, institutional context, and role (among other things). This category also provides elements that can be understood as falling into complex orthogonal interrelationships, describing the type and level of interactivity provided by the object, as well as the degree of concision of its contents. At the same time, this part of LOM has been criticized for its failure to address the educational characteristics of a learning resource in a substantial and flexible manner.
Rights	Uses four elements to indicate legal terms and conditions for the use of the learning object, but does not provide a clear way to accommodate emergent digital rights expression languages.‡
Relation	Also uses a small number of simply arranged elements to indicate the possible relations of a resource to other resources. Although this element is identified in LOM as equivalent to DC.Relation, the types of relations it describes differ from those identified in the DCMES.
Annotation	Employs only four elements to "enable educators to share their assessments, suggestions," and other "comments on the educational use of [the] learning object."**
Classification	Provides nine intricately structured elements (taxon source, taxon path, taxon identifier, taxon entry, and others) that can be adapted to the use of almost any classification or taxonomic purpose. Among the specific purposes recommended for this element group (as suggested by the recommended "vocabulary" values) are "ideas," "prerequisites," "educational objectives," "educational levels," and "competencies."

* Internet Mail Consortium, "vCard; The Electronic Business Card," version 2.1, 1998, http://www.imc.org/pdi/vcard-21.txt (accessed 6 August 2003).

† D. A. Wiley, M. M. Recker, and A. Gibbons, "In Defense of the By-Hand Assembly of Learning Objects," 2000, http://wiley.ed.usu.edu/docs/axiomatic.pdf (accessed 6 August 2003).

‡ Norm Friesen, Magda Mourad, and Robby Robson, "Towards a Digital Rights Expression Language Standard for Learning Technology: A Report of the IEEE Learning Technology Standards Committee Digital Rights Expression Language Study Group," 2002, http://ltsc.ieee.org/meeting/200212/doc/DREL_White_paper.doc (accessed 6 August 2003).

** Institute of Electrical and Electronics Engineers, IEEE P1484.12.2/D1, 2002-09-13, "Draft Standard for Learning Technology-Learning Object Metadata," 2002, http://ltsc.ieee.org/doc/wg12/LOM_1484_12_1_v1_Final_Draft.pdf (accessed 6 August 2003).

The LOM data elements are repeatable in different combinations, and on different levels within their hierarchical constructions. For example, on the lowest level in the hierarchy of elements in the Classification category, all elements should be repeatable as a group or category at least forty times. For each repetition on this level, at least fifteen different taxon paths can be specified; and for each of *these* repetitions, it should be possible to accommodate up to fifteen particular taxon identifiers and entries. This means that at a minimum, systems storing and processing LOM-compliant records should be able to accommodate at least 9,000 taxon identifier-value pairs.

Given the complex and demanding character of LOM, the task of adapting it to meet the specific and concrete needs of implementers and users requires interpretation, elaboration, extension, and perhaps especially, the simplification of both the technical demands and the myriad interpretive possibilities it presents.

LOM APPLICATION PROFILES

This task of interpretation and simplification has generally been understood as being the responsibility of application-profiling activities. In a document written jointly by representatives of the LOM and Dublin Core communities, an application profile is defined as "an assemblage of metadata elements selected from one or more metadata schemas and combined in a compound schema."[3] The numerous application profiles that interpret and adapt LOM may be separated into four general and not mutually exclusive groups:

1. Those that combine elements from LOM with elements from other metadata specifications and standards
2. Those that focus on the definition of element extensions and other customizations specifically for LOM
3. Those that emphasize the reduction of the number of LOM elements and the choices they present
4. Those that both simplify and undertake customized extensions of LOM

An example of the first, combinatory approach is provided by the Australian Le@rning Federation's Metadata Application Profile, which combines LOM elements with those from the DCMES, the Open Digital Rights Language, and other sources.[4] The second approach is prominently illustrated by the "CLEO Extensions" to both LOM data elements and controlled vocabularies developed jointly by Microsoft, IBM, Cisco, and Thompson NETg through the Customized Learning Experience Online Lab.[5] The third approach, focusing exclusively on the simplification of LOM, has been adopted by CanCore, and also characterizes the metadata profiling work undertaken by SingCore (http://www.ecc.org) and in the ADL SCORM reference framework.[6] The fourth approach, the simultaneous extension and reduction of the number of LOM elements, has been adopted by the Health Education Assets Laboratory and the United Kingdom's Curriculum Online project.[7]

CANCORE AND SEMANTIC INTEROPERABILITY

The approach taken by CanCore involves much more than a simple reduction in the number of elements recommended for use in LOM implementation. CanCore also places a great deal of emphasis on the refinement and precise definition of element and vocabulary *semantics,* applying wherever possible established and best practices from the larger metadata and cataloging communities.

CanCore has taken this approach with the intention of maximizing the potential for "semantic interoperability." Interoperability generally refers to "the ability of two or more systems or components to exchange information and to use the information that has been exchanged."[8] "Semantic interoperability" refers specifically to the meanings that are embedded in this exchanged information, and to the effective and consistent interpretation of these meanings. The systems or system components that carry out this interpretation, it should be emphasized, are generally human users rather than processing or transmission devices. For more about semantic interoperability as interpretive practice, see "Semantic Interoperability and Communities of Practice."[9]

CanCore's primary contribution to semantic interoperability takes the form of the Guidelines for Learning Object Metadata, a document in excess of 100 pages that is freely available from the CanCore website (http://www.cancore.org). This document provides a great deal of fine-grained information and guidance for each element and element group in LOM, including:

> explication and interpretation of element definitions and descriptions
>
> recommendations for element and vocabulary application based on existing best and common practices
>
> multilingual plain language and XML-encoded examples
>
> technical implementation notes

The notes, recommendations, examples, and interpretations that make up the CanCore guidelines contribute to semantic interoperability by reflecting consensus on common and best practices. In so doing, they also help to form a basis for further consensus on these practices. In this context, "common practice" refers to techniques and conventions—sometimes as simple as putting first personal name last, last name first—that are practical, widely understood, and can be consistently applied. Best practices, such as the use of LOM vocabulary values *in addition to* locally developed value sets, are typically demonstrably superior to other methods in optimizing interoperability.

For example, CanCore references a number of the recommendations, definitions, and practices developed by the Dublin Core Metadata Initiative and its communities of practice. In one specific instance, CanCore provides and recommends the use of Dublin Core definitions for DC.Source and qualified DC.Relation where an approximate or direct equivalence is suggested in LOM. In this way, CanCore leverages the semantic consensus already formalized in the DCMES and refined in the Dublin Core community to promote semantic interoperability among projects referencing the LOM, and also to work toward cross-domain interoperability through mutual reference to the DCMES.

CanCore also attempts to reflect and shape current practice by providing overviews of the interpretations of other application profiles in its guidelines documentation. Noting the convergence or divergence that some of this existing practice indicates, the CanCore guidelines often recommend interpretations and understandings that either mediate between this divergence or strengthen what appear to be emerging areas of consensus.

The first version of the CanCore guidelines was released in June 2002, and is based on version 1.2.1 of the IMS Learning Resource Metadata specification.[10] Since then these guidelines have been distributed and referenced internationally. They have, for example, been referenced extensively in the UK Common Metadata Framework and have been implemented in the LearnAlberta.ca repository initiative by Alberta Learning and in the EXPLOR@2 product by Technologies Cogigraph Inc. of Quebec.[11] While finding CanCore's guidelines and recommendations to be of great utility, some users and stakeholders have asked that the guidelines documentation be made simpler and more concise. Some have also encouraged CanCore to focus exclusively on LOM semantics, and to avoid the definition of custom vocabularies. These and other requests and revisions are being incorporated into the new version of the CanCore guidelines documentation, which is based exclusively on the new IEEE (Institute of Electrical and Electronics Engineers) LOM standard, and which will be presented in both print and dynamic web-based forms.

In both surveying and helping to form this emerging consensus, CanCore has received valuable input and assistance from a wide variety of projects and organizations.[12]

GUIDELINES FOR PRACTICE

The importance of "best practice" guidelines such as those developed by CanCore is generally recognized in the larger metadata community. Such guidelines have been developed for a variety of metadata specifications and implementations. Examples include the broadly based Using Dublin

Core guidelines, the CIMI Guide to Best Practice: Dublin Core developed for the museums community, and the Online Archive of California Best Practice Guidelines developed to support the Encoded Archival Description specification.[13] In the first of these documents, the purpose of the Dublin Core guidelines is described as follows:

> [An] important goal of this document is to promote "best practices" for describing resources using the Dublin Core element set. The Dublin Core community recognizes that consistency in creating metadata is an important key to achieving complete retrieval and intelligible display across disparate sources of descriptive records. Inconsistent metadata effectively hides desired records, resulting in uneven, unpredictable or incomplete search results.

A similar argument can be said to motivate each of the guidelines documents mentioned above.

In each case, as in the CanCore guidelines, brief definitions of the elements provided in the data model itself are augmented and refined. These guidelines also provide examples of how the elements would be used, and often highlight and attempt to resolve ambiguities that elements can present to implementers and record creators. Especially in the case of the CIMI (Consortium for the Computer Interchange of Museum Information) documentation, significant reference is also made to best practices as they have emerged in the field of cataloging and indexing, and as they are encoded in cataloging rules, such as the Anglo-American Cataloguing Rules (AACR2).

The complexity of Learning Object Metadata, as well as its widespread adoption, would seem to underscore the need for similar guidelines in the e-learning community. The apparent lack of publicly available, normative interpretation and explication of LOM elements represents a conspicuous gap existing across implementations and communities that CanCore hopes to address.

CanCore is also attempting to address these issues through its participation in the further standardization and development of LOM. CanCore has been actively participating in forums related to this standard, including the IMS Metadata Special Interest Group, the relevant working group in the IEEE Learning Technology Standards Committee, and ISO/IEC JTC1 SC36 (Subcommittee for Information Technology for Learning, Education and Training). It is in the context of the latter ISO group that significant international inputs are being gathered for further LOM development, and CanCore has been active in both supplying and gathering such inputs.[14]

APPROACHES TO SYNTACTIC INTEROPERABILITY

A second form of interoperability that is frequently emphasized in the literature, and that has played an important role in CanCore's development, is known as "technical" or "syntactic" interoperability. This form of interoperability is concerned with the technical issues and standards involved in the effective "communication, transport, storage and representation" of metadata and other types of information.[15] Its significance for CanCore can be said to lie less in any opportunities for simplification than in the importance of maintaining the full complexity of the LOM data model.

The LOM, like the DCMES, is dependent on data bindings for the interoperable representation, communication, and transport of metadata records. "Binding" refers to the expression of the LOM data model via a formal language or syntax for the purposes of effective data exchange and processing. In the case of both LOM and Dublin Core, the general standards used for creating these bindings include RDFS (Resource Description Framework Schema) and XMSL (Extensible Markup Schema Language). In the case of LOM, the specific way that the XML Schema Language is used to format or "bind" LOM data is itself the subject of standardization. In the summer of 2003, the XML binding for LOM was being standardized by the Institute of Electrical and Electronics Engineers to become part two of what will then be a "multipart" LOM standard.

Despite these and other efforts in support of technical interoperability for LOM, significant challenges and misunderstandings seem to persist.[16] Some of these problems arise from the intricacy and iteration that are a part of the hierarchical structures of the LOM data model. The complexity of these structures, while well suited to encoding and representation in XML, can be difficult to accommodate using common database techniques.[17] Specifically, the structures' number and iteration can be challenging to faithfully represent using the tabular and relational structures that are at the core of common database technologies. As a simple illustration, converting sample LOM records into common database file formats using automated routines will produce relational structures with forty or more tables.[18] Such a means of storing and accessing data can be, as Shanmugasundaram et al. put it, "unwieldy," to say the least. Compounding this problem is the fact that attractive alternatives to relational database technologies (for example, native XML databases) tend to be very costly, and are currently not available as mature open-source products.

This problem has placed considerable pressure on implementers to simplify LOM—to reduce the number of elements, element iterations, and other complexities in the LOM data model. In doing so, implementers would be able to greatly reduce the number of tables that are required for a relational database to reliably store LOM data. They might also be able to reduce the challenges of processing both XML and vCard encodings. In some cases, this has led implementers to develop simplified versions of the LOM XML binding, which specify limitations on element numbers and iterations. In other instances, it has presumably led to the development of application profiles that limit the use and iteration of LOM data elements.

However, attempts to simplify the LOM data model as it is implemented in databases and other infrastructure elements create other difficulties in the area of technical or syntactic interoperability. These difficulties arise from the fact that systems based on "simplified" LOM data models will not be able to reliably exchange and store metadata records that utilize particular parts, or even the whole, of the LOM data model. If systems are incapable of processing and storing anything less than the full LOM element set with *at least* the number of elements and iterations specified by LOM, there is a danger that these systems will truncate records from other systems they might receive, store, and then retransmit. With the prominence of metadata record-sharing strategies exemplified by the Open Archives Initiative's metadata harvesting protocol, the danger of such truncation is real, not hypothetical.[19]

As a result, in identifying a subset of recommended elements, the CanCore guidelines underscore the fact that this subset does *not* represent an acceptable minimum for transmission and storage infrastructures. To further support this point, this document provides recommendations and support for *all* of the elements in LOM—not just those in its element subset. The guidelines further emphasize that the CanCore subset, like any other simplification of the LOM data model, only applies to metadata record creation and display. In these particular contexts, it is often desirable to introduce even further simplifications and constraints than those explicitly recommended by CanCore.[20]

CONCLUSION

Metadata profiling efforts can provide significant guidance and support for the difficult task of implementing complex and abstract data models. In its Guidelines for Learning Object Metadata, CanCore goes further than other application profiles in interpreting and explicating element and vocabulary semantics, as well as reflecting and attempting to reinforce best and common practices. However, CanCore, like any other LOM application profile, is incapable of shielding technical implementers from the syntactic implications of the LOM data model. While application profiles can simplify, augment, and interpret the LOM data model to enhance *semantic* interoperation, providing similar support for *syntactic* interoperability is a different matter. The full set of elements and hierarchical interrelationships as outlined in LOM provide, by definition, the simplest common set of conditions for achieving technical interoperability. Speaking very broadly, both LOM and the DCMES, despite different approaches, can be said to present their respective communities not only with a common solution but also with a common set of problems or challenges. At the same time, whether in the areas of semantic, syntactic, or other forms of interoperability, these metadata standards also present the opportunity for the collaborative development of solutions, as well as their sharing and reuse across implementations.[21]

NOTES

1. Institute of Electrical and Electronics Engineers, IEEE P1484.12.2/D1, 2002-09-13, "Draft Standard for Learning Technology—Learning Object Metadata," 2002, http://ltsc.ieee.org/doc/wg12/LOM_1484_12_1_v1_Final_Draft.pdf (accessed 6 August 2003); ISO/IEC JTC1 SC36 WG4, "Resolutions of 2003-03 SC36/WG4 Meeting," 2003, http://mdlet.jtc1sc36.org/doc/SC36_WG4_N0020.pdf (accessed 6 August 2003).
2. Stuart Weibel, Renato Iannella, and Warwick Cathro, "The 4th Dublin Core Metadata Workshop Report," *D-Lib Magazine,* June 1997, http://www.dlib.org/dlib/june97/metadata/06weibel.html (accessed 6 August 2003).
3. Erik Duval, Wayne Hodgins, Stuart Sutton, and Stuart L. Weibel, "Metadata Principles and Practicalities," *D-Lib Magazine,* April 2002, http://www.dlib.org/dlib/april02/weibel/04weibel.html (accessed 6 August 2003).
4. Le@rning Federation, "Metadata Application Profile," 2003, http://www.thelearningfederation.edu.au/repo/cms2/tlf/published/3859/docs/Metadata_Application_Profile_1_2.pdf (accessed 6 August 2003).
5. Customized Learning Experience Online, "CLEO Extensions to the IEEE Learning Object Metadata," 2003, http://www.cleolab.org/CLEO_LOM_Ext_v1d1a.pdf (accessed 6 August 2003).

6. Advanced Distributed Learning, "SCORM Version 1.3, Application Profile Working Draft Version 1.0," 2003, http://www.adlnet.org/index.cfm? fuseaction=DownFile&libid=496&cfid=134102&cftoken=37120141&bc= false (accessed 6 August 2003).
7. Health Education Assets Library (HEAL metadata schema web page), http:// www.healcentral.org/metadata_schema.htm (accessed 2 December 2003); Curriculum Online (metadata guides page), http://www.curriculumonline.gov.uk/ Curriculum+OnLine/SupplierInfo/metadatadocs.htm?Nav=SupplierInfo (accessed 2 December 2003).
8. Institute of Electrical and Electronics Engineers, *IEEE Standard Computer Dictionary: A Compilation of IEEE Standard Computer Glossaries* (New York: Institute of Electrical and Electronics Engineers, 1990).
9. Norm Friesen, "Semantic Interoperability and Communities of Practice," in Global Summit of Online Learning Networks: Papers, ed. Jon Mason (Adelaide, Australia: Educationau, 2002), also available at http://www.educationau.edu.au/ globalsummit/papers/nfriesen.htm (accessed 6 August 2003).
10. IMS Global Learning Consortium, "IMS Learning Resource Meta-data Specification," 2001, http://www.imsglobal.org/metadata/index.cfm (accessed 6 August 2003).
11. Scott Wilson, "First Draft of UK Common Metadata Framework Released," 2003, http://www.cetis.ac.uk/content/20030523110919 (accessed 6 August 2003).
12. These projects and organizations have included, at various stages: Academic Technologies for Learning of the University of Alberta, Alberta Learning, Athabasca University, British Columbia Open University, Canadian Department of National Defense, Centre Recherché LICEF, CETIS UK, the Eisenhower National Clearinghouse, Electronic Text Centre of the University of New Brunswick, European Knowledge Network, Galbraith Media, Learning and Teaching Scotland, Library and Archives of Canada, Manitoba Education and Youth, Memorial University, Ontario Ministry of Education, The Open Learning Agency of British Columbia, TeleEducation New Brunswick, and the University of Calgary.
13. Diane Hillmann, "Using Dublin Core," 2001, http://dublincore.org/ documents/2000/07/16/usageguide/ (accessed 6 August 2003); Consortium for the Computer Interchange of Museum Information, "Guide to Best Practice: Dublin Core," 2000, http://www.cimi.org/public_docs/meta_bestprac_v1_1_ 210400.pdf (accessed 2 December 2003); Online Archive of California, "Online Archive of California Best Practice Guidelines," 2001, http://www.cdlib.org/ about/publications/oacbpg2001-08-23.pdf (accessed 2 December 2003).
14. Norm Friesen et al., "CanCore: Principles and Positions on Learning Object Metadata," 2003, contribution of the Canadian National Body to ISO/IEC JTC1 SC36 WG4, "Learning Resource Metadata," http://jtc1sc36.org/doc/ 36N0430.pdf (accessed 6 August 2003); Norm Friesen and Lassi Nirhamo, "LOM Survey Announcement," 2003, http://mdlet.jtc1sc36.org/doc/SC36_ WG4_N0029.pdf (accessed 6 August 2003).
15. Paul Miller, "UK Interoperability Focus," 2000, http://www.ukoln.ac.uk/ interop-focus/about/ (accessed 6 August 2003). See also Hewlett-Packard,

"Introduction to Semantic Web Technologies," 2003, http://www.hpl.hp.com/ semweb/sw-technology.htm (accessed 6 August 2003).

16. Steve Richardson and Andy Powell, "Exposing Information Resources for E-Learning—Harvesting and Searching IMS Metadata Using the OAI Protocol for Metadata Harvesting and Z39.50," *Ariadne* 34 (2003), http://www.ariadne .ac.uk/issue34/powell/ (accessed 6 August 2003); IMS Global Learning Consortium, "IMS Digital Repositories Specification," 2003, http://www .imsglobal.org/digitalrepositories (accessed 6 August 2003).

17. Jayavel Shanmugasundaram et al., "Relational Databases for Querying XML Documents: Limitations and Opportunities," in *Proceedings of the 25th Very Large Database Conference,* September 1999, http://www.cs.cornell.edu/people/ jai/papers/RdbmsForXML.pdf (accessed 6 August 2003).

18. Such a conversion from LOM XML formatting specifically to relational database structures can be easily undertaken. Sample XML records can be freely downloaded from the IMS Global Consortium website. (See note 10.) XML editing and validation software such as XML Spy can then be used to transform these metadata records into the complex relational structures (with dozens of tables) that are required for processing by relational databases. These relational structures can then be imported and viewed using database programs such as MySQL or Microsoft Access.

19. Richardson and Powell, "Exposing Information Resources."

20. Friesen et al., "CanCore: Principles and Positions."

21. Miller, "UK Interoperability Focus."

8

The Alexandria Digital Library Project: Metadata Development and Use

Linda L. Hill and Greg Janée

THE ALEXANDRIA DIGITAL Library (ADL) Project has the unique advantage of developing georeferenced digital libraries holding both textual and geospatial resources and providing services that provide geospatial description and access for all resources. The ADL Project evolved from the Map & Imagery Lab (MIL) of the University of California-Santa Barbara's Davidson Library and is today an operational part of the MIL.[1] The computer science, geography, and library science disciplines have been involved in ADL's development, which has been funded primarily by the National Science Foundation (NSF). The ADL's metadata structures and knowledge organization systems (KOS) are grounded in practices originating in traditional libraries, in geospatial and data clearinghouses, and in geographic information system (GIS) analysis environments. "Geospatially aware" digital library software, collections, and demonstration projects have emerged from this work that are freely available for wider use. This chapter presents a high-level view of ADL's metadata and KOS activities from the project's ten years of developing the infrastructure and components for *distributed* georeferenced digital libraries.

GEOREFERENCED DIGITAL LIBRARIES

There are two fundamental types of georeferencing: by place-names and by geospatial coordinates (primarily longitude and latitude, but also by grid reference such as the Universal Transverse Mercator, or UTM, system). Place-names are used in discourse and text, subject headings and index terms, labels on maps, and to identify administrative districts for addresses, statistics, and data. Geospatial coordinates are used to represent the location of features on the surface of the Earth and the coverage of maps, aerial photographs, remote-sensing images, and datasets of various kinds. Typically, the predominant use of place-name or coordinate place referencing has been associated with domains of information resources that have been treated by separate information management systems: text-based systems on the one hand and GIS on the other. Georeferenced digital libraries, by allowing users to pursue a place-based interest starting with either a place-name or a map location and retrieving both textual documents and geospatial data, bridge the gap between these types of information resources. This is achieved by integrating digital gazetteers into the system to translate between place-names and coordinate locations and by accommodating coordinate-based spatial referencing in basic metadata structures, data storage, data processing, and services.

In traditional libraries, geospatial documents and information services have been the focus of map collections and map librarianship.[2] This is again a form of the separation in treatment that generally exists for textual documents versus geospatial documents and data. Coordinate fields for MARC cataloging were developed by map librarians and are currently available in the 034 (coded cartographic data) and 255 (cartographic mathematical) fields.[3] As their names imply, these fields were intended for "cartographic" description and that is how they are used. It is not current practice to use these fields to catalog documents such as environmental impact reports that are also explicitly associated with coordinate-defined locations; place-name referencing using MARC field 651 (geographic name) and to some extent field 650 (topical term) is used instead.

Geographic information systems provide a rich modeling and analytical processing environment for geospatial data, with complex methods of geospatial referencing, data manipulation, and visualization. They also include place-name referencing in the form of labels for identified features within a GIS layer, e.g., the name for a lake in a hydrographic layer. In GIS, the coordinates are the primary focus and the place-names are secondary, the exact opposite of the text-based systems. Metadata documentation of the geospatial aspects of geographic datasets is very detailed to support both evaluation of fitness for use for particular purposes (e.g., can the data be used for navigation?) and for computer processing (e.g., geodetic datum, scale of resolution, level of certainty, scheme for coordinate representation).

Georeferenced digital libraries like ADL merge mathematical (coordinate representation) and textual (place-name references) georeferencing into an integrated system, where crossover in representation allows a user, using a single query, to find and accumulate information of all types that is associated with a geographic location and to visualize the results on a map. In addition, ADL is designed to be a distributed system of stand-alone or networked nodes. It is important to note that ADL's emphasis for metadata development has not been at the item level of description, but on metadata to support distributed searching and access across dissimilar collections, as well as on the design of KOS (i.e., gazetteers and thesauri) needed for georeferenced digital libraries. The ADL specification has no requirements for item-level description, but rather accommodates whatever item-level metadata the collection owner chooses to use through the mapping of searchable data elements to search indexes, as explained later in this chapter.

OVERVIEW OF ADL METADATA AND KOS DEVELOPMENTS

A full description of the ADL distributed library architecture is outside the scope of this chapter.[4] Briefly, ADL is structured as a set of distributed nodes (peers), each supporting one or more *collections* of *items*, subsets of which may be "published" (made visible) to other nodes. The combined *library* is the sum of all such collections. Collections are documented by collection-level metadata. Items are largely undefined by the architecture beyond the expectation that they are independent items documented by item-level metadata and that they are uniquely identified within a particular collection. While the contents of the distributed library may be heterogeneous, three features integrate the library into a uniform whole: (1) the ADL "bucket" system (a common model for search metadata), (2) a common format for collection-level metadata, and (3) a central collection discovery service that operates on indexes created from the collection-level metadata. Each ADL node is implemented as a Java web application that provides Java, HTTP, and RMI (Java remote method invocation) client interfaces. A second interface layer defines the interface between ADL nodes and collection implementations, or "drivers." ADL provides several drivers that support different collection implementation strategies, including relational databases, XML (Extensible Markup Language) document stores, and Z39.50 protocol services (experimental as of November 2003).

The Alexandria Digital Library Project website is the main access point for all ADL research and operational documentation and links to related resources.[5] To provide an overview for the discussion that follows, specific ADL metadata and KOS activities for distributed georeferenced digital libraries are listed here, with associated references.

Metadata include:

1. Support for search across dissimilar distributed collections through a common set of attributes that constitute search indexes[6]
2. Design of collection-level descriptions which support discovery of appropriate collections, and provide contextual and inherent information about collections for end users[7]
3. Design of metadata for access; i.e., standard views of item-level metadata describing what users/clients need to know to fetch and process it[8]
4. Development of a simple spatial geometry language, based on the Geometry Markup Language[9]
5. Collaborative development of the metadata design for the Digital Library for Earth System Education[10]
6. Development of a content standard for computational models[11]

Knowledge organization system activities include:

7. Design of protocols for the searching of distributed gazetteers and thesauri[12]
8. Design of a content standard for gazetteers[13]
9. Development of a Feature Type Thesaurus for gazetteers[14]
10. Use of concept spaces in support of undergraduate classroom education[15]

METADATA STRUCTURES TO SUPPORT DISTRIBUTED SEARCHING AND RETRIEVAL

Key metadata components of the ADL architecture are the search buckets, collection-level metadata, access metadata, standard reports, and browse image metadata. (See figure 8-1.)

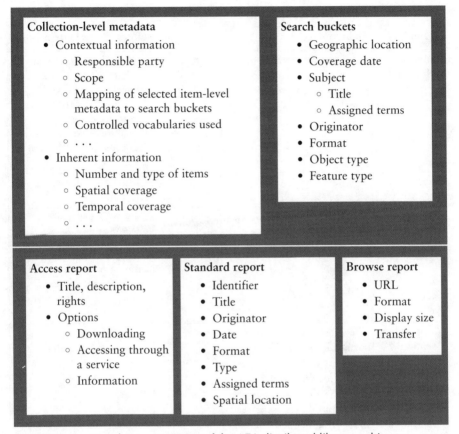

Collection-level metadata
- Contextual information
  ○ Responsible party
  ○ Scope
  ○ Mapping of selected item-level metadata to search buckets
  ○ Controlled vocabularies used
  ○ . . .
- Inherent information
  ○ Number and type of items
  ○ Spatial coverage
  ○ Temporal coverage
  ○ . . .

Search buckets
- Geographic location
- Coverage date
- Subject
  ○ Title
  ○ Assigned terms
- Originator
- Format
- Object type
- Feature type

Access report
- Title, description, rights
- Options
  ○ Downloading
  ○ Accessing through a service
  ○ Information

Standard report
- Identifier
- Title
- Originator
- Date
- Format
- Type
- Assigned terms
- Spatial location

Browse report
- URL
- Format
- Display size
- Transfer

FIGURE 8-1   Metadata components of the ADL distributed library architecture

The *search bucket* component is specifically designed to support common search indexes for distributed, heterogeneous collections (see table 8-1).[16] These search buckets are based on library practices and on common indexes to bibliographic databases, and they can be compared to the Dublin Core Metadata Initiative (DCMI) in that they are composed of high-level attributes common to most item-level descriptions.[17] A key feature of the ADL *search bucket* metadata structure is that it is composed of *typed* data elements for which specific *search constraints* can be defined. (See table 8-2.)

TABLE 8-1 Core ADL search buckets

Name	Definition	Data Type	Notes (DC = Dublin Core)
Subject-related text	Text indicative of the subject of the item, not necessarily from controlled vocabularies	textual	Title and assigned term buckets are sub-buckets to subject-related text. Mappings to this bucket can include abstracts, notes, free-text keywords, etc. Closest DC element: DC.Subject
Title	The item's title(s)	textual	Closest DC element: DC.Title
Assigned term	Subject-related terms from controlled vocabularies	textual	Closest DC element: DC.Subject
Originator	Names of entities related to the origination of the item	textual	Both persons and organizations; no particular syntax required. Closest DC elements: DC.Creator and DC.Publisher
Geographic location	The subset of the Earth's surface to which the item is related; expressed as a geometric region and defined in WGS84 latitude/longitude coordinates, expressed in an ADL-defined language	spatial	Closest DC element: DC.Coverage.Spatial
Coverage date	The calendar dates to which the item is relevant, expressed according to ISO 8601.	temporal	Closest DC element: DC.Coverage.Temporal
Object type	The intellectual type of the item	hierarchical	Closest DC element: DC.Type
Feature type	The type of the feature for gazetteers specifically	hierarchical	Closest DC element: DC.Type
Format	The physical type of the item	hierarchical	Closest DC element: DC.Format
Identifier	Names and codes that function as unique identifiers with, optionally, associated namespaces	identification	Closest DC element: DC.Identifier

TABLE 8-2   ADL search bucket types

Bucket Type	Value Type	Constraints	Example
Spatial	Any of several types of geometric regions defined in WGS84 latitude/longitude coordinates, expressed in an ADL-defined syntax	overlaps contains within	Find maps with coverage within this search region
Temporal	Range of calendar dates or single date in ISO 8601 syntax	overlaps contains within	Find aerial photos that have a date within the range of 1925 and 1935
Hierarchical	Term from a cited scheme; that is, a controlled vocabulary or thesaurus	*is a* relationship (hierarchical expand)	Find objects that are "images" and include objects that are *narrower terms* of "images" also
Textual	Text	any words (OR) all words (AND) phrase	Find place-names containing both "santa" and "barbara"
Numeric	Real number in standard scientific notation	<, =, >, . . .	Find populated places with population greater than 500,000
Identification	Identifier with an optional associated namespace	matches	Find a book with ISBN 0-201-63274-8

The types are spatial (coordinates), temporal, hierarchical term sets, textual, numeric, and identifiers. In addition to being typed, the buckets are semantically defined to ensure expected search results and to guide the mapping from the item-level metadata to the search buckets. There are no constraints or expectations for the metadata structure used to describe the items in the collections. Mappings from item-level metadata to the search buckets, which are done by the collection owner, are expected to meet the semantic definitions of the buckets, and the mappings themselves are documented explicitly in the collection-level metadata.

The Alexandria Digital Library's *collection-level metadata* provides a structure to describe the inherent and contextual attributes of a collection, here defined as any collection of items formally presented as a collection within a digital library.[18] Contextual information includes title, responsible party, scope and purpose, update frequency, etc. Inherent information is gathered from the collection itself, such as total number of items and subtotals by type, format, year and decade, and spatial coverage (which can be displayed on a map). Contextual information also includes the documentation of the mappings made from selected item-level metadata elements to the ADL search buckets. This mapping is very specific; for instance, MARC 21 fields 100 (main entry---personal name) and 110 (main entry---corporate name) have been mapped to the Contributor bucket. This collection-level documentation is useful in three ways. It provides:

> user understanding of the scope and origin of the collection;

> more specific search capability by querying item-level descriptive elements directly; that is, extending the search capability to a two-level process of searching first at the level of common, high-level search buckets and subsequently at the level of item metadata elements; and

> collection discovery by focusing queries on the collections most likely to contain the information needed.

The third metadata component for the distributed digital library architecture, the *access metadata,* is for the purpose of documenting intellectual property rights and what a user needs to know to retrieve library objects. It formalizes the description of the aspects of the item needed for downloading and processing.[19] Included are the basic descriptive elements of title, description, and rights, and the key attributes needed for downloading, accessing through a programmatic protocol or service, connecting to a web interface for more information, or obtaining an off-line item.

The fourth component is a metadata structure for *standard reports* so that the results obtained from heterogeneous collections are returned to the user or client in a predictable format. Standard reports reflect the reduced set of information about the item in the search buckets. Extended reports for the full item-level metadata are not specified by the ADL framework; the collection owner provides these according to the metadata structure used for the items or by local processes that create different metadata views of the item-level records.

A final metadata component required is one for describing the *browse images* that accompany items in the collections. These reduced images are included in the standard and extended reports to show the user a view of the object (see figure 8-2). The metadata for browse images includes an identifier and URL for the image and details about the format, display size in pixels, and transfer size in bytes.

In summary, the ADL Project has designed a distributed library architecture which includes metadata structures to support searching on core descriptive elements across heterogeneous collections, and collection-level metadata that defines the collections for human understanding and provides statistics and specifications needed for processing and collection discovery. These metadata components include geospatial representation as well as common core elements of item-level description, such as title, subject, and the persons, organizations, and dates associated with the item. Additional metadata structures are defined for accessing the items themselves, specifying standard reports, and describing the browse images that accompany image objects. All of these have been refined through the implementation of the operational Alexandria Digital Library.

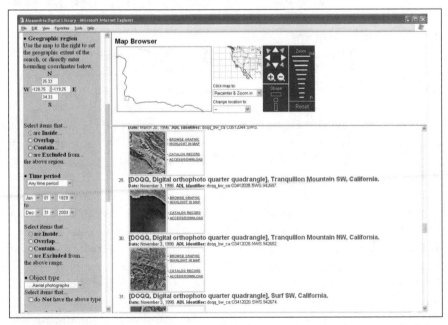

FIGURE 8-2   Screenshot of an ADL interface showing query parameters on the left, map browser on the top, and browse graphics with results for the search

METADATA STRUCTURES FOR SPECIAL PURPOSES

Metadata frameworks for representing geospatial data, at the item level, exist within and for the GIS community. The U.S. Federal Geographic Data Committee (FGDC) published version 1 of its Content Standard for Digital Geospatial Metadata in 1994 and the second version in 1998.[20] The Australia New Zealand Land Information Council (ANZLIC) published version 2 of its spatial information metadata guidelines in 2001.[21] The International Organization for Standardization's (ISO's) Technical Committee 211 (ISO TC 211) has recently released the Geographic Information Metadata standard that evolved from the FGDC and ANZLIC standards.[22] Profiles of the ISO standard will be developed to harmonize the earlier geospatial metadata standards with the ISO standard. Another source of geospatial metadata specifications is the Open GIS Consortium (OGC), "an international industry consortium of 258 companies, government agencies and universities participating in a consensus process to develop publicly available geoprocessing specifications."[23] The Geography Markup Language (GML) is "an XML grammar written in XML Schema for the modeling, transport, and storage of geographic information."[24]

These standards establish the framework for the item-level description of geospatial data. They are, however, developed for mapping and analysis, and for the reuse of geospatial data beyond the original purpose for the collection of the data. For use in digital library environments, something simpler is needed that preserves valid geospatial representation but simplifies the metadata structure. In collaboration with the Digital Library for Earth System Education and NASA, ADL developed a set of metadata elements to describe geospatial location as part of the ADN metadata framework.[25] This same set of geospatial elements was used for the Content Standard for Computational Models.[26] For the DCMI, Simon Cox developed a set of metadata elements to describe geospatial points and bounding boxes, with the same goal of encouraging the inclusion of geospatial referencing in metadata outside of the GIS environment.[27]

Greg Janée, lead software engineer for ADL, developed the following principles to guide the development of a new "simple geography language" that will be based on existing standards and will be suitable for use in digital library metadata:[28]

1. The number of different shapes supported by the language must be large enough to support both description of object footprints with reasonable fidelity and spatial searching over those footprints, but should be as small as possible to lessen the burden on users of the language. Simple shapes under consideration include points to represent point features (e.g., water wells); boxes as a simplified way to represent area features; disks (areas described by point and radius) to represent areas with uncertain location and extent; simple polygons (i.e., no donut shapes) to represent the shape of areas with greater fidelity than is possible with boxes; and polylines to represent linear features such as rivers. Aggregations of sets of shapes, either constrained to one kind of shape (e.g., set of points, set of polygons) or unconstrained, may also be needed.

2. The spatial reference system (SRS) in which primary shapes are defined (i.e., the coordinate system + datum) must not be mandated by the language, but should be declarable in a standard way. Mandating the use of a particular SRS places too high a burden on the users of the language, who would be forced to translate from an SRS used locally to the SRS mandated by the simple geometry language. Such translations can be mathematically complex and introduce unintended consequences.

3. The geometry language must provide a lingua franca that virtually all geometry consumers and producers can understand; in practice, due to simplicity of implementation and widespread support, this means that bounding boxes (also known as minimum bounding rectangles) must be encoded in parallel with all primary shapes. Such bounding boxes must be defined with respect to a spherical topology (i.e., there must be no discontinuity at the 180° meridian) and, notwithstanding principle 2, must be defined in a standard SRS, namely, WGS84 latitude/longitude coordinates. (SRS translations are generally not a problem when converting to simplified forms such as bounding boxes.)

In this statement, "datum" refers to the system of measurement and representation that defines the size and shape of the Earth and the origin and orientation of an Earth coordinate system. There are many of these definitions designed for different purposes. The World Geodetic System of

1984, or WGS84, is one such geodetic datum that is often used. The requirement that a bounding box be associated with each primary shape is needed to support base-level geospatial searching using "greater than" and "less than" comparisons of coordinate values in systems with limited geospatial query-matching capability.

The OGC's Simple Features–SQL specification and its XML companion specification, GML version 2, provide much of what the aforementioned principles require—with the exception of principle 3, mandating a simple lingua franca.[29] As of November 2003, a preliminary version of a "simple geography language," based on the GML specification, has been developed. Further development, implementation, and testing of the specification within ADL will continue before being published for general comment and use.

The metadata design challenge for non-GIS metadata is to incorporate a simplified representation of geospatial location that is consistent with the standards developed by the geospatial data community. There is an educational challenge as well: to help collection managers develop an understanding of geospatial location as a key representational component and a key place-based retrieval parameter across multiple domains of knowledge. The ability to find and accumulate information about a location, including the geography, climate, occurrence of biological organisms, cultural history and artifacts, remote sensing images, photographs (aerial and ground-based), social statistics, and descriptive documents, depends on meeting these challenges.

REPRESENTING NAMED GEOGRAPHIC PLACES

Toponymy is the "taxonomic study of place-names, based on etymological, historical, and geographical information," and the term is also used to mean the place-names for a region—e.g., the toponymy of El Salvador.[30] Toponymic authorities exist at national and state/province levels and apply established rules to designate the official names for geographic locations. In the United States, this authority is the U.S. Board on Geographic Names, which is an "interagency board established by public law to standardize geographic name spellings for use in U.S. Government publications."[31] At the United Nations, a permanent commission known as the United Nations Group of Experts on Geographical Names promotes the "consistent use worldwide of accurate place names" through cooperative efforts among countries.[32]

Place-names (e.g., Chicago, the Rocky Mountains, Coit Tower) are the dominant means of georeferencing outside of the geospatial data environment. Only some place-names are authorized for official use by toponymic authorities. Other names are known as colloquial names (e.g., "the Windy City" and "the Rockies"), or variant names. Different toponymic authorities can make different names official for the same place and, of course, place-names and other aspects of named geographic places change through time.

Gazetteers are dictionaries or indexes of named geographic features (places), and geospatially defined gazetteers contain entries in which geographic features are defined by both place-names and geospatial location. Such gazetteers can be used to translate from a place-name (official or not) to a map location. For example, a document or image or a query statement about Chicago can be linked to the map location of Chicago through the use of a gazetteer. Once the coordinate location is known, a spatial search for the geographic area of Chicago can be extended to retrieve relevant information that does not contain "Chicago" as a searchable place-name. Gazetteers, therefore, are key components of georeferenced digital libraries.

Each toponymic authority, atlas, GIS system, and gazetteer reference book uses its own ad hoc set of descriptive elements, data structures, and type categories for gazetteer data. The Alexandria Digital Library, therefore, developed a Gazetteer Content Standard (GCS) as a general descriptive standard for gazetteer data and used it to build a worldwide gazetteer of 4.4 million entries by combining the data from the two U.S. federal gazetteers, along with other datasets. A web-based client for the ADL Gazetteer, with a map browser for search and display, has been available since 1996 and is currently used to support a wide variety of applications worldwide.[33] The GCS is structured as an XML Schema. In the summer of 2003, a relational database model for version 3.1 of the GCS was developed and implemented in PostGreSQL, a freely available database-management system with support for spatial data. In addition to the GCS, a specification for the ADL Gazetteer Protocol has been published and implemented to support searching across distributed gazetteers of various structures.[34]

These descriptive structures—the GCS and the protocol's standard report—represent two ends of the spectrum from complex to simple (see figure 8-3).

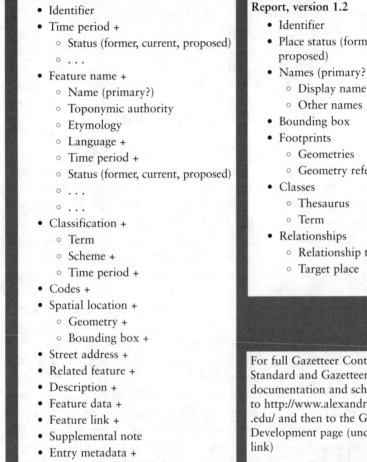

ADL Gazetteer Content Standard

- Identifier
- Time period +
  - Status (former, current, proposed)
  - . . .
- Feature name +
  - Name (primary?)
  - Toponymic authority
  - Etymology
  - Language +
  - Time period +
  - Status (former, current, proposed)
  - . . .
  - . . .
- Classification +
  - Term
  - Scheme +
  - Time period +
- Codes +
- Spatial location +
  - Geometry +
  - Bounding box +
- Street address +
- Related feature +
- Description +
- Feature data +
- Feature link +
- Supplemental note
- Entry metadata +

ADL Gazetteer Protocol Standard Report, version 1.2

- Identifier
- Place status (former, current, proposed)
- Names (primary?) (status)
  - Display name
  - Other names
- Bounding box
- Footprints
  - Geometries
  - Geometry references
- Classes
  - Thesaurus
  - Term
- Relationships
  - Relationship type
  - Target place

For full Gazetteer Content Standard and Gazetteer Protocol documentation and schemas, go to http://www.alexandria.ucsb.edu/ and then to the Gazetteer Development page (under KOS link)

FIGURE 8-3   Top-level view of the ADL Gazetteer Content Standard with comparison to the report specification of the ADL Gazetteer Protocol, to illustrate the complexity of one and the simplicity of the other

The GCS is structured to accommodate:

   complexity of place-names

   authoritative vs. colloquial names

multilingual representations

variant spellings

explanation of the origin of the name (etymology)

uncertainties of our knowledge about ancient place-names

varying geospatial representations of location (e.g., points, bounding boxes, and polygons and geospatial data from various sources)

primary and secondary type categories from specified typing schemes

complexity of time periods for name use, geospatial extent, and administrative relationships

The GCS is also designed to attribute pieces of information about a place to a particular source of that information, so that a single entry can be composed of information gathered from multiple sources.

The Gazetteer Protocol, on the other hand, uses an abstract model of a gazetteer containing the key descriptive components needed to support distributed searching (similar to the ADL search bucket approach). The protocol can be used with any structure for the gazetteer data.

The ADL GCS is a *metadata-like* or catalog approach to representing named geographic places. That is, there are *records* representing each named geographic place, and within each record, explicit relationships can be declared with other gazetteer entries. For example, the record for Chicago, Illinois, can include the fact that it is *part of* the state of Illinois (another entry in the gazetteer). The spatial footprints for Chicago and Illinois also establish this fact spatially; the explicit statement establishes it administratively. The two U.S. federal gazetteers use a catalog record approach,[35] as does the ISO draft standard for gazetteers, Spatial Referencing by Geographic Identifiers.[36]

There are other familiar structures used for gazetteers. One is the hierarchical thesaurus structure, as used by the Getty Thesaurus of Geographic Names.[37] In a thesaurus structure, the administrative hierarchy is the organizing principle for the *whole-part* hierarchy. New places are inserted into the hierarchy by the editorial staff. Other structures are the simple list, or the authority list, which may not include the geospatial location; the table of *feature labels* for a GIS data layer linked to polygons or points; and the index by place-name in the back of an atlas linked to map numbers and grid references.

There are several advantages to the catalog approach to gazetteers. One is that the hierarchical relationships can be more extensive than just the administrative hierarchy. A place can be said to be *part of* a watershed or a geological basin or an economic zone in addition to the administrative hierarchy. The catalog approach is also more suited to *open contribution* models, since new places do not have to be inserted into an existing hierarchy. For some purposes, however, the thesaurus approach based on administrative relationships is most suitable.

Other applications for the gazetteer model have become apparent since its development. It can also be applied to the description of other *named entities* having *spatial-temporal* definitions. One application is for the description of named time periods (e.g., the Iron Age or the Cretaceous Period), where the primary definition is a range of dates rather than geospatial coordinates. Another application is for the description of named spatial-temporal events, such as hurricanes or expeditions, where both the time range and the spatial coordinates are key components of the definitions.

DEVELOPING THESAURI AND CONCEPT SPACES

This book and this chapter are focused on metadata developments, but some mention should be made of the development of knowledge organization systems (KOS) that are used with the metadata structures to describe information objects. For ADL, this includes the development of the Feature Type Thesaurus (FTT), the ADL Thesaurus Protocol, and the development and use of concept spaces to represent important scientific reasoning and knowledge concepts for undergraduate teaching purposes.[38]

The FTT formalizes a set of terms (e.g., "populated places," "mountains," "towers") within a hierarchical structure and is used to categorize gazetteer entries. It was developed because no shared set of such categories existed—only the ad hoc set of classes used by individual gazetteer creators. The FTT terms are used as *values* for the *class* element in the GCS, and the FTT has been adopted or adapted for other purposes as well.

The ADL Thesaurus Protocol is designed to support the searching of multiple, distributed thesauri. It defines an abstract model of thesauri and the search operations that can be performed on them. By summer 2003, this protocol had been implemented on a test basis only and was one of several such approaches being evaluated in a search for a general solution to the problem of integrating a variety of KOS resources into digital libraries.[39]

The concept-based approach to teaching and learning has been prototyped at the University of California-Santa Barbara by developing an undergraduate course in physical geography and presenting it in two academic terms.[40] This approach integrates a collection of illustrations and models with the domain-specific concept space and with lecture composer software. The end result is a multiscreen presentation that can be navigated with either the two-dimensional concept space or the lecture outline during classroom presentations. The components are also available to students for out-of-class study. It is a potentially powerful way to transmit to students the important concepts and the structure of a field of knowledge. Evaluation of the effectiveness of this approach is continuing.

LESSONS LEARNED

The Alexandria Digital Library Project, through its two phases of NSF digital library funding and its implementation as an operational georeferenced digital library, has provided a rich testing environment for digital library development. Along with software for distributed digital libraries and collection building, the project has accumulated a wealth of experience in designing and implementing metadata structures and KOS resources for georeferenced digital libraries. The research, development, and implementation process continues, but at this point in time some observations can be made about what succeeded and how the ADL approach differs from other metadata and digital library initiatives.

The ADL Project has demonstrated how geospatial description and access can be integrated into digital libraries to provide users with access to all types of information and data about a geographic location—overcoming not only data format differences and operationally distinct information services, but also hindrances such as multilingual, multicultural, multitemporal, and colloquial place-name variances.

In the process of developing software and metadata support for a distributed digital library architecture, ADL demonstrated the need to create metadata structures specifically designed for searching across dissimilar collections. Formal specification of collection-level metadata permits discovery of collections likely to have information relevant to a query. In the ADL search buckets and the gazetteer and thesaurus protocols, data typing and associated search constraints support a high level of search capability across collections that can be very diverse.

ADL's creation of metadata structures for interoperability across dissimilar collections demonstrates that the benefits of interoperability can be achieved without specifying a particular metadata standard for item-level description. However, it is also clear that customization of item-level metadata for the requirements of a particular set of objects should be based, as much as possible, on the use of shared metadata element sets, successful metadata design practices, and shared KOS resources in order to make interoperability more successful. Increasingly, metadata structures will be composed of element sets that have been developed as components to cover certain aspects of description. Geospatial representation is one of those areas.

The ADL Project has used standards from formal standards bodies when stable standards exist and can be adopted. At the same time, ADL has formalized and published the metadata, KOS, and distributed library structures developed through the course of the project as an informal standards effort. A key to success for these efforts is that the resulting product has incorporated the best of what is already in place and is consistent with or uses the emerging frameworks for the Web and knowledge organization. A measure of the value of the informal standards process is the extent to which the resulting frameworks are adopted or adapted by emerging communities of practice. Both formal and informal standards development are needed. In areas of emerging practice, the informal path moves quicker and is informed by actual prototyping and test conditions.

It is a simplistic expectation that everyone is capable of creating good metadata or KOS resources, but it is one that has been prevalent to the detriment of predictable search and retrieval across distributed collections. The drive to create metadata and term lists automatically is also misguided if it doesn't include a "human in the loop" for quality assurance and feedback to the system so that it can improve. Metadata and KOS design and creation must be a team effort where the expertise of domain experts and computer engineers is integrated with the expertise of metadata and information retrieval experts. This implies, among other adjustments, a shifting of educational requirements and employment opportunities for the profession of librarianship.

The ADL Project consists of multidisciplinary teams meeting on the common ground of digital library development: primarily computer scientists/engineers, geographers, and library/information specialists. This is a challenging environment where knowledge, assumptions, expectations, and language use are often not shared but are implicitly expected. It is a creative environment, absolutely required for digital library development, but the difficulties should be acknowledged. One problem is that terms with shades of meaning or explicit specification in one domain are sometimes used generically outside of that domain. To relieve the frustration, some mutual learning needs to happen and, if necessary, troublesome terms need to be used only with definition.

CONCLUSIONS

Geospatial access to and analysis of data and information is a key discriminating factor in many fields: biodiversity, national security, transportation, social science, politics, cultural history, urban planning, epidemiology, natural resource exploration, and emergency management. Metadata and information service design and implementation are at a critical juncture where these activities must integrate geospatial georeferencing with traditional practices so that users can locate place-based information from documents and data, from libraries and data centers, and from museums and web pages. Two paths to doing this are (1) to incorporate coordinate representation directly into metadata instances for all types of information objects and into distributed digital library services, and (2) to develop distributed gazetteer services to translate place-names in subject headings and text documents into coordinate locations, either as an aid to cataloging (metadata creation) or as a component of information retrieval services. Implementing geospatial access services in cataloging and information retrieval services through the translation of place-name references to coordinate references using gazetteer services is an obvious development path. With sufficient development, such services will ease the cost and level of effort of extending geospatial access to all types of information.

Acknowledgments

The ADL Project has been funded primarily by the National Science Foundation as part of its digital library initiative: NSF IR94-11330 (phase

I) and ISI-98-17432 (phase II). ADL metadata development is a team effort involving members of the ADL Implementation Team and the staff of the Map & Imagery Lab, Davidson Library, University of California-Santa Barbara.

NOTES

1. Alexandria Digital Library Project (operational home page), http://www.alexandria.ucsb.edu/adl/ (accessed 9 September 2003).
2. M. L. Larsgaard, *Map Librarianship: An Introduction*, 3rd ed. (Englewood, Colo.: Libraries Unlimited, 1998).
3. Library of Congress, Network Development and MARC Standards Office, "MARC Standards," 2003, http://lcweb.loc.gov/marc/ (accessed 9 September 2003).
4. G. Janée and J. Frew, "The ADEPT Digital Library Architecture," paper given at the ACM-IEEE Joint Conference on Digital Libraries, Portland, Ore., 14–18 July 2002.
5. Alexandria Digital Library Project (home page), http://www.alexandria.ucsb.edu (accessed 9 September 2003).
6. G. Janée et al., "The ADL Bucket Framework," paper given at the Third DELOS Workshop on Interoperability and Mediation in Heterogeneous Digital Libraries, Darmstadt, Germany, 8–9 September 2001.
7. Alexandria Digital Library Project, "ADL Collection Metadata," 2003, http://www.alexandria.ucsb.edu/~gjanee/collection-metadata/ (accessed 9 September 2003).
8. G. Janée, J. Frew, and D. Valentine, "Content Access Characterization in Digital Libraries," 2003, paper given at the ACM-IEEE Joint Conference on Digital Libraries, Houston, Tex., 27–31 May 2003.
9. G. Janée, "Principles for a Simple Geometry Language for Use in Digital Library Metadata," 2003, internal document for the Alexandria Digital Library Project, University of California-Santa Barbara.
10. Digital Library for Earth System Education, "ADN Metadata Framework," 2003, http://www.dlese.org/Metadata/adn-item/index.htm (accessed 20 September 2003).
11. S. J. Crosier et al., "Developing an Infrastructure for Sharing Environmental Models," *Environment and Planning B: Planning and Design* 30 (2003): 487–501; L. L. Hill et al., "A Content Standard for Computational Models," *D-Lib Magazine*, June 2001, http://www.dlib.org/dlib/june01/hill/06hill.html.
12. G. Janée and L. L. Hill, "ADL Gazetteer Protocol," version 1.1, Alexandria Digital Library Project, 2002, http://www.alexandria.ucsb.edu/gazetteer/protocol/ (accessed 2 May 2003); G. Janée, S. Ikeda, and L. L. Hill, "ADL Thesaurus Protocol," version 1.0, Alexandria Digital Library Project, 2003, http://www.alexandria.ucsb.edu/thesaurus/protocol/ (accessed 9 September 2003).
13. L. L. Hill, "Guide to the ADL Gazetteer Content Standard," version 3.1, 2003, http://www.alexandria.ucsb.edu/gazetteer/ContentStandard/version3-1/GCS3-1-guide.doc (accessed 20 September 2003).

14. L. L. Hill, "Feature Type Thesaurus," Alexandria Digital Library Project, 2002, http://www.alexandria.ucsb.edu/gazetteer/FeatureTypes/FTT_metadata.htm (accessed 20 September 2003).
15. T. R. Smith et al., "The ADEPT Concept-Based Digital Learning Environment," 2003, paper given at "Research and Advanced Technology for Digital Libraries," 7th European Conference on Digital Libraries, Trondheim, Norway, 17–22 August 2003; T. R. Smith, M. L. Zeng, and ADEPT Knowledge Team, "Structured Models of Scientific Concepts for Organizing, Accessing, and Using Learning Materials," 2002, paper given at the Seventh International Society for Knowledge Organization Conference, Granada, Spain, 10–13 July 2002.
16. Janée et al., "ADL Bucket Framework."
17. Dublin Core Metadata Initiative (home page), http://www.dublincore.org/ (accessed 11 September 2003).
18. L. L. Hill et al., "Collection Metadata Solutions for Digital Library Applications," *Journal of the American Society for Information Science* 50, no. 13 (1999): 1169–81.
19. Alexandria Digital Library Project, "ADL Access Report DTD," 2003, http://www.alexandria.ucsb.edu/middleware/dtds/ADL-access-report.dtd (accessed 9 September 2003).
20. U.S. Federal Geographic Data Committee, "Content Standard for Digital Geospatial Metadata," version 2, 1998, http://fgdc.er.usgs.gov/metadata/contstan.html (accessed 1 June 2003).
21. Australia New Zealand Land Information Council–Spatial Information Council, "ANZLIC Metadata Guidelines," version 2, 2001, http://www.anzlic.org.au/download.html?oid=2358011755 (accessed 20 September 2003).
22. International Organization for Standardization, Technical Committee 211, "Geographic Information—Metadata," 2003.
23. Open GIS Consortium (home page), http://www.opengis.org/ (accessed 20 September 2003).
24. Open GIS Consortium, "Geography Markup Language Implementation Specification," version 3, http://www.opengis.org/techno/documents/02-023r4.pdf (accessed 9 September 2003).
25. Digital Library for Earth System Education, "ADN Metadata Framework."
26. Crosier et al., "Developing an Infrastructure"; Hill et al., "Content Standard for Computational Models."
27. S. Cox, "DCMI Box Encoding Scheme: Specification of the Spatial Limits of a Place, and Methods for Encoding This in a Text String," Dublin Core Metadata Initiative, 2000, http://dublincore.org/documents/2000/07/28/dcmi-box/ (accessed 26 April 2003); S. Cox, "DCMI Point Encoding Scheme: A Point Location in Space, and Methods for Encoding This in a Text String," Dublin Core Metadata Initiative, 2000, http://dublincore.org/documents/dcmi-point/ (accessed 26 April 2003).
28. Janée, "Principles for a Simple Geometry Language."
29. Open GIS Consortium, "OpenGIS Simple Features Specification for SQL," 1999, http://www.opengis.org/docs/99-049.pdf (accessed 13 November 2003); Open GIS Consortium, "OpenGIS Geography Markup Language Implementation

Specification," version 2.1.2, 2002, http://www.opengis.org/docs/02-069.pdf (accessed 13 November 2003).

30. *Encyclopaedia Britannica,* entry for "toponymy," http://www.britannica.com/eb/article?eu=74822 (accessed 3 November 2003).

31. U.S. Board on Geographic Names (home page), http://geonames.usgs.gov/bgn.html and http://earth-info.nima.mil/gns/html/bgn.html (accessed 3 November 2003).

32. United Nations Group of Experts on Geographical Names, http://unstats.un.org/unsd/geoinfo/englishUNGEGN.pdf (accessed 3 November 2003).

33. Hill, "ADL Gazetteer Content Standard"; Alexandria Digital Library Project, "ADL Gazetteer Client," 2003, http://www.alexandria.ucsb.edu/clients/gazetteer (accessed 20 September 2003).

34. Janée and Hill, "ADL Gazetteer Protocol."

35. U.S. National Imagery and Mapping Agency, Geonet Names Server, http://164.214.2.59/gns/html/ (accessed 20 September 2003); U.S. Geological Survey, Geographic Names Information Service (home page), http://mapping.usgs.gov/www/gnis/ (accessed 20 September 2003).

36. International Organization for Standardization, "Geographic Information: Spatial Referencing by Geographic Identifiers," 2002.

37. Getty Information Institute, "Getty Thesaurus of Geographic Names On Line," 2003, http://www.getty.edu/research/tools/vocabulary/tgn/ (accessed 20 September 2003).

38. Janée, Ikeda, and Hill, "ADL Thesaurus Protocol"; Hill, "Feature Type Thesaurus"; Smith, "ADEPT Concept-Based Digital Learning Environment."

39. L. L. Hill et al., "Integration of Knowledge Organization Systems into Digital Library Architectures," 2002, paper given at the Thirteenth ASIS&T SIG/CR Workshop on "Reconceptualizing Classification Research," Philadelphia, 17 November 2002.

40. Smith, "ADEPT Concept-Based Digital Learning Environment"; Smith, Zeng, and ADEPT Knowledge Team, "Structured Models of Scientific Concepts."

9 Distributing and Synchronizing Heterogeneous Metadata in Geospatial Information Repositories for Access

Elaine L. Westbrooks

IN 1998 THE Albert R. Mann Library created the Cornell University Geospatial Information Repository (CUGIR), a web-based repository providing free access to geospatial data and metadata for New York State.[1] Since its inception, CUGIR has undergone a series of changes and upgrades in response to emerging standards and technologies in the field of geospatial information systems (GIS) and digital library research. Its continuous adoption of new library and GIS standards and developments has made CUGIR increasingly more accessible to users within Cornell University and beyond.

The Cornell University Geospatial Information Repository has a number of characteristics that pose unique challenges for digital library developers. First, most GIS repositories manually distribute data and metadata via CD-ROM, whereas CUGIR freely distributes data and metadata via the World Wide Web, making it a true digital library. Second, it is rare to have a geospatial repository whose invention, support, and subsequent development occur within an academic research library. Academic GIS repositories or units are typically under the jurisdiction of urban planning, architecture, or geography departments. Because CUGIR is positioned in a library environment, it embraces standards and practices associated with the preservation, retrieval, acquisition, and organization of information. The library community has always been concerned with the archiving and version control of information, and believes that consistent application of standards will increase interoperability. The library community also believes that metadata, though costly and difficult to create and manage, adds value to whatever it describes. The GIS community is most concerned with creating data efficiently, easing the burden of metadata, and distributing data according to user requests. Generally speaking, GIS data are qualitatively different and more problematic than most digital library objects, including moving images.[2] More importantly, perpetual updating, versioning, and "editioning" of data at the owner's request makes GIS data management and metadata management difficult.[3] CUGIR reserves a position in two communities, library and GIS, requiring the CUGIR team to embrace the standards of both.

This sum of CUGIR's unique characteristics led the team to ask the following questions: if one were to create a perfect and heterogeneous metadata management system for a digital library, like CUGIR, what characteristics would it possess? How would it behave? What problems would it solve? The CUGIR team set out to create a system characterized by automatic metadata updating and digital object permanence. The system would be designed to behave in a predictable fashion, reduce work and costs, and increase access. The CUGIR metadata model is not a perfect metadata management system, but it is efficient. This is largely because it is a hybrid system embracing the standards, research, and practices of the library community while adopting the GIS community's most attractive feature, its software.

In striving for metadata management perfection, the CUGIR team became keenly aware of the shortcomings in the way GIS software manages digital objects and metadata, primarily the lack of version control for objects and preservation for metadata. Subsequently, these shortcomings were examined under the lens of the Functional Requirements for Bibliographic Records (FRBR) conceptual data.[4] This set of requirements was sponsored by the International Federation of Library Associations and Institutions' (IFLA's) section on cataloging to address the changes in cataloging processes. The FRBR addresses three groups of entities, but for CUGIR's purposes the first group, which outlines the primary relationships between works, expressions, manifestations, and items, is most critical. In particular, FRBR's use of the concept *work* was examined in the context of CUGIR, and it was through this lens that the team began to view the differences among metadata surrogates or *entities* within CUGIR.

Similarly, the weaknesses of the typical digital library metadata model, particularly its disregard for automation, were addressed in two ways. First, the storage of surrogate records for multiple *manifestations* of the same *expression* was eliminated. Second, the automatic metadata-creation tools unique to GIS software applications were exploited to increase efficiency. These changes proved to be a step in the right direction toward improved management of heterogeneous metadata.

The purpose of this chapter is to introduce the CUGIR metadata management model, whose primary goal is access. This model specifically attempts to address the following problems that can hinder access:

1. Management of multiple metadata schemas, i.e., FGDC, MARC, and DC, that occur in multiple manifestations and expressions in CUGIR
2. The lack or absence of fixity and persistence or permanence of geospatial digital objects[5]
3. The creation and maintenance of metadata that is typically difficult, costly, and time-consuming
4. The lack of tools to automate the creation and management of metadata, in particular, metadata synchronization

It was the goal of the CUGIR team to take the best of both worlds (digital libraries and GIS applications) and merge them to make a powerful system from which both communities could benefit. Although this model was chiefly designed for geospatial data and metadata, it can be applied to other types of digital libraries.

BACKGROUND

CUGIR is a clearinghouse and repository that provides unrestricted access to geospatial data and metadata, with special emphasis on those natural features relevant to agriculture, ecology, natural resources, and human-environment interactions in New York State. Staff at the Albert R. Mann Library of Cornell University began looking at ways to disseminate geospatial data from Mann's collections via the Web in 1995, and in 1998 they established a web-based clearinghouse for New York State geospatial data and metadata. Building a clearinghouse entailed creating partnerships with local, state, and federal agencies; understanding how to interpret and apply the Federal Geographic Data Committee (FGDC) Content Standard for Digital Geospatial Metadata (CSDGM); and designing a search and retrieval interface, as well as a flexible and scalable data storage system.[6]

The CUGIR team consists of five regular members, each coordinating work within their areas of specialty. Primary responsibility for the overall coordination of clearinghouse development rests with the GIS librarian. This team provides for the management, preservation, organization, and storage needs of datasets that are distributed in CUGIR, but which are owned by various departments in New York State governmental agencies as well as Cornell-affiliated departments, agencies, and researchers.[7] Although the CUGIR team strives to make access better, the biggest responsibility of the team is adding value to the data within CUGIR.

The Cornell University Geospatial Information Repository is one of 250 international nodes within the National Geospatial Data Clearinghouse that contain searchable metadata records describing geospatial datasets. All nodes are located on data servers using the Z39.50 information retrieval protocol. As a result, nodes can be linked to a single search interface where the metadata contents of all nodes, or any subset in combination, can be searched simultaneously. The Cornell repository, like most clearinghouse nodes, has its own website with customized browsing and searching interfaces. Usage statistics indicate that CUGIR's utility and popularity continues to grow. Since 1998, CUGIR data requests have increased by at least 40 percent each year. In fact, it is projected that CUGIR will record over 100,000 requests in 2004, the most for any single year since the repository was established in 1998.[8]

CUGIR Data

Currently CUGIR freely distributes online over 7,000 datasets produced by ten data partners, and their data come in seven unique proprietary and nonproprietary formats. [9] In many cases, one dataset is produced in multiple formats. For example, the dataset "Minor Civil Divisions, Albany County" is available in ArcExport as well as in shapefile format. Each format has unique characteristics that make it more or less desirable for certain uses and purposes. Unlike most digital library files that require little more than Internet connectivity and web browser software, geospatial data require technical expertise in the use of sophisticated and powerful GIS software applications. In addition, users must also understand cartographic and geographic concepts related to GIS.

CUGIR Metadata

In 1994 the Federal Geographic Data Committee established the Content Standard for Digital Geospatial Metadata for describing the content and function of geospatial data. There are 334 different elements in FGDC's CSDGM, 119 of which exist only to contain other elements.[10] These elements are organized within seven main sections and three supporting sections that describe different aspects of data that potential users might need to know: Identification Information, Data Quality Information, Spatial Data Organization Information, Spatial Reference Information, Entity and Attribute Information, Distribution Information, and Metadata Reference Information. For more extensive information about geospatial metadata, see Hart and Phillips's Metadata Primer.[11]

The Content Standard for Digital Geospatial Metadata is detailed, hierarchical, and complex. A high percentage of CUGIR geospatial metadata is provided by the data producer, and all of it is reviewed and enhanced by the metadata librarian to make it fully FGDC-compliant. Figure 9-1 is an example of a CUGIR record entitled "Minor Civil Divisions, Albany County." Note that the "Online_Linkage" element links users to the Dublin Core (DC) record where the data can be downloaded.

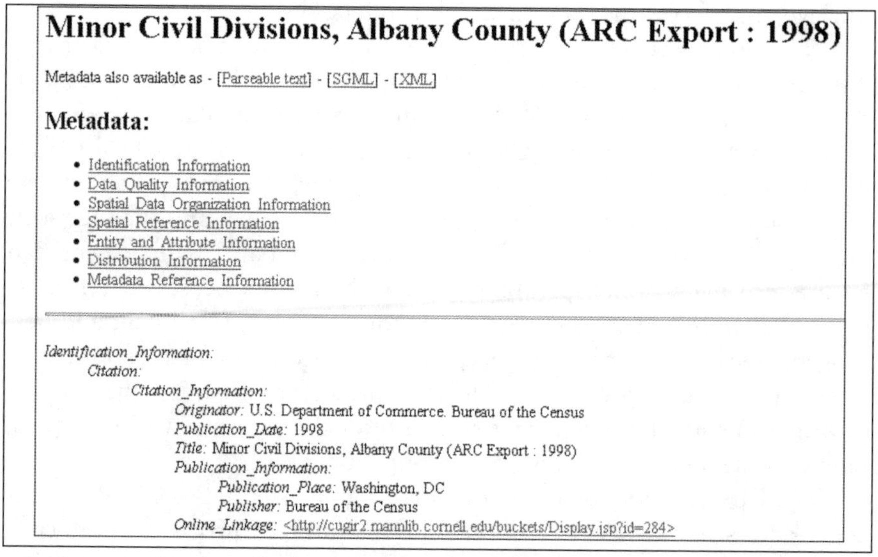

Minor Civil Divisions, Albany County (ARC Export : 1998)

Metadata also available as - [Parseable text] - [SGML] - [XML]

Metadata:

- Identification Information
- Data Quality Information
- Spatial Data Organization Information
- Spatial Reference Information
- Entity and Attribute Information
- Distribution Information
- Metadata Reference Information

Identification_Information:
  Citation:
    Citation_Information:
      Originator: U.S. Department of Commerce. Bureau of the Census
      Publication_Date: 1998
      Title: Minor Civil Divisions, Albany County (ARC Export : 1998)
      Publication_Information:
        Publication_Place: Washington, DC
        Publisher: Bureau of the Census
      Online_Linkage: <http://cugir2.mannlib.cornell.edu/buckets/Display.jsp?id=284>

FIGURE 9-1 Geospatial/FGDC metadata record in CUGIR. From this record, one may download the dataset from the online linkage.

Of the 7,117 datasets in CUGIR, 7,111 are accompanied by FGDC-compliant metadata. CUGIR metadata are created and stored as ASCII text, HTML, SGML, and XML. Online users may view any metadata record in any syntax of their choice.

CUGIR METADATA MANAGEMENT

Today the term "metadata management" is increasingly being used by librarians, computer scientists, information scientists, and the e-commerce community.[12] Although libraries managed metadata long before it was known as metadata, the term "metadata management" has not been completely defined. Some practitioners indicate that it is an organizational process that can or cannot be automated, but the author takes the term one step further: "In a broad sense and in the case of CUGIR, metadata management implies the implementation of a metadata policy (i.e., principles that form the guiding framework within which metadata exists) and adherence to metadata standards."[13] Furthermore, metadata management is the process of acquiring and maintaining a controlled set of metadata, with or without automation, in order to describe, discover, preserve, retrieve, and access the data to which it refers.[14]

As problems arose in the development of CUGIR, it became clear that although the CUGIR team and its data partners had been creating metadata for years, there had never been a metadata policy that was explicitly articulated for them. This oversight was exposed when the CUGIR team began to approach preservation—since preservation policy should rest heavily on metadata policy. Although metadata policy and management are not panaceas for digital library woes, metadata management can ensure efficiency, interoperability, extensibility, and cost effectiveness through a clear and concise plan. The more complex, relational, and heterogeneous CUGIR metadata became, the more it became necessary to adopt a metadata policy as well as a preservation policy that would inform a metadata management system to deal with preservation, access, data and metadata versioning, and redundancy.

The CUGIR team identified one major area essential to CUGIR's success—access. It was clear to the team that Cornell University's core constituency of faculty, students, and staff were not sufficiently utilizing CUGIR's geospatial resources. In order to make geospatial information resources more accessible to users who might not otherwise encounter them, CUGIR's FGDC records were converted to MARC and added to the library's online catalog and OCLC's FirstSearch. In addition, FGDC records were converted to Dublin Core (DC) and subsequently harvested by the Open Archives metadata harvester.[15]

Another identified problem was the prevalence of redundant metadata records that differed only in syntax, i.e., HTML or XML (Extensible Markup Language). The storage of metadata in HTML, XML, SGML, and ASCII text was difficult to manage when changes were necessary. Similarly, the repetition of metadata elements or fields in those metadata also demonstrated inefficient use of storage space. In order to address these problems, the CUGIR team set out to introduce a more accessible and efficient management system, based on the notion of one canonical metadata work.

Canonical CUGIR Metadata

In order to minimize the amount of data lost as a result of crosswalking among multiple schemas, the metadata schema-conversion process began with the core, or canonical, FGDC record that is assembled on-the-fly. The FGDC record is considered the "native" and most complete source of information in one of the most flexible exchange syntaxes, XML. With no existing tools to convert FGDC XML to MARC XML, this was quite a challenge. Elizabeth Mangan of the Library of Congress created an FGDC-to-MARC 21 crosswalk that was a useful beginning, but a new and customized FGDC XML-to-MARC XML crosswalk had to be created to suit our purposes.[16] The MARC XML is also derived from the canonical form and is produced on-the-fly.

What makes the use of the canonical record even more important is the upcoming introduction of International Organization for Standardization (ISO) geospatial metadata. The ISO metadata, when implemented, will harmonize the FGDC Metadata Standard (FGDC-STD-001-1998) with the ISO's Geographic Information/Geomatics Technical Committee (TC) 211 Metadata Standard 19115.[17] The standard will be expressed as a multilingual XML Schema designed to be extensible, multilayered, and modeled in Unified Modeling Language (UML).[18] In addition, it will be integrated with other ISO standards such as Dublin Core (ISO 15836:2003) and Codes for the Representation of Names of Languages (ISO 639-2).[19]

This harmonization process is a powerful step in the right direction because it not only addresses many known deficiencies in FGDC CSDGM, but also enables interoperability while providing additional support for the functions of metadata. Embracing XML-encoded FGDC is the CUGIR team's way of preparing for the upcoming changes. Given the metadata tools and practices we have in place, we expect a predictable and effortless transition from FGDC to ISO. Thus CUGIR will be poised to make an early transition, instead of waiting for proprietary metadata tools to emerge. The canonical record is stored in a database and is produced on-the-fly. This method allows for the introduction of some efficiencies; for example, each data partner has standard contact information (e.g., address, telephone number). Instead of repeating such information in each and every metadata record, it is stored once and rendered dynamically. Figure 9-2 illustrates the CUGIR metadata conversion process.

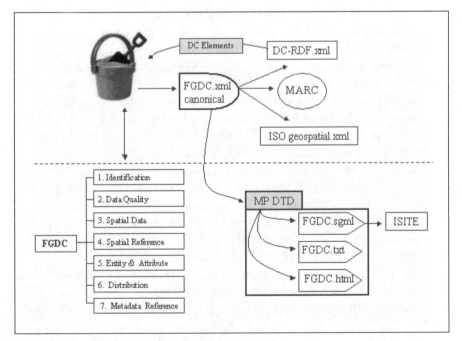

FIGURE 9-2   CUGIR metadata conversion process

As shown in the figure, the FGDC metadata is stored within a relational database and links to the bucket that is populated by Dublin Core. In addition, the activities above the line represent the new way of managing the metadata, and the activities below the line represent the old way of producing metadata records manually.

Resource Description Framework for Open Archives Initiative and the Semantic Web

The Open Archives Initiative (OAI) Metadata Harvesting Protocol was the only metadata-sharing tool, outside of CUGIR and the National Geospatial Data Clearinghouse, that was used to enhance access to CUGIR.[20] The minimum requirement for metadata in OAI is simple Dublin Core.[21] The CUGIR team chose to use the Resource Description Framework (RDF) for a number of reasons, the first being the convenient use of OCLC's Connexion to export OAI-ready DC in RDF with little effort.[22] As the metadata project progressed, we favored a less OCLC-centric approach to metadata creation. Moreover, we discovered that DC-compliant RDF records (in XML) could be easily created with XML stylesheets (XSL) coupled with Extensible Stylesheet Language Transformations (XSLT).[23] The use of RDF can be justified by its integral role in the Semantic Web.

Metadata Management with MARC

The contribution of MARC 21 records to OCLC makes CUGIR data internationally accessible to WorldCat users. Additionally, other libraries on the OCLC network get the opportunity to utilize full-level MARC records. The integration of CUGIR data into the Cornell University OPAC made it possible for library users to discover geospatial resources as they typically discover journals, books, and online databases. In sum, the transformation from FGDC to MARC 21 enabled the CUGIR team to do the following:

1. Gain bibliographic control over CUGIR metadata records outside of CUGIR.
2. Enhance access to geospatial records via the OPAC.
3. Share MARC 21 records with libraries worldwide via WorldCat.

A CUGIR MARC 21 record is based on the XML-encoded FGDC records and transformed on-the-fly using XSLT. See figure 9-3 for an example of a MARC 21 record in the Cornell University Library's OPAC based on the FGDC record shown in figure 9-1.

While the team was already creating multiple metadata schemas, it seemed only natural to include some of the latest developments in metadata, such as the Metadata Object Description Schema (MODS).[24] The addition of MODS into the metadata framework forced the team to create an FGDC-to-MODS crosswalk, stylesheet, and transformation, since none existed.[25] The MODS schema is a flexible XML-based descriptive standard which can be combined with other XML-based standards, including the Metadata Encoding and Transmission Standard (METS).[26] METS, a standard for encoding descriptive, administrative, and structural metadata regarding objects within a digital library, fills in essential components needed to manage a digital library. Since any descriptive metadata that is part of CUGIR can be part of METS objects, we anticipate that the next step will be to investigate how well METS can handle geospatial information.

Minor Civil Divisions, Albany County

Database: Cornell University Library
Title: Minor Civil Divisions, Albany County [electronic resource].
Published: Washington, DC : Bureau of the Census, 1998.
Description: Scale not given.
Electronic Access: http://cugir2.mannlib.cornell.edu/buckets/Display.jsp?id=284
Summary: These files are an extract of selected geographic and cartographic information from the 1995 TIGER/Line files detailing county subdivisions. This dataset includes minor civil divisions and other statistical entities.
Notes: Mode of Access: World Wide Web.
System Requirements: Some files require desktop Geographic information Systems (GIS) software such as MAPInfo, ARC/Info, ArcView, or Adobe Acrobat Reader, for storing, modifying, querying, analyzing, and displaying various forms of geospatial data on Windows, MAC or UNIX platforms. Additionally, some files require desktop extraction utilities such as Winzip to handle compressed or archived files.
Restrictions: Access Constraints: None.
Rights Access: None. Acknowledgement of the U.S. Bureau of the Census would be appreciated for products derived from these files. TIGER, TIGER/Line and Census TIGER are trademarks of the Bureau of the Census.

FIGURE 9-3   MARC record in the Cornell University Library online catalog. Notice how the Electronic Access (MARC 856) field is identical to the link, no. 284, found in figure 9-1.

Metadata Editing and Automatic Metadata Creation and Synchronization

CUGIR currently uses a suite of software produced by the Environmental Systems Research Institute (ESRI), commonly used in geospatial information analysis, to manage and store CUGIR data and metadata. These include the software components ArcGIS, an Internet Mapping Service (ArcIMS), and a Spatial Data Engine (ArcSDE). ArcGIS contains a data management tool known as ArcCatalog, which is a data exploration and management application used to preview metadata as well as a dataset's geographic and tabular data. It automatically creates metadata for datasets stored in the geodatabase if none exists. Some of the automatically generated metadata describe the data's current properties, i.e., coordinate system, entity, and attribute information. Every time the metadata librarian views the metadata, ArcCatalog automatically updates or synchronizes dataset properties with its most current values. The synchronization ensures that the metadata is perpetually up-to-date according to the changes in the dataset. Automatic synchronization is invaluable, but it brings forth a host of problems associated with archiving and bibliographic control. Making distinctions between and among metadata versions, editions, and updates is crucial for any type of digital library with archiving responsibilities such as CUGIR. The inability of the synchronizer to differentiate a version of a metadata record from an edition or update brought forth a new set of challenges.

FUNCTIONAL REQUIREMENTS FOR BIBLIOGRAPHIC RECORDS OVERVIEW

When the CUGIR team needed to determine the key issues in distinguishing and classifying CUGIR metadata, it was clear that the FRBR entity hierarchy could provide some guidance. CUGIR, like most digital libraries, organizes data linearly. There is a one-to-one relationship between CUGIR datasets and metadata. The metadatabase system in ArcCatalog displays bibliographic information in hierarchical ways, yet the a priori relationships are not fully captured. Fortunately, CUGIR's Smart Object Dumb Archive (SODA) architecture alleviates the problem by displaying alternate expressions of datasets, but SODA cannot fully capture the hierarchical relationship inherent to the data. The intricate details of the SODA model have been well documented by its creator, Michael Nelson.[27] The similarities and differences among expressions, manifestations, and items pose unique challenges for the archiving, preservation, and organization of CUGIR data.

In some cases, changes to the intellectual content of the dataset (e.g., datum) are reflected in its respective metadata. Similarly, a change in the way a particular dataset is packaged (e.g., compression) can also be handled under synchronization. On the other hand, there are often changes to the data that are not necessarily recognized by the synchronizer. For example, a change in a keyword would not be apparent to the metadata synchronizer, but represents nonetheless a key access point change in the metadata. The CUGIR team works frequently with data partners that are more familiar with the world of GIS than with theory and research regarding the intellectual organization of information. Geospatial information practitioners do not make distinctions between intellectual content and physical packaging, but in the world of libraries such issues are viewed as critical. These relationships, nuances, and embodiments of CUGIR metadata records should be examined under the FRBR lens in order to secure clarity over what should be and should not be synchronized.

FRBR and CUGIR Metadata

The FRBR model can assist in determining what should be the appropriate unit of storage for the organization, discovery, preservation, and description of CUGIR data. Any substantial changes to the canonical FGDC record means that the derivative records (DC-RDF, MARC 21, MODS) must be changed as well. The design of the CUGIR metadata model is in concert with Jenkins et al.'s assertion: "Automatic metadata generation would appear to be an essential pre-requisite for widespread deployment of RDF based applications."[28] The application of the FRBR model to CUGIR records is shown in figure 9-4.

The CUGIR team is still negotiating methods by which the synchronizer can be programmed to form an FRBR-like hierarchy when metadata needs to be changed. Since the synchronizer does not understand the difference between an intellectual and physical change, the metadata records were parsed in such a way as to require a command that dictates: <when field 1.1.2 (thesaurus field) changes in FGDC record, do not synchronize metadata because it has intellectually changed>. Although the entire

Minor Civil Divisions   *[Work]*
   Shapefile   *[Expression]*
      DC-RDF (XML)   *[Manifestations]*
      FGDC   *[Manifestations]*
         XML
         HTML
         SGML
         ASCII Text
      MARC   *[Manifestations]*
         MARC 21
         MARC XML
         MODS (XML)
   ArcExport   *[Expression]*
      DC-RDF (XML)   *[Manifestations]*
      FGDC   *[Manifestations]*
         XML
         HTML
         SGML
         ASCII Text
      MARC   *[Manifestations]*
         MARC 21
         MARC XML
         MODS (XML)

FIGURE 9-4   CUGIR metadata conceptualized in the FRBR work entity framework

analysis of CUGIR data is incomplete, it is clear that CUGIR data does not fit neatly into the FRBR model.

LESSONS LEARNED

During the course of any metadata-intensive project, the tools (software), knowledge, and the metadata schemas will change. In hindsight, there is little that the CUGIR team could have done to improve the metadata management model. This is because changes to the software, the team's knowledge set, and the metadata standards happened unpredictably throughout the implementation of the metadata management system.

Metadata. When the project began, CUGIR utilized the existing metadata standard, FGDC. Currently, ISO metadata, in an XML Schema, has been approved and destined to replace FGDC. This transition from FGDC to ISO was one of the biggest catalysts that forced the team to expand their use of metadata standards.

Software. The software and tools that were developed for the project changed as the standards and understanding changed. When the CUGIR metadata management project was conceived, it was designed to deal with metadata in SGML (Standard Generalized Markup Language), not XML. Because CUGIR was using the Isite software, which required SGML, the team was working with the assumption that ISITE and SGML, respectively, would be used for indexing CUGIR metadata for three more years.[29] It became clear that SGML was too cumbersome, so the team was forced to re-create the tools with XML in mind. In addition, the CUGIR data was migrated to the proprietary software package produced by the GIS leader ESRI, eliminating the last remaining need for SGML.

Knowledge. Probably the most important and underestimated factor that had an impact on the progress of the project was the knowledge base of the team. As the programmer and the librarians involved became more knowledgeable about the utility of RDF, their ideas began to shift. The placement of RDF within the model happened as the team became exposed to more information about RDF, the Semantic Web, and ontologies.

OUTCOMES OF CUGIR METADATA FRAMEWORK

The CUGIR metadata framework proved successful in reaching its primary goals: increasing access and implementing an efficient metadata management system. But clearly the test of the system's effectiveness is in the question of whether more users discovered CUGIR as a result of the metadata framework.

When the framework was implemented, referrer data, which indicated the web page that a user visited in order to access the bucket, was captured and stored in a database. The IP addresses of the hosts were also collected. To preserve the privacy of users, the IP addresses were encrypted and the subnets dropped from the statistics database. As a result, the domain name rather than the unique address of the computer has been stored. These data identify whether users encountered a bucket from OAI, the

Cornell OPAC, or OCLC's FirstSearch as their entry into CUGIR. Since the metadata framework has been in place over 12,000 buckets have been accessed from a variety of locations. The results indicate that less than 5 percent of our users discover CUGIR metadata via the Cornell OPAC. Less than one percent of our users discover CUGIR metadata via FirstSearch. Almost 95 percent of our users discover CUGIR metadata from CUGIR's home page.

If only 5 percent of our users discovered CUGIR as a result of this metadata framework, was it worthwhile? Although the statistics do not indicate "success" in regard to access, the work and process of formulating the metadata-sharing framework forced us to document all metadata processes, streamline workflows, and create more metadata with less effort. In terms of data management, the metadata framework reduced the number of metadata files that had to be managed and stored. CUGIR no longer stores each metadata schema in multiple formats. In the past, we stored nine metadata files per dataset; now we only store one.

CONCLUSION

We are confident that our work to make CUGIR more accessible will pay off in the long run. Furthermore, the proliferation of web mapping services will expose GIS data to even more users. Increasingly diverse and sophisticated interactive mapping websites, allowing instant creation of customized maps, exemplify the most dynamic aspects of GIS usage. Many repositories are beginning to offer interactive mapping websites where one can create maps based on large census, Environmental Protection Agency, or U.S. Geological Survey databases of information.

Finally, the value of the CUGIR metadata framework is promising when one examines the growing importance of standards in the GIS community. Consortia such as the Open GIS Consortium are aimed at growing interoperability for technologies involving spatial information and location, so that benefits from geographic information and services can be made available across any network, application, or platform.[30] With this in mind, analysis of data on the use of the CUGIR metadata management system yields some interesting insights:

1. In spite of the vast efforts to make CUGIR data accessible across metadata schemas and information systems, users who know

about CUGIR overwhelmingly prefer to acquire data from the FGDC metadata records on the CUGIR home page. This may always be the case no matter how much metadata sharing persists.

2. The OPAC provides discovery but minimal means for access for users who might not otherwise discover geospatial data.

3. The addition of MARC 21 records in OCLC has not significantly increased access to CUGIR, but other libraries in the OCLC network have access to full-level MARC records and may find them useful.

4. The application of the FRBR model helped the team make clearer distinctions among metadata surrogates, but it did not necessarily solve the problems that GIS software presents to digital libraries.

The fundamental value of the library is the organization of information as the foundation through which information resources can be utilized. Centuries of library research support this claim. The same principles are not routinely being applied to digital libraries. The CUGIR team embraces metadata as the first-order prerequisite to establishing a complete geospatial repository. Furthermore, it should be clear that library standards and theory as well as GIS standards and software must be applied in concert, in order to produce open, interoperable, efficient, and robust digital libraries.

NOTES

1. Cornell University Geospatial Information Repository (home page), http://cugir .mannlib.cornell.edu (accessed 16 December 2003).

2. Geospatial data are typically born digital and by definition are digital representations of real-world features that describe objects and relations among them. Additionally, GIS data include spatial reference information, contain both geometric and thematic data, come in many different formats, support a wide range of applications, and offer more flexibility than hard-copy maps. When it became clear that GIS data was being lost (e.g., the 1968 New York Land Use Study), the CUGIR team looked to long-standing library standards and practices in preservation to prevent more data loss. The CUGIR team was unaware of major preservation initiatives, in part because GIS practitioners are more focused on building resources than on saving older versions of data for posterity. For many GIS practitioners, GIS data are ephemeral, but for libraries, preservation is paramount. Through our discussions about preserving CUGIR data, we began to focus on what makes GIS data unique and problematic. Some of the information gathered about GIS data was presented at Cornell University Library's conference on "Digital Preservation Management: Implementing Short Term Strategies for Long Term Problems," Ithaca, N.Y., August 2003.

3. By "editioning," I refer to metadata records that are updated and become first, second, or third editions of the same work. This concept must be distinguished from "versioning," which typically pertains to the information that accompanies the format of the data that the metadata is describing.

4. IFLA Study Group on the Functional Requirements for Bibliographic Records, *Functional Requirements for Bibliographic Records: Final Report* (Munich: K. G. Saur, 1998).

5. Fixity is used to ensure that the particular content information object has not been altered in an undocumented manner, according to "Preservation Metadata and the OAIS Information Model, A Metadata Framework to Support the Preservation of Digital Objects: A Report by The OCLC/RLG Working Group on Preservation Metadata," June 2002, http://www.oclc.org/research/projects/pmwg/pm_framework.pdf (accessed 23 November 2003). To quote John Kunze, researcher at the University of California at San Francisco's Library Center for Knowledge Management: "Permanence of electronic information, namely, the extent to which structured digital data remains predictably available through known channels, is a central concern for most organizations whose mission includes an archival function" (http://www.nii.ac.jp/dc2001/proceedings/product/paper-27.pdf; accessed 15 December 2003). Michael Nelson and B. Danette Allen also talk about object persistence in their article, "Object Persistence and Availability in Digital Libraries," *D-Lib Magazine*, January 2002, http://www.dlib.org/dlib/january02/nelson/01nelson.html (accessed 15 December 2003).

6. Philip Herold, Thomas D. Gale, and Thomas Turner, "Optimizing Web Access to Geospatial Data: The Cornell University Geospatial Information Repository," *Issues in Science and Technology Librarianship* (winter 1999), http://www.library.ucsb.edu/istl/99-winter/article2.html (accessed 24 January 2003).

7. Herold, Gale, and Turner, "Optimizing Web Access."

8. CUGIR, "CUGIR Statistics Database," http://cugir.mannlib.cornell.edu/about_cug/ (accessed 7 March 2004).

9. As of 2003, CUGIR file formats included ArcExport, shapefile, CAD, geoTIFF, PDF, ArcInfo Grid, and DEM. More information about them can be found at "CUGIR Help Files," http://cugir.mannlib.cornell.edu/help/help.html (accessed 5 April 2003).

10. Peter Schweitzer, "Frequently Asked Questions on FGDC Metadata," http://geology.usgs.gov/tools/metadata/tools/doc/faq.html (accessed 2 February 2003).

11. D. Hart and Hugh Phillips, "Metadata Primer—'How To' Guide on Metadata Implementation," 2001, http://www.lic.wisc.edu/metadata/ metaprim.htm (accessed 10 August 2001).

12. OCLC: Online Computing Library Center, "Metadata Management and Knowledge Organization," 2003, http://www.oclc.org/research/projects/metadata_management.htm. (accessed 19 December 2003). In the private sector, a host of companies are devoted to this endeavor, including Metadata Management Corp. and Agilense, Inc. See also Diane I. Hillmann, "Metadata Management," 2002, http://metamanagement.comm.nsdl.org/cgi-bin/wiki.pl (accessed 23 November 2003).

13. Elaine L. Westbrooks, "Distributing and Synchronizing Heterogeneous Metadata for the Management of Geospatial Information in DC-2003," in *Proceedings of the International DCMI Metadata Conference and Workshop,* Seattle, Wash., 28 September–2 October 2003, http://www.siderean.com/dc2003/204_Paper78.pdf (accessed 7 March 2004).

14. Intra-Governmental Group on Geographic Information Working Group, "Principles of Good Metadata Management," 2002, in *Intra-Governmental Group on Geographic Information, Working Group on Metadata Implementation Guide,* http://www.iggi.gov.uk/achievements_deliverables/pdf/Guide.pdf (accessed 17 July 2003).

15. Carl Lagoze et al., "The Open Archives Initiative Protocol for Metadata Harvesting," 2001, http://www.openarchives.org/OAI/openarchivesprotocol.html (accessed 1 March 2003).

16. Elizabeth Mangan, "Crosswalk: FGDC Content Standards for Digital Geospatial Metadata to USMARC," 1997, http://alexandria.sdc.ucsb.edu/public-documents/metadata/fgdc2marc.html (accessed 12 December 2000); Elaine L. Westbrooks, "FGDC Content Standards for Geospatial Metadata to MARC and MODS Crosswalk," 2003, http://metadata-wg.mannlib.cornell.edu/elaine/fgdc/fgdc2mod4.html (accessed 7 March 2004).

17. Federal Geographic Data Committee, "FGDC/ISO Metadata Standard Harmonization," 2003, http://www.fgdc.gov/metadata/whatsnew/fgdciso.html (accessed 4 November 2003).

18. Federal Geographic Data Committee, "FGDC/ISO Metadata Standard Harmonization."

19. The Dublin Core Metadata Element Set ISO 15836:2003(E) was approved to be an ISO standard on 4 August 2003. See http://www.niso.org/international/SC4/n515.pdf (accessed 15 December 2003); Library of Congress, Network Development and MARC Standards Office, "Codes for the Representation of Names of Languages—Part 2," 2003, http://www.loc.gov/standards/iso639-2/ (accessed 15 December 2003).

20. According to the Federal Geographic Data Committee, the National Geospatial Data Clearinghouse "is a collection of over 250 spatial data servers that have digital geographic data primarily for use in GIS, image processing systems, and other modelling software. These data collections can be searched through a single interface based on . . . metadata." See http://130.11.52.184 (accessed 16 December 2003).

21. Carl Lagoze et al., "Open Archives Initiative Frequently Asked Questions," 2002, http://www.openarchives.org/documents/FAQ.html (accessed 1 March 2003).

22. Connexion is OCLC's online cataloging service that is used to create and edit bibliographic and authority records, as well as harvest metadata from online resources. For more information, see OCLC: Online Computing Library Center, "Connexion—Cataloging and Metadata," 2003, http://www.oclc.org/connexion/ (accessed 15 December 2003). For more information about Dublin Core expressed within the Resource Description Framework (DC-RDF), see Dave Beckett, "Expressing Simple Dublin Core in RDF/XML," http://dublincore.org/documents/2002/04/22/dcmes-xml/index.shtml (accessed 15 December 2003). See also Stefan Kokkelink, "Expressing Qualified Dublin Core in

RDF/XML," http://dublincore.org/documents/2001/08/29/dcq-rdf-xml/index .shtml (accessed 12 December 2003).

23. Extensible Stylesheet Language (XSL) defines how data are presented, while Extensible Stylesheet Language Transformations (XSLT) is designed for use as part of XSL.

24. Library of Congress, Network Development and MARC Standards Office, "MODS: The Metadata Object Description Schema" (home page), http://www.loc.gov/standards/mods/ (accessed 12 February 2003). Rebecca Guenther, senior networking and standards specialist at the Library of Congress, adds: "MODS should complement other metadata formats and should provide an alternative between a very simple metadata format with a minimum of fields and no or little substructure [i.e., Dublin Core] and a very detailed format with many data elements having various structural complexities such as MARC 21."

25. Elaine L. Westbrooks, "FGDC to MODS Crosswalk," 2003, http://metadata-wg.mannlib.cornell.edu/elaine/fgdc/ (accessed 30 April 2003).

26. Library of Congress, "METS: Metadata Encoding and Transmission Standard," http://www.loc.gov/standards/mets/ (accessed 6 May 2003).

27. Michael L. Nelson, "Buckets: Smart Objects for Digital Libraries," 2000, unpublished Ph.D., Old Dominion University, Norfolk, Va.; Michael L. Nelson, "Smart Objects and Open Archives," *D-Lib Magazine*, February 2001, http://www.dlib.org/dlib/february01/nelson/02nelson.html (accessed 15 January 2002); Michael L. Nelson, "Smart Objects, Dumb Archives: A User-Centric, Layered Digital Library Framework," *D-Lib Magazine*, March 1999, http://www.dlib.org/dlib/march99/maly/03maly.html (accessed 19 December 2003).

28. Charlotte Jenkins et al., "Automatic RDF Metadata Generation for Resource Discovery," *Computer Networks* 31 (1999): 1305–20.

29. Federal Geographic Data Committee, "Federal Geographic Data Committee FAQs: What Is the Isite Software and What Do Each of the Components Do?" 2003, http://clearinghouse4.fgdc.gov/fgdcfaq/showquestion.asp?faq=3& fldAuto=13 (accessed 16 December 2003).

30. Open GIS Consortium, "About the Open GIS Consortium," 2003, http://www.opengis.org/ogcAbout.htm (accessed 2 May 2003).

10

The Internet Scout Project's Metadata Management Experience: Research, Solutions, and Knowledge

Rachael Bower, David Sleasman, and Edward Almasy

THE INTERNET SCOUT Project (Scout), part of the University of Wisconsin-Madison's Computer Sciences Department, began in 1994 with a grant from the National Science Foundation (NSF).[1] The goal was straightforward: to provide education and research communities with an effective method of discovering newly created online materials. Since then, Scout has matured into a multifaceted group of digital library and metadata-related projects, including online publications and web-based services as well as software. Through research, experimentation, and self-examination, Scout project managers have gleaned knowledge that may offer solutions and suggestions applicable to any digital library project.

Central to Scout's growth has been its relationship to metadata, particularly metadata for learning communities. From the critical analysis of online resources in our publications to software designed to help other projects bring their resources to the Web, metadata is the common thread that runs through every project. The Internet Scout Project struggles with many of the same issues—e.g., funding, outreach, project management, staffing, standards, and technology—faced by all digital libraries and research projects. These fundamental administrative and research issues have shaped our approach as we have worked through the challenges that they present. It is our hope that the Internet Scout Project's experiences may inform any project's metadata planning, as well as the building and maintenance of a digital collection.

BACKGROUND

In the early 1990s, much of the education community was facing a new problem: how to stay aware of online developments and new materials on the Web in a timely manner. The original *Scout Report* was developed to meet this need.[2] First published 29 April 1994 and using a format similar to print newsletters, the *Scout Report* had a readable tone and manageable scope; approximately twenty Internet resources were reviewed in each issue. The report was delivered via e-mail every Friday afternoon. *The Report*'s aim was to make resource discovery effortless for readers.

The original *Scout Report* concept was expanded in the mid- and late 1990s to include a broader range of discovery tools such as *Net-Happenings* and an array of subject-specific *Scout Reports*, including the current reports focused on specific content on the Web (life sciences, physical sciences, and math, engineering, and technology).[3] This experimentation with creating web services has continued, resulting in projects like LearningLanguages.net and the *NSDL Scout Reports*.[4]

As Scout's service projects continued to grow, so did the project's body of resource descriptions. With this expansion came the opportunity to offer the resources in a searchable and well-organized online database. This idea presented Scout with the possibility of creating an information hub, or portal, to share and distribute its critical reviews of online materials, providing an alternative to nonselective automated search engines and web directories. Debuting in 1997, the Scout Archives were designed to follow the general pattern established by print libraries for organization, access, and presentation in online catalogs.[5]

Having developed a successful in-house archive, Scout started to consider research initiatives that would build on this experience. As there was interest from the field in searching disparate portals simultaneously, Scout worked to develop technology such as the Isaac Network and the iMesh Toolkit that would allow users to search transparently across portals like the Scout Archives.[6] Concurrently, Scout began recognizing the difficulties that potential collection developers were having in finding appropriate software with which to build their portals. The idea of a Scout Portal Toolkit (SPT) emerged in 1999 as a remedy for this situation. The goal of this project was to design software that would allow groups with collections of information and metadata (and limited technical and financial resources) to share that information with others via the World Wide Web.[7] By 2002 the Scout Portal Toolkit had delivered a turnkey software package that could be installed with minimal technology and with few metadata barriers.

Scout has continued to explore new applications for its tools and services, most recently through participation in the NSF's National Science Digital Library (NSDL) initiative.[8] This effort combines the lessons learned and skills acquired during past projects with new ideas to develop tools and services for the NSDL. These new products include the *NSDL Scout Reports,* Access NSDL, and the Collection Workflow Integration System (CWIS), a focused extension of SPT.[9] As the Web evolves, so do Scout's mission and projects. Relationships with members of the digital library, education, and research communities continue to broaden, and it is hoped that other projects will benefit from this analysis of the successes and struggles of the Internet Scout Project.

Even in the rapidly changing landscape of the online world, some things remain constant. No matter how much information management is mechanized and automated, people are still at the core of every effort. Over the past ten years the Scout team has learned a few lessons about interactions between people, computers, and metadata, and how best to manage those interactions in the course of a digital library project. The sections that follow will focus on the areas of standards and technology, workflow and procedure, durability and change, and community and collaboration.

STANDARDS AND TECHNOLOGY

Standards and technologies are key to keeping a digital house in order, making collections easier to use, and seamlessly sharing data among projects. Throughout Scout's history, and central to its research and development efforts, has been an underlying commitment to high-quality metadata and the effective use of that metadata in Scout service projects and software tools.

The decision about which standards are right for an individual project or organization must be based on project needs, end-user needs, and the latest technology. From the Scout perspective, focusing on the right mix of standards and technology has resulted in the delivery of high-quality services and software that consistently meet user and community needs. The proper mix not only improves production efficiency, but also allows for a product to develop and change.

Plan Ahead, Carefully, and in Detail

In the early stages of any online collection project, detailed planning and a careful examination of needs are central to success in tackling the issues surrounding metadata, standards, and technology. These issues will be at the core of how collections operate and how they provide services for information consumers, both human and automated.

Decisions in metadata planning can have a ripple effect throughout the life of a project. Standards, as well as in-house practices, project staffing levels, and timelines, need to be carefully planned. When transitioning from a brick-and-mortar environment to a digital system, the existing services, practices, and standards should be examined so that conscious decisions are made about sustaining those same services or building similar services in an online environment. Planning ahead can help the project team consider the possible uses of the metadata beyond the project at hand.

The choice to use the emerging Dublin Core Metadata Element Set (DCMES) in the mid-1990s as Scout's metadata framework for resource description was made primarily because of its flexibility, simplicity, and modest requirements.[10] Since the DCMES specifies no syntax or specific vocabulary, Scout decided to draw upon established library standards such as the Anglo-American Cataloguing Rules (AACR2), Library of Congress Classification (LCC), and Library of Congress Subject Headings (LCSH) to control values and vocabularies in order to maintain consistency.[11]

This early planning and decision-making served Scout well. The Scout Archives debuted successfully in 1997 and included many of the same functions as a traditional library online catalog: hyperlinked subject headings and names to collate like resources, fielded search and retrieval mechanisms, and administrative metadata documenting record creation and maintenance. Early consideration of the technical constraints that Scout faced, careful planning, and the decision to use standardized metadata has meant that many of the original Scout Archives' components and features are still in place. The archive continues to thrive and develop, and with each change Scout tries to consider the future and plan accordingly.

Try Not to Reinvent the Wheel, Just Oil It

It is important to know how to apply standards—when to adopt established standards, how to adapt them to fit a project's needs, and when to create internal standards that only apply to your project. Sometimes recognized standards may not appear to be exact fits for your needs, but that does not mean a completely new solution is required. Evaluate which parts fit well "as is" when applying or using standards, and consider adapting other pieces or using a standard in innovative ways to meet your needs.

One example of this strategy was Scout's development of a browsing interface for the Scout Archives. Initially, the Library of Congress Classification was used as a browsing mechanism: readers could scroll through the LCC (which was listed alphabetically by classification order) and click on a classification to see associated resources. This approach was ultimately abandoned because it required Scout Archives users to have an understanding of the LCC in order to locate entries effectively. A second approach involved the in-house development of a completely new faceted browsing scheme. Although promising, full deployment of the system would have required extensive reworking of the archive's software and also reclassification of existing database records. Further, use of this homegrown classification system would have limited effective resource sharing with other digital library projects and placed additional maintenance demands on an already stretched staff. The solution ultimately implemented is based on Library of Congress Subject Headings broken apart at each subdivision to make them usable as a browsing hierarchy. This is an unconventional approach by library standards, but one that has worked well, providing end users with a browsable taxonomy without requiring a large in-house outlay of resources. Also, because LCSH is a recognized taxonomy, it allows metadata sharing with other digital library projects.

Reuse can also apply to in-house guidelines and other internal products. The Scout editorial staff had their own set of editorial guidelines that predated the Scout Archives. When the archive was created, a new set of separate standards was written to support both collection development and cataloging. The older editorial guidelines, based in part on the *Chicago Manual of Style*, were effective for publication, but were not intended for cataloging. Ultimately, staff realized that generating useful collection records from the *Scout Report* required melding existing Scout editorial guidelines with established cataloging practices, in part because traditional cataloging did not typically incorporate editorial description. The resulting Scout in-house style guide minimized reediting, and provided a more general document to use as a starting point for future service projects. This new guide pulled together the best of both sets of materials, incorporating standard library cataloging tools like AACR2 and the Library of Congress Subject Cataloging Manual to provide general guidance in areas like authority control and construction of subject headings. The practical result has been faster cataloging of Scout Archives records and more consistent descriptions of resources. The guidelines' ability to support consistency of resource descriptions is of particular importance for the archive because a keyword search of the archive utilizes the description text. Consistency in how resources are described, focusing on including descriptive keywords and appropriate professional terminology, helps users find resources that truly match their needs. And from a workflow perspective, using a hybrid set of guidelines has helped facilitate communication and coordination between coworkers and accelerate the process of training new staff.

For Scout, melding existing editorial guidelines with established cataloging practices significantly lowered the maintenance burden for the Scout Archives. The adaptation of an LCSH-based taxonomy also made the resulting collection more useful for end users, many of whom were already familiar with searching in traditional library catalogs. Attempting to solve either of these problems from scratch would have significantly delayed the archive's introduction or resulted in a collection that could be difficult to maintain. For projects like LearningLanguages.net, the Scout style guide provided a foundation for training content editors to use cataloging concepts to describe a resource directly with only minimal supervision from a professional cataloger for quality assurance.

Understand the Difference between Emerging and Established Standards

Both a blessing and a curse, standards and practices are a moving target in the world of digital libraries. It is important to remember that there are critical differences between a well-established standard and a standard in development. Sometimes it takes a while for well-established standards to be updated to support technological changes. For example, during the early days of the Scout Archives, chapter 9 of the *Anglo-American Cataloguing Rules,* "Electronic Resources," had not yet been updated to describe online resources effectively. Scout had to make decisions about description based on experience and publishing practices. At other times, a brand new standard arrives at just the right point where a project can make use of it. For Scout, adoption of the emerging DCMES standard provided consistent and useful metadata and the ability to rapidly adopt emerging harvesting protocols like the Open Archives Initiative (OAI). However, there can be a down side to being an early adopter. Scout has had to respond as DCMES evolved, sometimes revising metadata and refining in-house practices to match the standard's evolution and eventually needing to revise software developed at Scout to incorporate these changes.[12]

When developing software for the digital library community, Scout's adherence to established standards became critical. Many portal developers have little or no knowledge of metadata and may not have access to librarians or metadata specialists. The Scout Portal Toolkit comes complete with support for common underlying technical standards (e.g., OAI, RSS) and with metadata management and workflow capabilities based on established digital library standards (e.g., DCMES).[13] Making sure that SPT complied with these standards has made the toolkit easier for collection developers to use because it allowed them to easily import existing metadata and share that metadata with others.

Use Appropriate Technology and Be Willing to Change It

Database and web server stability, functionality, and scalability can all be important factors in determining the success of a project. A collection may start out small, with few users, but will the technical infrastructure support the expected growth and beyond? Will the infrastructure provide the flexibility to interoperate with other projects? When something goes wrong, is technical support (or at least support information) available?

Of course, the need for awareness of these technological issues does not end with the initial selection of software. As technology evolves, so must your technical infrastructure, to insure the ability to build new features and increase efficiency while maintaining consistency of service. Making sure that someone on your team stays abreast of these new tools will likely pay off in increased group productivity in the long run. Being aware of the state of the art in metadata and collection management tools can also significantly increase your chances of funding, both by helping to demonstrate the innovative nature of your project to a potential funding agency and by presenting a wider range of possibilities for collaborative projects.

The evolution of the Scout technical infrastructure over the past decade illustrates the consequences of attention and inattention to the impact of technological choices. At the time of the archive's inception, experienced technical staff were in short supply and most desktops at Scout were home to Apple Macintosh computers. Primarily because of these two factors, the original platform for the archive was a commercial FileMaker database for Macintosh personal computers. Seen as an inexpensive solution with a limited life span, it performed admirably at first, with some amount of tweaking and the addition of custom code patched together to achieve more functionality.

Unfortunately, insufficient consideration was given to long-term needs, and as the Scout Archives and Scout user base grew, FileMaker quickly began to show its limitations. By the time the archive was relocated to an SQL database several years later, the response time on the FileMaker-based system had become agonizingly slow and the process for transferring the annotations from a single *Scout Report* into the archive had grown to almost fifty steps.[14] Today the Scout Archives, using the Scout Portal Toolkit software, is on a Linux system running Apache and MySQL. Despite the continued growth of the Scout Archives and Scout user base (now up to 3 million hits per month and 350,000 readers per week, respectively), searching is almost instantaneous and transferring the *Reports* into the archive now takes a single step.[15]

WORKFLOW AND PROCEDURE

Metadata standards benefit users, but they also exist to help collection developers and catalogers collect and catalog resources. They can provide consistency and help in creating workflow patterns that allow for graceful and timely execution of procedures. Many metadata schemas have elements that can be used to address administrative and workflow issues.

Understand (and Leverage off) Workflow and Collection Development Issues

Any collection project will encounter its own unique challenges as it sets about the task of resolving workflow and collection development issues. In terms of planning, workflow, and collection development, a collection with a finite number of resources is very different from an ongoing aggregation project.

Traditional libraries have divisions of labor based on established professional roles, while in the digital community functional divisions are not always apparent. Constraints or workflow direction are sometimes determined by the nature of the project—its scope, budget, and content. The Scout Archives' workflow is determined in great part by the Scout publication schedule. New records are created from the Scout's weekly and biweekly reports and then added to the archive, requiring coordination between the Scout editorial and cataloging teams.

The resource records in the Scout Archives have been collected as a result of Scout publications being generated weekly and biweekly, with each publication's editorial team providing criteria for inclusion and review. This approach to collection development has naturally resulted in a less coherent collection in terms of scope and depth than is typically the result of traditional library collection building. However, the loss of consistency of coverage is somewhat offset by the gains in steady and predictable production. From a metadata and cataloging point of view, this workflow model from publications to archive offers a known quantity of records entering the database at a constant rate, ultimately making the tasks of estimating and forecasting staff time and other resource demands easier. In the long term, Scout's workflow model also provides an easy measure for production goals and collection growth.

Decisions about how to handle the flow of resources in the Scout Project, particularly in regard to cataloging and staff responsibilities, have changed over time. Currently, for example, Scout uses local administrative metadata elements, e.g., Date Record Checked, Release Flag, and Added By to facilitate workflow and maintain the integrity of the Scout Archives. The Release Flag element is a recent addition and has improved flexibility in workflow, allowing more initial cataloging to be done by content specialists, with a final check and release done by a professional cataloger.

In addition to archive workflow issues, Scout has had to adapt to collection development issues that have arisen in the course of software development projects. During development of the CWIS software, determining how to handle administrative metadata became an issue for portal developers, who were often unfamiliar with its application. Alpha testing of the initial software release revealed some confusion among users in understanding the difference between metadata about the resource and the administrative metadata fields intended to aid in collection management. The importance of clearly separating these elements, which had been lumped together in the original design, became more obvious to developers through user feedback. Changes were made to reflect this important separation, and to clarify how descriptive and administrative data should be used when exposing metadata for OAI harvesting.

Plan for Ongoing Maintenance and Documentation Efforts

If metadata is to be sustained over the long term, maintenance planning and clear documentation are essential. Even with in-house collections, servers move or are retired, institutional and information technology policies are updated, and the advance of technology can necessitate change. An array of technological options exists to ease this burden, but manual intervention and attention are often needed. In addition, the descriptive integrity of metadata needs to be examined and adjusted to guide maintenance. When has a resource been updated and when is it new? When does the original description no longer apply? Planning for these decisions and documenting them as they happen is an essential part of creating and maintaining a digital library.

Accurate, long-range planning is difficult, but a little project management applied consistently can go a long way in maintaining your collection. The Scout team has learned to ask the following questions:

What is the projected work plan for the next few weeks or months?

What are the goals for that time frame?

How much staff time will be required to meet those goals?

Do multiple projects overlap with intersecting deadlines?

Can any of the tasks be automated or made more efficient with technology?

All of this does not mean that Scout has a perfectly systematic approach. But maintaining the archive and continuing to update it requires ongoing effort. An important aspect of keeping the archive up-to-date is keeping its documentation current.

In the initial phase of Scout's history, when the in-house archive was created, the decision had been made to use professional librarians to do the cataloging. Over time, this proved to be too expensive to maintain.

Scout eventually changed staffing and workflow patterns and adopted a different staffing configuration: one professional librarian supported by one or more library and information science graduate students. The librarian defines policy and oversees quality assurance, while the students get hands-on experience and education. Documentation created originally to suit professional librarians shifted to more explicit materials designed to support the inexperienced graduate students. Scout strives to document internal policies and procedures early and update them often, believing that outdated documentation is often worse than no documentation at all.

The burden of ongoing maintenance applies not only to metadata and documentation but also to supporting software and technical infrastructure, i.e., installing updates, replacing outdated systems, and providing for changing staff needs. While a team may not be directly responsible for those tasks, maintenance of any type requires time and resources, and taking that expenditure into account will help keep a project on track.

DURABILITY AND CHANGE

Working in an online environment means that change is inevitable. Project managers must consider how metadata can help support the long-term needs of both users and the project. This may include thinking about which parts of a project or collection should be retained in-house, and, if funding ends, who might receive the metadata or resources if they cannot be retained. This type of planning and consideration will ease transitions and help conserve valuable resources.

Understand the Needs of Both the User and the Project

In tandem with project planning and standards selection, there should be a careful review of project needs. Special attention should be given to collection goals, staffing, and the overall life cycle of the project, as all of these areas will likely affect long-term planning and choice of standards. Metadata standards vary considerably in complexity and purpose, and some are directed toward specific information communities. Over time the needs of both the information consumers and the collection developers will change. New ideas and approaches will evolve and new services will be developed, often as the result of the developers' gaining a better understanding of user needs. This was the case with the development of CWIS, which extended the usefulness of the Scout Portal Toolkit by customizing it to fit the needs of the NSDL user community. It is helpful to clearly determine the initial needs of a project, at all levels, and to try to build systems, both technical and otherwise, that are flexible enough to accommodate change.

For Scout's core metadata standard, a subset of the DCMES was chosen, with local additions for website presentation, database administration, and accommodation of publication process idiosyncrasies. The DCMES standard appealed to Scout because it was easily applied, flexible, and did not impose restrictions by requiring specific fields. In addition, the standard allowed local extensions and accommodated a variety of vocabularies. DCMES offered the extra appeal of not specifying syntax or vocabulary for each field, which, for catalogers, meant the ability to experiment with granularity and vocabularies within the metadata fields in order to ultimately enhance benefits for users in terms of precision and retrieval.

Ask Whether the Collection (or Which Pieces) Should Be Sustained

It is natural to assume, after years of collecting resources and carefully creating high-quality metadata, that the results are all equally valuable. Creating and maintaining metadata is costly, and when a funded project becomes a legacy project (i.e., is no longer being sustained financially through grants or a parent institution), trying to support metadata production or maintenance can put a strain on resources better allocated to currently funded projects. Careful consideration of options when dealing with legacy projects may result in keeping what can be maintained without financial strain and passing the metadata that cannot be maintained along to digital library projects, parent institutions, or professional associations. Look for new uses of legacy project metadata: repurposing can extend the useful life of metadata far beyond the initial project for which it was created.

Part of the strategy in laying out the Scout Archives was to make it easy and inexpensive to maintain. As a project winds down, Scout integrates any appropriate metadata created for the project into the archive, preserving it for end users and insuring its availability for future projects. Legacy issues may also be an integral part of initial project plans. For the

NSDL Scout Reports, published as part of the National Science Digital Library initiative, the intention from the start has been that the generated metadata will eventually be passed on to the NSDL community.

COMMUNITY AND COLLABORATION

Realize That Your Audience May Be Wider Than You Think

Having a clear picture of the intended audience for any project is important, but be aware that project resources may serve a much wider community than originally intended. Planning to make your website, services, and products inclusive while thinking about access and resources for groups with different backgrounds and needs is increasingly important as adoption of the Americans with Disabilities Act and other accessibility legislation becomes more widespread.

Although metadata may not yet play a definitive role in making websites more accessible to users with disabilities, consistent metadata application will make websites more accessible to all.[16] Making websites more accessible means designing them with a variety of paths of access, along with more conventional steps toward accessibility, such as adding Alternative Text (alt text) tags to describe images and adding captioning to audiovisual resources. Scout has relied on the World Wide Web Consortium's Web Accessibility Initiative's Web Content Accessibility Guidelines to assure that our websites, materials, and software are accessible to users and developers with disabilities.[17]

Considering a wide audience is helpful in relation to taxonomies and resource descriptions. A survey of our report readership in 2000 showed that Scout has readers from many communities. Its commitment to keeping descriptions readable by defining acronyms and avoiding the use of jargon has meant that a publication originally created for the higher education community can become a useful resource-discovery tool for a more diverse audience. When Scout began working on projects that included a focus on resources for children, such as LearningLanguages.net, it became clear that the project needed to create a simpler taxonomy and change the perspective used for resource descriptions. Simultaneously, we needed to plan for the integration of these resources into the Scout Archives, so crosswalks between the new taxonomies and LCSH were created for future use. This means that if future funding is not secured for an individual Scout portal project, the resource records created for that project can be seamlessly integrated into the Scout Archives, and can be maintained as part of Scout's permanent collection.

Be Open to Collaboration—One Plus One Can Equal More Than Two

In the online world, the more eyes you have on your page, the more valuable it is. Being open to collaboration means working with partners and having the ability to share resources. Scout has had good experiences in its collaborations, with the most recent effort being the large National Science Digital Library project. As part of this enterprise, Scout has benefited from networking opportunities, by helping to set policy and procedure, and by working with like-minded colleagues on pertinent issues. Collaboration also requires projects to share their metadata and resources. Scout editorial policy has actively encouraged the use of resource reviews by anyone in education or research, provided they assign credit to Scout. Rich Site Summary and OAI channels harvest and distribute Scout metadata effortlessly. Because of this openness to sharing and collaboration, Scout publications are read by more than 350,000 readers each week.

How, and to what extent, metadata is shared can even have an impact on audience size. For example, online databases are sometimes inaccessible to search engines because they lack an infrastructure based on persistent links. Scout's use of LCSH as stable links for browsing resources has made the Scout Archives much easier to "spider" by search engines such as Google.

CONCLUSION

Digital collections and projects face many difficult decisions related to metadata. Deciding which underlying technologies to employ, which metadata standards to follow, and determining the best workflow practices are just a few of the issues that confront a project. Adding to the complexity of decision making is the environment of the Web itself, a new information territory with its own evolving standards, technologies, and communities. The Internet Scout Project has been providing services and web-related software to the education and research communities since the inception of the Web in the early 1990s. We have learned much along the way, and we hope that the information provided in this chapter will help other projects avoid a few pitfalls, and make the process of creating and sharing their resources and metadata a little smoother.

NOTES

1. Internet Scout Project (home page), http://scout.wisc.edu (accessed 11 December 2003).
2. Internet Scout Project, *Scout Report,* http://scout.wisc.edu/Reports/ScoutReport/Current/; back issues available at http://scout.wisc.edu/Reports/ScoutReport/Archive/ (accessed 11 December 2003).
3. *Net-Happenings,* once published by the Internet Scout Project, is now hosted by Classroom Connect. Founded in 1993 by web education expert Gleason Sackmann, *Net-Happenings* distributes announcements about the latest Internet resources, with an emphasis on education-related topics.
4. As part of the National Science Digital Library project, the Internet Scout Project's *NSDL Scout Reports* offer high-quality information about online resources. As with Scout's flagship publication, the *Scout Report,* the Scout team of professional librarians and content experts locates, researches, and annotates resources for academics, researchers, librarians, and K–12 teachers and students. More information on *NSDL Scout Reports* is available at http://scout.wisc .edu/Projects/NSDLReports/ (accessed 17 October 2003). LearningLanguages .net (home page), http://www.learninglanguages.net (accessed 11 December 2003).
5. Scout Archives (home page), http://scout.wisc.edu/Archives/ (accessed 11 December 2003).
6. Both Isaac Network and iMesh were projects related to developing federated searching of digital libraries using lightweight protocols. Information on them is available at http://scout.wisc.edu/Projects/PastProjects/ (accessed 17 October 2003).
7. Scout Portal Toolkit (home page), http://scout.wisc.edu/Projects/SPT/ (accessed 17 October 2003).
8. Funded by the National Science Foundation, the National Science Digital Library seeks to develop an integrated digital library of works in mathematics and the sciences for students in kindergarten through adulthood. The NSDL can be found at http://nsdl.org/.
9. Access NSDL project staff are providing the NSDL community with recommendations, tools, and resources to guide the development of a universally designed infrastructure and accessible services and content. The project design leverages work currently under way within the CPB/WGBH National Center for Accessible Media and the Internet Scout Project, and utilizes resources available at the IMS Global Learning Consortium and the Web Accessibility Initiative at the World Wide Web Consortium. More information on Access NSDL is available at http://accessnsdl.org/ (accessed 11 December 2003). The Collection Workflow Integration System is a turnkey software package to allow collections to put their materials online and integrate them with the NSDL Core Infrastructure (CI) quickly and easily. CWIS software is being created in tight

coordination with the NSDL CI, and in collaboration with existing NSDL collections and services. By supporting the inclusion of materials created by smaller institutions or organizations, CWIS will bring collections with more diverse materials, in many cases created by and for underserved populations, into NSDL. CWIS information and software are available at http://scout.wisc.edu/Projects/CWIS/ (accessed 11 December 2003).

10. Dublin Core Metadata Initiative, "Dublin Core Metadata Element Set," version 1.1, http://dublincore.org/documents/dces/ (accessed 11 December 2003).
11. American Library Association, *Anglo-American Cataloguing Rules,* 2d ed., 1998 revision (Chicago: Canadian Library Association; Chartered Institute of Library and Information Professionals; American Library Association, 1998).
12. The Open Archives Initiative Protocol for Metadata Harvesting provides an application-independent interoperability framework based on metadata harvesting. Version 2.0 of the protocol is available at http://www.openarchives.org/OAI/openarchivesprotocol.html (accessed 11 December 2003).
13. Rich Site Summary (RSS) is an XML based web content syndication format. The RSS 0.92 specification is available at http://backend.userland.com/rss092/ (accessed 17 October 2003).
14. MySQL Open Source Database (home page), http://www.mysql.com/ (accessed 11 December 2003).
15. Apache Software Foundation (home page), http://www.apache.org/ (accessed 11 December 2003).
16. Dublin Core Metadata Initiative, Accessibility Working Group (home page), http://dublincore.org/groups/access/ (accessed 11 December 2003).
17. World Wide Web Consortium, Web Accessibility Initiative, "Web Content Accessibility Guidelines," version 1.0, http://www.w3.org/TR/WCAG10/ (accessed 11 December 2003).

11 Lessons Learned from the Illinois OAI Metadata Harvesting Project

Timothy W. Cole and Sarah L. Shreeves

FOR ANY PROJECT involving the creation of metadata records, the selection of metadata semantics, vocabularies, and content-creation rules will depend on a number of factors. Most often the requirements of the immediate local environment and user community for which the metadata records are generated will dominate these decisions. However, almost always, an assumed benefit of and motivation for creating metadata is the supposition that good metadata will facilitate interoperability with other collections and other projects. Rich metadata records are seen as a way to help ensure the long-term usefulness and reusability of collections—even in contexts other than those originally envisioned.[1]

This chapter describes our experiences over the course of a two-year research and demonstration project designed to test this assumption and to assess the utility of an aggregation of metadata in the domain of cultural heritage. While the overall outcome of our project is encouraging, our experience suggests that there are wide variations in current practice when it comes to the creation of metadata. These differences affect how well the metadata supports interoperability. Some difficulties were anticipated, such as those that occur when mixing descriptive methodologies as fundamentally different as the Dublin Core (DC) metadata schema and the Encoded Archival Description (EAD) metadata schema. Dublin Core is designed to describe individual information objects independently. Encoded

Archival Description is designed to describe collections and provides information about individual information objects only within the context of a hierarchical collection description. Strategies and best practices continue to evolve for creating indexes and interfaces that allow end-user searching across an aggregation containing both DC and EAD metadata.

Other, unanticipated issues also emerged. Some end users were confused by the wide diversity of content and different levels of granularity in the descriptions retrieved during searches of aggregated metadata. Our metadata aggregation revealed wider than anticipated variations in the use of DC elements. For instance, academic libraries—institutions with strong traditions of descriptive cataloging—made surprisingly infrequent use of the "subject" element. Meanwhile, the way many DC elements were used by metadata authors appeared to hinge on whether an author set out to describe a work itself or a representation of a work. Few used standard controlled vocabularies when authoring metadata, even for basic elements such as "type," "format," and "date."

Our research suggests that metadata normalization and well-designed search interfaces can reduce the negative impact of these variations on end users. However, our work also indicates that improvements in metadata quality and uniformity are desirable. Results suggest that the use of simple or unqualified Dublin Core alone may be insufficient to achieve adequate interoperability among projects that encompass a range of communities and institution types. The flexibility and lack of precision inherent in simple DC also allow its inconsistent application. Our experience corroborates earlier work suggesting that ongoing efforts to map subject terminologies and harmonize ontologies are necessary to achieve a high level of functional interoperability.[2] At the very least, communities need basic agreement on the application of vocabularies and content-creation rules. Arguably, the wider use of more precise and expressive schemas, e.g., qualified DC, could be helpful.

APPROACH TO INTEROPERABILITY AND PROJECT OBJECTIVES

The Open Archives Initiative Protocol for Metadata Harvesting (OAI-PMH), version 1.0, was publicly released on 23 January 2001 in Washington, D.C., as part of an event called "OAI Open Day for the U.S." The current release of the protocol is version 2.0.[3] The result of a multiyear grassroots effort led by Carl Lagoze and Herbert Van de Sompel and underwritten by the Digital Library Federation, the Coalition for Networked Information, and the National Science Foundation, OAI-PMH is a prescription for sharing descriptive metadata.[4] A technically low-barrier approach to interoperability, OAI-PMH is premised on a "harvest" model of interoperability—that is, it divides the world into *data providers* (also known as *content providers*) and *service providers*. Data providers make available discrete collections of content and the metadata describing those collections. Service providers harvest and aggregate metadata from a range of data providers in order to offer high-level services, such as single-point search and discovery services across multiple collections of content held by widely distributed data providers. This latter approach is reminiscent of old-style library union catalogs and of services offered by cataloging utilities like the Online Computing Library Center, OCLC. It contrasts with broadcast search services, sometimes referred to as federated search systems or cross-system search services. Broadcast search services enable an end user to simultaneously query multiple data providers in real time. The difference between the two approaches centers on where the metadata resides and who does the searching (e.g., the aggregator in a central locale or the data providers in a distributed fashion). The ANSI/NISO Z39.50 standard is an example of a popular approach to broadcast searching.[5]

In June 2001, the Andrew W. Mellon Foundation funded seven research and demonstration projects, all of which were designed to assess the usefulness and potential of OAI-PMH.[6] The Illinois OAI Metadata Harvesting Project (http://oai.grainger.uiuc.edu/), undertaken by the University of Illinois Library at Urbana-Champaign from June 2001 through May 2003, was designed to test the efficacy and utility of OAI-PMH in the domain of cultural heritage. Its primary objective was to design, implement, and study the utility of a suite of tools and services for OAI-PMH–based metadata-harvesting tools and services intended to facilitate the discovery and retrieval of scholarly information resources in the cultural heritage domain. In particular, we set out to create OAI-PMH tools and software, including an OAI-PMH harvesting utility that would also be used by the Mellon-funded project at the University of Michigan; examine how to integrate and present metadata originally created in a range of schemas, including MARC, simple and qualified DC, and EAD; investigate how variations in metadata authoring practices affect a harvesting service's ability to search metadata aggregations effectively; and identify normalization and interface design techniques that could enhance the searching of metadata aggregated from heterogeneous sources.

We focused on descriptive metadata, search interoperability, and the reuse of metadata across organizations, metadata schemas, and application profiles. Structural metadata was not investigated, nor was the administrative metadata associated with rights management, preservation, or the technical characteristics of objects described. The only administrative metadata of interest were those elements required by OAI-PMH itself, namely a persistent OAI metadata record identifier and a date stamp element containing the date that the record was created, deleted, or last modified. The OAI-PMH specification prescribes that metadata be shared using XML (Extensible Markup Language), so the metadata record syntax was a given. The protocol also specifies the use of simple DC as a lowest common denominator, but we made a point of also obtaining metadata in project-native schemas, so that crosswalks and normalization techniques could be explored.

CHARACTERISTICS OF HARVESTED METADATA

By the end of our project we had gathered more than one million item-level metadata records from thirty-nine data providers. Because a number of the providers harvested were themselves aggregators, these metadata records described a mix of analog and digital items held by more than 500 cultural heritage institutions worldwide. Harvested metadata records were stored as discrete XML files on our servers and encoded according to the semantics of simple DC (validated according to the XML Schema Definition Language document maintained by OAI, available at http://www.openarchives.org/OAI/2.0/oai_dc.xsd). Files were indexed and made searchable using an implementation of the University of Michigan Digital Library Extension Service's XPat database management system (http://www.dlxs.org/).

More than 600,000 of the metadata records collected were harvested directly from data providers in simple DC using OAI-PMH. Repeat harvests were performed periodically during the course of the project to refresh the records. No harvests occurred during interface testing and analysis, from late 2002 through early 2003.

Approximately 4,500 additional metadata records were obtained from data providers on a one-time-only basis using techniques other than OAI-PMH, typically file transfer protocol (FTP). These metadata "snapshots" were given to us in various schemas and syntaxes, including MARC records and as tables from relational database management systems. We then processed the snapshot collections and created surrogate OAI provider services on our servers in order to make the records accessible to our harvester according to the OAI-PMH specification. Processing these snapshot collections involved transforming records received in other schemas into simple DC. To transform MARC records, we implemented the MARC-to-DC crosswalk maintained by the Library of Congress (http:// www.loc.gov/marc/marc2dc.html). We also obtained item-level metadata records in the Visual Resources Association Core, in local schemas unrelated to any standard, and in variations of simple and qualified DC. (For example, http://imlsdcc.grainger.uiuc.edu/schemas/cdp_dc_test.xsd.) We developed new, unique crosswalks to transform metadata in these schemas into simple DC as required for export via OAI-PMH. Once processing had made the snapshot metadata records available via OAI-PMH, the records were treated the same as those harvested directly from OAI-PMH–compliant providers. Unlike the directly harvested metadata, the snapshot metadata did not change over the life of the project.

Finally, we obtained more than 8,000 EAD online finding aids in XML or SGML syntax from ten data providers, including the Online Archives of California, which provided EAD files from fifty institutions within the state. These files were obtained via FTP or via HTTP if web-accessible. Each of these finding aids described hundreds to thousands of items in a given manuscript archive or other special collection. We developed an algorithm to decompose the individual nodes of the finding aids into item-level descriptions in simple DC. In doing so we preserved relationships to immediate parent nodes in the EAD structure and included pointers (using XML XPointer syntax) to the location of each node in the original EAD file.[7] We then made these derived item-level metadata records available to our harvesting system. This process yielded an additional 1.6 million item-level records.

The metadata harvested via OAI-PMH and obtained by the other means represented a heterogeneous collection of content held by a wide range of institutions. Figures 11-1 and 11-2 show breakdowns of the categories of institutions providing the metadata and of the categories of content described by the metadata.

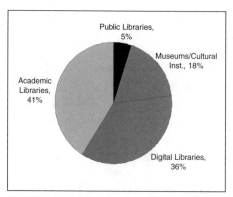

FIGURE 11-1 Types of institutions (39 total) providing metadata for the Illinois OAI Metadata Harvesting Project as of October 2002

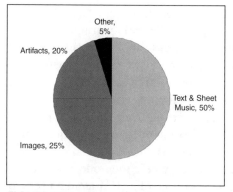

FIGURE 11-2 Types of content represented by 1.1 million records in the Illinois OAI Project as of October 2002

ENCODED ARCHIVAL DESCRIPTION AND DUBLIN CORE

Archival finding aids describe collections of content (e.g., letters, working papers, or other documents associated with an individual or organization). They offer context and structure that are useful for understanding and making use of the collection's individual objects. The Encoded Archival Description specification for encoding the metadata of an archival finding aid in digital form is hierarchical and is designed to capture structure in a way that facilitates efficient machine processing and presentation. It allows considerable flexibility in the number of levels and in what each level represents. For example, the "co3" level may represent a box, a folder, or an individual letter, according to the specifics of the archival collection being described. Because of this flexibility, difficulties can arise when trying to perform searches across multiple EAD finding aids. This problem is exacerbated when trying simultaneously to search an aggregation of metadata from EAD finding aids (describing collections of information objects) and DC metadata records (each created to describe a single information object).

Most existing EAD-to-DC crosswalks link DC elements to only the collection-level descriptive elements of EAD, and thus can be used only to create collection-level records (http://lcweb.loc.gov/ead/ag/agappb.html#sec3). The rest of the finding aid, including detailed description of subordinate (item-level) components, is discarded. When the intent is to help the end user locate individual information objects, much of the information that could facilitate searching is lost.

We examined new approaches that would allow us to represent individual information objects in EAD finding aids in our metadata index. To develop an alternative EAD-to-DC crosswalk that could make use of subordinate components, we considered three issues: which nodes in the finding aid to treat as items worthy of an individual DC record; how much information from parent, child, or sibling nodes to repeat in multiple derived DC records; and how to best preserve the context and structure provided by the finding aid.

The transformation we implemented created multiple DC metadata records for each EAD file. The transformation was designed to retain item-level descriptive information and simultaneously to preserve, at least for presentation purposes, the archival context expressed by the finding aid.[8] One DC metadata record was created to contain the EAD file header metadata. Additional records were created for each component node in the description of subordinate component elements (e.g., "co1," "co2," "co3," etc.) having textual content (e.g., in the "component unit title" element). Thus DC records were created for both terminal (leaf) nodes and for all intermediate nodes in the EAD hierarchy that contained useful content for searching—regardless of how many hierarchical levels were in the finding aid. Each DC record contained a pointer to its immediate parent concatenated with the component unit title string from the parent node in a DC "relation" element. Each record also included an identifier which provided the URL to a complete copy of the EAD finding aid and included a reference in XPointer syntax that identified where the node appeared in the finding aid's hierarchical structure. A sample of a DC metadata record created for a specific node in an EAD file is provided in figure 11-3.

DIVERSITY OF CONTENT AND GRANULARITY

Analog versus Digital Primary Content

As mentioned earlier, the decomposition of the EAD records into DC metadata records describing both collection and individual component information added 1.6 million records to the Illinois repository. The majority of these records describe analog (physical) objects or groups of objects. While the vast majority of records describing analog content were

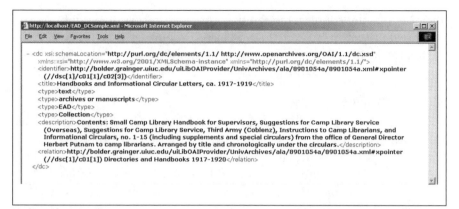

FIGURE 11-3   Sample item-level DC record derived from an EAD finding aid

derived from finding aids, some came from other data providers as well. In fall 2002, we conducted usability tests on the repository's search portal with a group of twenty-three college students in a University of Illinois honors-level curriculum and instruction course.[9] The students were instructed to use the repository to find supporting materials for a lesson plan on a specific topic. Metadata records that described physical objects lacking digital surrogates frustrated these users. Their expectation of instant access to the resources described in a finding aid, and their lack of familiarity with the value of archival collections in general, meant that these end users often disregarded this set of results.

While we recognized that other end users familiar with archival collections might well find the inclusion of records derived from EAD finding aids useful, we saw a need for an option to exclude metadata that described analog content. For this purpose we provided a search option that allowed users to limit their results to "online resources." We also designed search results that would indicate hyperlinks to online content and digital representations of primary content differently from hyperlinks to finding aids or other forms of information about content not available in digital form. Unfortunately, inconsistencies in the use of DC "identifier" and "relation" elements produced unpredictable results. The search and discovery interface frequently was unable to programmatically distinguish records describing digital content from those describing analog content. In addition, many data providers chose not to provide direct hyperlinks to their own digital content. Instead they provided generic hyperlinks to top-level search web pages on their websites, requiring that users then re-search the local collection for records of interest.

Granularity Issues

The size and scope of objects described varied considerably, making it difficult for users to have consistent expectations when approaching the search portal. Several data providers included metadata describing archival collections without including the specific content of those collections. Since these metadata records were harvested as simple DC records using OAI-PMH, we could not break down these archival records into component parts. Similarly, websites were described by some providers as single, discrete information objects.

Indexed alongside these types of collection-level metadata were records describing individual items ranging from letters to coins, photographs, and entire texts. One data provider even included records that described segments within a video. Table 11-1 shows the range of information resources described by single DC metadata records.

Even within a single data provider, the granularity of the information objects described might vary. Thus, metadata from one data provider included records that described individual photographs, groups of related images, and websites. As mentioned earlier, archival collections are traditionally described first as a collection, then as boxes and folders, and finally as individual items. Museums may inventory each of their holdings individually, even if there are a large number of similar items. A moving

TABLE 11-1   Granularity of resources described by metadata harvested for the Illinois OAI Project

Collections	Individual Items	Parts of Items
Archival collections Websites Groups of photographs	Letters Individual photographs Coins Museum artifacts Books (in their entirety) Videos (moving images)	Segments of videos

image available on the World Wide Web may be stored in segments in order to give users more control over download times. Each segment may have a separate metadata record. The impact on the aggregator and end users of the aggregating service is not well understood. For some purposes it might be desirable to have a separate description record for every coin in a collection, even if those records only differ in the detail of a museum's accession number. On the other hand, for search and discovery purposes, how useful is it to retrieve dozens of records, each of which describes a single coin, when the records vary only in one detail: the coin's accession number? Would it be more useful to have a single record describing a group of similar coins? These questions deserve further study.

USE OF DUBLIN CORE AS THE LOWEST COMMON DENOMINATOR

The Open Archives Initiative Protocol supports the use of any metadata schema for which a schema written in XML Schema Definition Language is readily available (from the data provider or a trusted third party). This feature provides flexibility but does not ensure minimum interoperability across OAI projects. To accomplish this second objective, OAI-PMH requires that data providers must support, at a minimum, simple Dublin Core. Harvesting services can therefore count on being able to harvest simple DC records from any OAI data provider. In the months preceding the release of OAI-PMH 2.0, the OAI Technical Committee discussed whether to retain this requirement and whether simple DC was the best choice as the minimal required schema. The requirement was retained.[10] While the requirement has ensured minimum interoperability, it has tended to focus many implementers on simple DC exclusively and has led many to blur the distinction between OAI-PMH and DC. The protocol does support the use of schemas other than simple DC, but initial OAI offerings from commercial vendors (e.g., ContentDM and ENCompass) support only simple DC in their OAI data provider implementations. For this project, we chose as well to focus exclusively on simple DC.

Early in our project it became clear that the decision to index simple DC metadata represented something of a compromise. Dublin Core usage practice varies widely. Table 11-2 illustrates this point by showing the range of practice in how often elements were used by the different communities of

TABLE 11-2   Use of DC elements by community (records collected natively in DC)

Element Name	Museums and Cultural / Historical Societies (6 total, 255,800 records)		Academic Libraries (7 total, 235,294 records)		Digital Library Projects (10 total, 122,719 records)	
	% records containing element	Average times used per record	% records containing element	Average times used per record	% records containing element	Average times used per record
Contributor	45%	1.91	2%	1.93	2%	1.13
Coverage	69%	3.41	41%	1.01	51%	1.00
Creator	37%	1.02	79%	1.03	93%	1.22
Date	64%	1.08	52%	1.06	63%	1.33
Description	93%	1.64	13%	2.24	36%	1.88
Format	33%	1.77	42%	1.05	14%	1.38
Identifier	100%	1.55	100%	1.13	100%	1.06
Language	46%	1.00	33%	1.01	44%	1.00
Publisher	97%	1.30	45%	1.06	59%	1.19
Relation	79%	1.43	11%	1.55	8%	1.03
Rights	83%	1.50	48%	1.00	50%	1.07
Source	21%	1.00	4%	1.00	4%	1.06
Subject	93%	2.75	15%	3.22	78%	2.26
Title	77%	1.05	66%	1.93	100%	1.01
Type	100%	3.49	39%	1.03	97%	2.34

data providers. Of interest in the table is the very sparse use of the DC "subject" element by academic libraries. Clearly, metadata authors in the academic libraries sampled are not following the same content creation rules they use for creating catalog records describing their print collections. This suggests that different models of descriptive cataloging are being evaluated, perhaps in part for economic reasons, by metadata librarians working in the digital library environment.

Our DC metadata sample also showed wide disparities in how and for what purpose various DC elements were utilized. Encodings used in even standard elements such as "date," "coverage," "format," and "type" varied significantly. Metadata authors had different interpretations as to the purpose of specific DC elements. This is a well-recognized issue in the community of DC users.[11] For our project, the discrepancies observed seemed in part to relate to whether the metadata author chose to focus on describing a given work itself or on describing the digital surrogate of a given work. This in turn appears to be traceable to the nature of the original environment or project for which the metadata was created. This is not a new problem—similar issues have arisen when considering how to describe an image and have been discussed extensively within the Dublin Core Metadata Initiative (the "one-to-one" rule).[12]

Table 11-3 illustrates this discrepancy through excerpts of metadata from two different data providers. Each record describes a coverlet. Each record contains a hyperlink to a digital image of a coverlet in the "identifier" element (not shown). The record from Provider A, created specifically for a database of images from a museum, focuses on the digital image surrogate. The "format" and "type" elements apply to the image, not the physical object depicted in the image. Three of the four instances of the "date" element apply to the image. The brief contents of the "description" element indirectly describe the coverlet, but most of the essential information about the coverlet resides only in the "source" element. The "coverage" element is not used. The record from Provider B, however, ignores the digital image surrogate altogether (except to provide a hyperlink to it in the "identifier" element) and describes the coverlet itself—its dimensions and weight ("format"), the date of its creation ("date"), and its "type." The "description" element describes the coverlet in detail and does not mention the image. The "source" element is not used. The record from Provider B was derived from a content management system for a museum collection, which explains the primacy of the actual physical object over the digital surrogate. A variety of valid reasons related to local implementation will influence how individual data providers choose to describe the attributes of a digital information resource. The problem for the metadata harvester is to cope with the varying levels of representation that result when an aggregator harvests from a wide range of data providers.

TABLE 11-3 Excerpt of metadata records describing coverlets harvested from Data Providers A and B

Dublin Core Element	Data Provider A	Date Provider B
Description	Digital image of a single-sized cotton coverlet for a bed with embroidered butterfly design. Handmade by Anna F. Ginsberg Hayutin.	Materials: Textile-Multi, Pigment-Dye: Manufacturing Process: Weaving-Hand, Spinning, Dyeing, Hand-loomed blue wool and white linen coverlet, worked in overshot weave in plain geometric variant of a checkerboard pattern. Coverlet is constructed from finely spun, indigo-dyed wool and undyed linen, woven with considerable skill. Although the pattern is simpler, the overall craftsmanship is higher than 1934. 01.0094A. – D.S., 11/19/99 This coverlet is an example of early "overshot" weaving construction, probably dating to the 1820's and is not attributable to any particular weaver. – G.S., 10/9/1973
Source	Materials: cotton and embroidery floss. Dimensions: 71 in. x 86 in. Markings: top right hand corner has 1 1/2 in. x 1/2 in. label cut outs at upper left and right hand side for head board; fabric is woven in a variation of a rib weave; color each of yellow and gray; hand-embroidered cotton butterflies and flowers from two shades of each color of embroidery floss - blue, pink, green and purple and single top 20 in. bordered with blue and black cotton embroidery thread; stitches used for embroidery: running stitch, chain stitch, French knot and back stitches; selvage edges left unfinished; lower edges turned under and finished with large gray running stitches made with embroidery floss.	-

Format	Epson Expression 836 XL Scanner with Adobe Photoshop version 5.5; 300 dpi; 21-53K bytes. Available via the World Wide Web.	228 x 169 x 1.2 cm (1,629 g)
Coverage	-	Euro-American; America, North; United States; Indiana? Illinois?
Date	Created: 2001-09-19 09:45:18 Updated: 20011107162451 Created: 2001-04-05 Created: 1912-1920?	Early 19th c. CE
Type	Image	Cultural; physical object; original

NORMALIZATION AND INTERFACE DESIGN TO FACILITATE SEARCH OF METADATA HARVESTED

The variability in metadata authoring practices noted above was problematic for both the construction of a functional search service and the end user's interaction with the metadata. Where possible, we employed strategies designed to minimize these variations. These strategies included normalization of selected elements and organization and indexing of metadata by type of resource.

Metadata records harvested were normalized or modified on a per-contributor basis to account for peculiarities of practice. We used XPat to supply pointers to the holding institution and collection website in the display of the metadata; often this information was not included in the metadata itself. We also focused on the temporal aspect of the "coverage" element and the "date" element for normalization. Through an analysis of the harvested metadata, we had discovered that these two DC elements were often used interchangeably and that dates and other temporal information were inputted in many different ways.[13] We were specifically concerned with the dates associated with the described object itself (not the date the digital object was created or the date the metadata was created). We mapped the appropriate date information (in either the "coverage" or "date" element) to a standard date "normalization vocabulary" developed specifically for this purpose. This normalized vocabulary was then added to the metadata record and was clearly marked as coming from the University of Illinois project. We were then able to build a "limit by date range" function into the search interface.

We also organized and indexed our metadata by type of resource described. We had initially indexed the metadata by the data provider. For both technical and usability reasons, we decided that grouping the metadata by type of resource (e.g., image, text, archive) would be a better choice. Because the "type" element was inconsistently used by data providers, we examined each data provider and, where possible, the sub-collections or sets of each data provider, and attempted to categorize them by type of resource. In some cases, we had to categorize a data provider by the type of resource described by the majority of its metadata. Usability testing validated this choice; we found that our end users did not base decisions about what metadata to view by the holding institution.[14] Although some end users did not understand how to navigate through the groupings of metadata, those that did reported liking the ability to view just images or to skip viewing archival collections.

An interesting result of the usability testing was that end users held the search service responsible not only for the functionality of the search service, but for the quality and usability of the metadata itself. We were somewhat surprised by this finding, as we had spent a session with the class explaining the concept of aggregated metadata. This finding (though not generalizable due to the pilot nature of the study) could have obvious ramifications for metadata aggregators, as well as for where the responsibility lies in cleaning up metadata available for harvest via OAI—with the data providers or with service providers.

CONCLUSIONS AND IMPLICATIONS FOR FUTURE WORK

The two-year project described in this chapter raises more questions than it answers, but clearly it suggests lines of further inquiry that hold promise. Based on observations made during this project, we are exploring a number of new and more sophisticated approaches in our ongoing work with OAI-PMH and metadata aggregation. Digital technologies are blurring the boundaries between traditional cultural heritage institutions. While we remain optimistic that metadata contributed by different communities of content providers (e.g., libraries, museums, and archives) can be searched in aggregate to good effect, we continue to struggle with a lack of consistency in practice. Overall our work suggests that if metadata interoperability is a desired objective, more care should be given by metadata authors to defining and following community best practices and taking into account other considerations that will facilitate interoperability. More work to develop enhanced mappings and crosswalks between metadata schemas is needed. Metadata authors should consider factors of granularity and should strive to describe both the representation and the primary source work in adequate detail. Consideration should be given to using metadata schemas that are more expressive and prescriptive than simple DC (e.g., MARC, MODS, or qualified DC or some variant). We are finding it useful at the search and discovery level to further isolate and segment metadata aggregations, not only by subject domain and resource type, as was done in the project described, but also as to whether the metadata harvested describes digital or analog resources.

The release of OAI-PMH has led to the emergence of several new models for digital library interoperability at the metadata level. A number of other community and discipline-based metadata aggregators are in development. Of particular note is the work being done as part of the National Science Foundation-funded National Science Digital Library and the Open Language Archives Community.[15] It is of interest to note that implementers involved in both these projects have found it necessary to prescribe some additional metadata content-creation rules and to augment the simple DC schema in order to achieve desired levels of interoperability. More study is also needed to better understand how data providers create, maintain, and use metadata internally and how end users might most effectively utilize metadata aggregations. A new project at the University of Illinois (http://imlsdcc.grainger.uiuc.edu), funded by the Institute of Museum and Library Services (IMLS) and designed to create a collection registry and item-level metadata repository for digital content associated with past and current IMLS National Leadership Grant projects, will feature a research component to further investigate these issues.

NOTES

1. Priscilla Caplan et al., "A Framework of Guidance for Building Good Digital Collections," 2001, http://www.imls.gov/pubs/forumframework.htm (accessed 12 May 2003).

2. Dennis Nicholson, Dunsire Gordon, and Susannah Neill, "HILT: Moving towards Interoperability in Subject Terminologies," *Journal of Internet Cataloging* 5, no. 4 (2002): 97–111; Martin Doerr, Jane Hunter, and Carl Lagoze, "Towards a Core Ontology for Information Integration," *Journal of Digital Information* 4, no. 1 (2003), http://jodi.ecs.soton.ac.uk/Articles/v04/i01/Doerr/ (accessed 12 May 2003).
3. Carl Lagoze et al., "The Open Archives Initiative Protocol for Metadata Harvesting," 2002, http://www.openarchives.org/OAI/openarchivesprotocol.html (accessed 12 May 2003).
4. Carl Lagoze and Herbert Van de Sompel, "The Making of the Open Archives Initiative Protocol for Metadata Harvesting," *Library Hi-Tech* 21, no. 2 (2003): 118–28.
5. For more information, visit the official Z39.50 web page maintained by the Library of Congress Network Development and MARC Standards Office, http://www.loc.gov/z3950/agency/ (accessed 12 August 2003).
6. Donald J. Waters, "The Metadata Harvesting Initiative of the Mellon Foundation," *ARL Newsletter* 217 (2001), also available at http://www.arl.org/newsltr/217/waters.html (accessed 12 May 2003).
7. Christopher J. Prom and Thomas G. Habing, "Using the Open Archives Initiative Protocols with EAD," in *Proceedings of the Second ACM/IEEE-CS Joint Conference on Digital Libraries, July 14–18, 2002,* ed. Gary Marchionini and William Hersch (New York: Association for Computing Machinery, 2002), 171–80.
8. Christopher J. Prom, "Reengineering Archival Access through the OAI Protocols," *Library Hi-Tech* 21, no. 2 (2003): 199–209.
9. Sarah L. Shreeves et al., "Utility of an OAI Service Provider Search Portal," in *Proceedings: 2003 Joint Conference on Digital Libraries, May 27–31, 2003,* ed. Catherine C. Marshall, Geneva Henry, and Lois Delcambre (Los Alamitos, Calif.: Institute of Electrical and Electronics Engineers, 2003), 306–8.
10. Lagoze and Van de Sompel, "Open Archives Initiative Protocol."
11. Doerr, Hunter, and Lagoze, "Towards a Core Ontology."
12. Sara Shatford Layne, "Some Issues in the Indexing of Images," *Journal of the American Society for Information Science* 45, no. 8 (1994): 583–88; Stuart Weibel and Juha Hakala, "DC-5: The Helsinki Metadata Workshop," *D-Lib Magazine,* February 1998, http://www.dlib.org/dlib/february98/02weibel.html (accessed 25 July 2003).
13. Sarah L. Shreeves, Joanne Kaczmarek, and Timothy W. Cole, "Harvesting Cultural Heritage Metadata Using the OAI Protocol," *Library Hi-Tech* 21, no. 2 (2003): 159–69.
14. Shreeves et al., "OAI Service Provider Search Protocol."
15. William Y. Arms et al., "A Case Study in Metadata Harvesting: The NSDL," *Library Hi-Tech* 21, no. 2 (2003): 228–37; Gary Simons and Steven Bird, "Building an Open Language Archives Community on the OAI Foundation," *Library Hi-Tech* 21, no. 2 (2003): 210–18.

12

Community-Based Content Control

Harriette Hemmasi

WHETHER ONE ASKS by humming, drumming, nodding, knocking, blinking, speaking, or keying, the asking is for content. Content, whether it is melody, rhythm, color, concept, shape, date, formula, frame, scene, or pixel, begs for context. Context provides a framework for understanding and interpreting content and is shaped by individual and community knowledge. This knowledge can be further refined through a set of imposed controls or tracking mechanisms. These controls are embodied in community-defined rules, a shared logic for these rules, and a common set of labels, or vocabulary, that must be communicable across humans and computers. Web-based search and retrieval processes demand the engagement of total content, i.e., data, metadata, schema, and ontology. Community-specific content control exercised at the points of describing, organizing, and searching helps put content into context and ultimately improves retrieval. The purpose of this chapter is to demonstrate how the music community, illustrative of other domain-specific communities, is attempting to improve the definition and management of its content, and to examine what additional steps might be needed to accomplish these goals. Many of the challenges faced by the music community are common to other communities. It is hoped that this discussion will not only lead to more self-awareness among the music community, but may also serve as a useful example or basis of comparison for those communities embarking on or already involved in the process of community-based content control.

COMMUNITY-BASED ONTOLOGY

By their very nature, communities loosely or strictly generate either implicitly or explicitly a common set of rules, a shared logic for applying those rules, and a collective vocabulary or set of labels derived from that content and its contextual environment. Together these rules, logic, and labels comprise the fundamentals of a community-specific knowledge base or ontology. While the emergence of a knowledge base can be thought of as a natural evolution within an established group, domain, or discipline, a knowledge base is not usually recognized as such and is rarely documented, even informally. To improve communication both within a given community and among other communities in the web environment, it is critical to formalize domain-specific knowledge into a domain-specific ontology.

A domain- or community-based ontology serves as the conceptual backbone for providing, accessing, and structuring information in a comprehensible and comprehensive fashion. Building ontologies is a social process wherein different stakeholders need to agree on shared classes, terminology, relationships, and constraints. In the online environment, ontologies provide the foundation for processing resources based on the meaningful interpretation of their content rather than simply on their physical structure or metadata surrogates. Ontologies define a common vocabulary for researchers who need to share information within and beyond a given domain. In addition, ontologies include machine-interpretable definitions of basic concepts within the domain, established properties and restrictions of each concept, and delineated relationships among the concepts. Ontologies facilitate the understanding of the structure of information among a community and software agents. They enable the reuse of domain knowledge; document and explicate assumptions shared by a community; separate domain knowledge from operational knowledge; and promote the analysis of domain knowledge.[1]

By definition, ontologies contain rules, logic, and labels that are communicable across people and computers. Because of the integral role that ontologies play in interpreting content, they become an essential and ultimately inseparable part of content. As it is collectively the medium *and* the message that create meaning, so, too, ontologies must represent both content and context in order to express and explicate the complete digital resource.[2]

THE MEANING OF "CONTENT"

Expressions of intellectual and artistic content could hardly be more multifarious than what we find in today's commercial, educational, and research markets. Simplicity is replaced by multiplicity on every level. In addition to "just text," there are objects of art and architecture, printed and recorded works of music, endless statistics and geospatial representations, videos, photographs, files, slides, and all manner of learning and commercial objects that are presented as viable candidates for description, identification, retrieval, and preservation. Users expect that if "it" exists (or existed) either online or in print, they should be able to find it, any part of it, and everything about it, depending on where and how precisely they search. As a result, information specialists are expected to assemble, save, and serve mass quantities of content as well as tiny bytes of information, ad infinitum. The amount and variation of content, and the fact that searchable content may extend beyond traditional cataloging records or metadata to include the artifact, create major challenges for information technologists.[3]

Therefore, the meaning of "content," i.e., what *is* (or was) and what *is sought,* can no longer be limited to the descriptive surrogate or even the surrogate plus object. Instead, a more complete definition of content encompasses the data (i.e., document, artifact, etc.); accompanied by its descriptive, structural, and technical metadata; the schema that defines the metadata; and also the ontology that provides an explicit framework for interpreting the data and metadata. An even more comprehensive statement of content, particularly when considering long-term preservation, would include not only the multilayered artifact-metadata-schema-ontology compound, but also the original software design and operating system used to support the object's transmission, retrieval, and analysis. For the purposes of this chapter, the author defines "content" as the combination of artifact, metadata, schema, and ontology. Together, these four components comprise layer upon layer of intrinsic, potentially identifiable, and ultimately preservable content. Each element representing this expanded definition of "content" is an expression of the community's rules, logic, and labels.

COMMUNITY-BASED CONTENT: THE MUSIC DOMAIN

Works of Music

The music domain's primary content is comprised of works of music, i.e., compositions that may be manifested on the printed page, in recorded sound, or in live performance; and works about music, meaning text-based and multimedia works written about music, musicians, and related topics. As the music community is attempting to increase the accessibility of this content, it is also attempting to improve the definition and management of music-related content. Deceptively simple, the most fundamental "physical" elements of music that are transmitted and understood are sound and its production. This is like saying that visual art is nothing more than color and shape, or literature nothing more than words. The richness of music, as with other arts, is its intricate interweaving of these basic elements into a myriad of patterns and variations. The results are an artistic complexity worth pursuing and worth preserving.

Organizing sound into patterns results in musical composition, with sound occurring either singularly (melody) or simultaneously (harmony) and according to a measured or unmeasured beat (rhythm). Compositions may be written or unwritten and thus may or may not be ascribed to a particular composer, time, or place. Musical performance is the "sounding" of organized patterns, either precisely or imprecisely at the will or ability of the performer. Lastly, there are multiple physical manifestations of compositions and their performances in various forms of notated scores, recordings, and live performances. Together, these four broad attributes—composer, composition, performer, and manifestation—represent what are commonly known as "bibliographic" elements. Taken together with the physical elements of sound and sound production (such as melody, harmony, rhythm, instrumentation, musical form, etc.), they generate a complex array of multidimensional and deeply interrelated content for which the community must develop explicit rules, logic, and labels.

All aspects and pursuits in Western music, whether artistic, academic, or commercial, center on these basic bibliographic and physical attributes. They serve as the touchstones for upcoming and experienced performers, musicologists (regardless of area of expertise), and the commercial and entertainment industries. Composer, composition, performer, and manifestation are the most common attributes provided in a surrogate describing the "contents" of music, while melody, harmony, and rhythm are the most common elements found in actual musical content. Despite the frequency with which these elements are used, there is little consistency in how various members of the music community, much less the general public, name these attributes and relate them within a given composition or among groups of compositions.[4] Examples of such inconsistencies were documented in an article in the *New York Times* about Apple's new music service, iTunes.[5] The author states that iTunes has "10 different listings for Tchaikovsky, from Piotr Ilytch to just plain Peter"; the title for Saint-Saen's First Cello Concerto is listed as "Violincello [sic] in A major, Op. 33, No. 1"; and the only "artist" (i.e., performer) cited for this selection is the cellist, Mstislav Rostropovich (totally disregarding the participation of the symphony orchestra and its conductor). Disparities in naming conventions and incomplete or inadequate identification of roles and relationships among the composer, work, and performers continue to be major barriers to successful music information retrieval (MIR).

Works about Music

In addition to establishing improved access to works, performances, and manifestations *of* music, there are also community concerns about improving access to text-based and multimedia works *about* music. While writings about music may concentrate heavily on musical elements and ideas, these texts are likely to include musical examples (e.g., score, sound, video), and they are often highly interdisciplinary in nature. The literature of Western historical musicology, theory and analysis, performance practice, ethnomusicology, etc., addresses not only purely musical ideas but also the rich cultural, social, and political environment from which music evolved and in which it existed and influenced its surroundings. Likewise, writings and multimedia works emanating from other disciplines often allude to and at times focus on musical matters. These multimedia, multicultural, and multidisciplinary works about music present complex representational and retrieval problems for music information retrieval, for bibliographic description, and for the general searcher. For effective retrieval in the web environment, works about music also need an explicit set of rules, logic, and labels.

COMMUNITY EFFORTS TOWARD CONTENT CONTROL

Music information retrieval is a growing research community involving audio engineers, musicologists, music theorists, computer scientists, lawyers, librarians, and others who are concerned with content identification and control.[6] Music representation languages are in the early stages of facilitating the isolation and tracking of both individual and combined physical elements of a musical work, such as melody, harmony, rhythm, instrumentation, and text (when present), and addressing the rules, logic, and labels that apply to these elements. While much progress has been made, an enormous amount of work clearly remains to be done in developing effective MIR systems.[7]

Stephen Downie, professor in the Graduate School of Library and Information Science at the University of Illinois at Urbana-Champaign and a leader in music information retrieval, highlights two major concerns in MIR research: system evaluation and user studies. According to Downie in his 2003 overview of music information retrieval, "Each contributing discipline brings to the MIR community its own set of goals, accepted practices, valid research questions, and generalizable evaluation paradigms."[8] Communicating across disciplines can be problematic, and Downie believes that a lack of standardized evaluations is one of the biggest obstacles. He and others have called for the creation of standardized test collections, queries, and relevance judgments to help stabilize the evaluation process and advance MIR research.

Closely related to system evaluation is the concern for usability studies, or community analysis, both online and offline. Among the ten central questions for MIR research, Downie cites eight in his overview that deal with system capability and two that represent fundamental questions about usability: (1) what do "real" users of MIR systems actually want the systems to do, and (2) how will "real" users actually interact with MIR systems?

The continuing need to answer these rudimentary questions about what users want demonstrates the lack of explicit rules and logic about how the music community conceives of and connects musical elements, whether bibliographic or physical. It is not uncommon for researchers and practitioners to launch system development before gaining a clear understanding of what users want. Additionally, researchers and practitioners may prematurely establish what they believe to be a satisfactory manner of anticipating users' searching behavior. This approach is typical of many research projects and creates a major stumbling block to the successful communication and retrieval of information. The music community has the opportunity and the responsibility to lay a solid foundation in user studies that will enable future sharing and reuse of information about music. To construct this framework, the community must analyze not only this information's content and context but also its constituents.

A major MIR research project is Variations2, the Indiana University Digital Music Library project funded by the National Science Foundation and the National Endowment for the Humanities through the Digital Libraries Phase 2 program.[9] This project is comprised of an interdisciplinary research team working together to coordinate innovations in system design, usability, metadata, intellectual property, music instruction, and networking. The team has made advances in establishing a digital music library test-bed system supporting multiple formats: audio, video, score images, and score notation. During each phase of the project's development, special care has been taken to gather and respond to users' reactions. Based on user feedback, the Variations2 team has established explicit relationships among composer, work, performer, and manifestation in its data model, similar to the Functional Requirements for Bibliographic Records.[10]

The Variations2 data model is work-centered (a change from the container-centered, static object representation of traditional library cataloging records), strengthening the links between individual works and their associated properties. The data model clearly links and identifies the role of each contributor (composer, performer, editor, etc.) to each work and facilitates both the collocation of and distinction among the many manifestations or versions of individual works within the database.[11] The data model is comprised of a set of music-specific metadata encoded in XML (Extensible Markup Language) format for scores and sound recordings and is supported by a robust search and retrieval system developed for digitized works of music, with the capability of synchronized playback and display of sound and scores files. Efforts are also under way to establish a representative music vocabulary, particularly for form or genre and musical instruments, based in part on terminology found in the Library of Congress Subject Headings (LCSH).[12] The long-term value of Variations2 will be measured by user response and by the extensibility of the project beyond its current use at Indiana University and the handful of satellite sites.

A COMMUNITY FACING CHANGES

The music community, like other specialized communities, has an uneven understanding and acceptance of emerging technologies and the enormous impact these technologies have on music resources as well as search and retrieval processes. Some community members continue to cling to outgrown but long-standing traditions. Many of these traditions are still at least partially functional, and some are deeply embedded in and prized by both the community and society at large. Among such traditions are widespread inconsistencies in naming conventions that would be difficult, if not impossible, to codify (e.g., multiple spellings of "Tchaikovsky"); and the use of stale, imprecise, and incomplete "controlled" vocabulary and classification schemes such as those contained in the LCSH, the Library of Congress Classification, and the Dewey Decimal Classification (e.g., limited representation of many styles of music, particularly in the areas of popular and ethnic music). Also problematic is the already-mentioned lack of explicit relationships between composer, composition, performer, and manifestation, as propagated by the Anglo-American Cataloguing Rules (AACR2), the MARC record, online public access catalogs, commercial databases, and the World Wide Web.[13] The acceptance, and possibly even the advancement of technology is impeded by the continuing use of print publications—such as thematic indexes—for processes that could be accomplished much more efficiently via a search engine. By contrast, over-reliance on what is available on the Web, a trusting acceptance of the Web's limited search strategies, and the assumption that going to Google is an adequate replacement for going to the library also represent barriers to sophisticated music information retrieval. As in other disciplines, there is a sense of community pride in and protection of the expertise held by certain individuals or groups within the music community (e.g., "only the finest Beethoven scholar can answer your question," or "only expert catalogers are able to establish the correct form of a name") that can inhibit the willingness to entrust an equivalent level of knowledge or skill to computer programs. In addition, the academic music community strongly supports individualism: finding one's own answers the best way possible, even if it is the hardest way; and pursuing one's own research project without sufficient regard to how the project might meet broader needs or fit into the community's more comprehensive research agenda.

Even when the need for change is clear, such as the need for metadata beyond the traditional bibliographic descriptions of scores and sound recordings supported by AACR2 description and MARC encoding, reaching consensus and obtaining community endorsement is a tedious and time-consuming process. The Music Library Association, for instance, has only tentatively begun to examine the possibility of expanding metadata for digitized musical scores and sound recordings beyond the confines of the MARC bibliographic record.[14] Yet it is precisely this group, with its extensive experience and knowledge of describing and accessing works of and about music, which should be among the leaders of music metadata reform. Instead, individual research projects, commercial companies, and web search engine designers are setting the agenda for the next generation of music metadata and music retrieval.

For many years the music community has clearly expressed the need for improved subject access to works of and about music.[15] Several attempts, both within the United States and internationally, to create a music thesaurus have fallen by the wayside due to lack of community coordination and adequate funding.[16] Gathering, documenting, organizing, and sharing domain-specific terminology (descriptors, names, and works) would be an enormous contribution to the music community, as well as to other communities. No less significant than the development of the Art and Architecture Thesaurus which flourished under the J. Paul Getty Trust sponsorship, identifying and arranging the vast array of scholarly and popular musical terms, both foreign and English, would be invaluable.[17] The potential impact of providing and maintaining a standardized searching and indexing vocabulary that could be applied across academia, the Web, and the commercial and entertainment sectors argues for a more concerted community effort and more serious consideration by potential funding agencies.

CROSS-COMMUNITY COMMITMENT

In order to facilitate large-scale knowledge integration, ontologies need to be viewed from a highly interdisciplinary perspective. The ability to share and reuse parts of formalized bodies of knowledge is vital to the management and preservation of knowledge. While the ability to transparently handle variations in content and the meanings of content is needed, it is neither realistic nor practical to seek interoperability through the adoption of a single standard or a single vocabulary. Instead, developing domain-specific schemas and vocabularies are essential first steps toward improving cross-community knowledge sharing. Harmonization of metadata vocabularies through the use of schemas that consist of data elements drawn from one or more namespaces seems to offer an optimal approach.[18] The cost of building and maintaining such systems must be weighed against the value of the content. It is the quality of content *and* control that must guide community efforts and that will bind our commitment to the future.

CONCLUSION

Music, like other specialized communities, has a well-developed but largely undocumented knowledge base. Even though the basic physical and bibliographic attributes of music are seemingly apparent and may be considered to be widely known and recognizable, they lack the necessary formalization of explicit rules, logic, and labels. Reliance on informal rules, implicit logic, and variant name forms for the same concept, object, work, or person results in insurmountable gaps in communication and accessibility, particularly as the amount of information and breadth of distribution increase. The many variations and intricate interweaving of musical elements generate a set of complexities that require an expanded view of content in order to improve information retrieval both within the music community and beyond. For successful music information retrieval, the texts and artifacts (data) must be wrapped in community-developed metadata, a community-endorsed metadata schema, and a community-specific ontology. This total framework for content will ensure that it is communicable across people and computers.

The MIR research community is making strides in isolating, identifying, and presenting basic elements of musical content for search and retrieval. Meanwhile, there are still fundamental questions about what users want and need from a music information retrieval system. The music community has yet to do a thorough self-analysis, to lay a solid foundation in user studies. While the outcome of such studies is unlikely to be one of consensus, user input, however varied, is critical to system development and to documenting the community's rules, logic, and labels.

Even as segments of the music community are eager to make advances in information retrieval, there remain pockets within the community who are either satisfied or willing to live with the current state of affairs, no matter how inadequate. Widespread and persistent education about the need for change and the advantages of collaboration and cooperation in forming a common set of rules, logic, and labels cannot be overestimated. Building a common understanding of the goals and projecting the potential results of achieving these goals are important steps toward involvement, endorsement, and ultimate success.

NOTES

1. Natalya F. Noy and Deborah L. McGuinness, "Ontology Development 101: A Guide to Creating Your First Ontology," http://protege.stanford.edu/publications/ontology_development/ontology101-noy-mcguinness.html (accessed 21 September 2003).
2. Marshall McLuhan, *The Gutenberg Galaxy: The Making of Typographic Man* (Toronto: University of Toronto Press, 1962).
3. Carl Lagoze, "From Static to Dynamic Surrogates: Resource Discovery in the Digital Age," *D-Lib Magazine*, June 1997, http://www.dlib.org/dlib/june97/06lagoze.html (accessed 21 September 2003).
4. R. Smiraglia, "Musical Works as Information Retrieval Entities: Epistemological Perspectives," in *Proceedings of the 2nd Annual International Symposium on Music Information Retrieval: ISMIR 2001* (Bloomington: Indiana University Press, 2001), 85–92, available at http://ismir2001.indiana.edu/pdf/smiraglia.pdf (accessed 21 September 2003).
5. "Adventures in Downloading Haydn," *New York Times*, June 15, 2003, Arts section.
6. Music Information Retrieval (home page), http://music-ir.org (accessed 21 September 2003).
7. J. Stephen Downie, "Music Information Retrieval," chapter 7 of *Annual Review of Information Science and Technology 37*, ed. Blaise Cronin (Medford, N.J.: Information Today, 2003), 295–340, also available at http://music-ir.org/downie_mir_arist37.pdf (accessed 21 September 2003).
8. Downie, "Music Information Retrieval."
9. Variations2: Indiana University Digital Music Library (home page), http://www.dml.indiana.edu/index.html (accessed 21 September 2003).
10. IFLA Study Group on the Functional Requirements for Bibliographic Records, "Functional Requirements for Bibliographic Records," http://www.ifla.org/VII/s13/frbr/frbr.pdf (accessed 21 September 2003).
11. Harriette Hemmasi, "Why Not MARC?" in *Proceedings of the 3rd Annual International Conference on Music Information Retrieval: ISMIR 2002* (Paris: Pompidou Centre, 2002), 242–48, also available at http://ismir2002.ismir.net/Proceedings/02-FP08-3.pdf (accessed 21 September 2003).
12. Library of Congress Program for Cooperative Cataloging, "Library of Congress Subject Headings," http://www.loc.gov/catdir/pcc/ (accessed 21 September 2003).
13. Library of Congress Classification, http://lcweb.loc.gov/catdir/cpso/lcco/lcco.html (accessed 21 September 2003); Dewey Decimal Classification, http://www.oclc.org/dewey/ (accessed 21 September 2003); American Library Association, *Anglo-American Cataloguing Rules*, 2d ed., 1998 revision (Chicago: American Library Association, 1998); Library of Congress, Network Development and MARC Standards Office, "MARC Standards," http://www.loc.gov/marc/ (accessed 21 September 2003).

14. The Music Library Association Metadata Standards Working Group was charged and appointed in September 2003. (The author is a member of this group.)
15. Mark McKnight et al., "Improving Access to Music: A Report of the Music Thesaurus Project Working Group," *NOTES* 45 (1989): 714.
16. Harriette Hemmasi, "The Music Thesaurus: Function and Foundations," *NOTES* 50, no. 3 (1994): 875–82.
17. Getty Research Institute, "Art and Architecture Thesaurus Online," http://www.getty.edu/research/tools/vocabulary/aat/ (accessed 21 September 2003).
18. Carl Lagoze and Jane Hunter, "The ABC Ontology and Model," *Journal of Digital Information* 2, no. 2 (2001), http://jodi.ecs.soton.ac.uk/Articles/v02/i02/Lagoze/lagoze-final.pdf (accessed 21 September 2003).

13
Building an Open Language Archives Community on the DC Foundation

Steven Bird and Gary Simons

THE RAPID GROWTH of ubiquitous computing as well as the multilingual and multimedia Internet is stimulating the development of a new generation of language technologies. Speech processing, translation, information extraction, and document summarization, among others, unlock the information content of large unstructured collections of text and speech, opening the door to more natural human-computer interfaces. At the same time, inexpensive hardware for digital capture and mass storage is stimulating widespread efforts to digitize and preserve the world's endangered linguistic heritage. All of these efforts depend on language technologies and language data. Yet as these language resources proliferate, it is becoming increasingly difficult to locate and reuse them.

In December 2000, a new initiative based on Dublin Core (DC) and the Open Archives Initiative (OAI) was founded, with the following statement of purpose:[1]

> The Open Language Archives Community is an international partnership of institutions and individuals who are creating a worldwide virtual library of language resources by: (i) developing consensus on best current practice for the digital archiving of language resources, and (ii) developing a network of interoperating repositories and services for housing and accessing such resources.

At the time of writing there are twenty-five participating repositories and several proposed standards and recommendations under review by the Open Language Archives Community (OLAC; http://www.language-archives.org). The framework for OLAC's operation is provided by three standards: OLAC Metadata, OLAC Repositories, and OLAC Process.[2] This chapter charts the community-based development of these standards and shows how, in each case, initial models that proved too cumbersome to implement were simplified over time through the adoption of ideas and practices originating in the Dublin Core community.[3]

LAUNCHING A METADATA COMMUNITY

The Open Language Archives Community grew out of a collaboration between three international linguistic service organizations: the Linguistic Data Consortium (LDC), SIL International, and LINGUIST List. The LDC supports language-related education, research, and technology development by creating and sharing linguistic resources. To date it has published over 200 linguistic databases and distributed more than 15,000 copies to research institutions worldwide.[4] SIL International serves the peoples of the world through research, translation, and literacy; at present it is facilitating language-based development in over 1,000 languages worldwide.[5] LINGUIST List is the home of linguistics on the Web, currently hosting 2,000 pages of content, 100 mailing lists, and serving 20,000 subscribers worldwide.[6]

These three organizations could hardly be more different in their goals and constituencies, yet all three found themselves managing digital language documentation and developing software infrastructure and educational materials. Moreover, all three organizations were independently developing systematic methods to archive, catalog, and disseminate these resources, while helping their associated communities to do likewise. Joining forces, the trio of organizations became a microcosm of the language resources community. With timely sponsorship from the National Science Foundation, the group explored an OAI- and DC-based solution to the needs of the community, making rapid progress on implementation owing to the simplicity and generality of these standards. This exploration quickly matured into a high-level vision and detailed low-level requirements.[7] The high-level vision described "seven pillars of open language archiving" and presented the simple model of resource discovery shown in figure 13-1.

As shown in the figure, individual users would be able to access the data, tools, and advice they need by visiting a single gateway to access aggregated metadata. The operation of the system would be governed by a small set of standards, and the provision of high-quality content would be encouraged by peer review within the community.

Corresponding to this high-level vision were thirty-six low-level requirements covering the needs of five special interest groups:

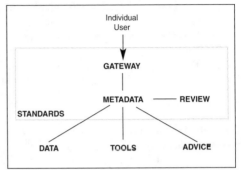

FIGURE 13-1 Vision of community infrastructure

1. *Users,* the people who want to access language materials which have been stored away in archives
2. *Creators,* the people who create the language materials that get archived
3. *Archivists,* the people who manage the process of acquiring, maintaining, and accessing the information resources stored in archives
4. *Developers,* the people who create data models, tools, and formats for storing and manipulating digital language documentation
5. *Sponsors,* the organizations that fund the creation of information resources and their maintenance in archives

Each requirement consisted of three statements: the desired state, the situation we wanted to avoid, and how OLAC would meet the requirement once it was functioning. The first two user requirements are shown in figure 13-2.

These two documents—the high-level vision and the low-level requirements—were augmented with a survey of language archives, a white paper showing how OLAC could be built on DC metadata and the OAI Protocol for Metadata Harvesting, and a mock-up demonstration of an OLAC service provider.[8] All of these components were presented at the Workshop on Web-Based Language Documentation and Description, held

What users want	What users don't want	How OLAC meets the requirement
There is a single site on the Web where any user can go to discover what language information resources are available, regardless of where they may be archived.	The only way to discover language resources on the Web is to visit all the individual archives or to hope that the resources one is interested in have been indexed in an intuitive way by one's favorite general purpose search engine.	Linguist List (www .linguistlist.org) will host a combined catalog of all participating archives.
All language resources (regardless of where they may be archived) are catalogued with a consistent set of metadata descriptions, so that the user can ascertain all the basic facts about a resource without having to download it.	The only way to get a good idea about a resource contains, who is responsible for it, or what are its terms of availability is to retrieve it.	Every holding in the combined catalog is described using the OLAC metadata set. Since that metadata set includes all the elements of the Dublin Core, it offers enough breadth to handle all the basic facts about a resource.

FIGURE 13-2   Examples of user requirements

in Philadelphia in December 2000. Present at this meeting was a very broad cross-section of the language resources community representing work in Africa, Asia, Europe, Australia, and North and South America. Over the course of the three-day workshop, which included working group sessions and consultations with geographical and domain representatives, a strong consensus was built. In the closing session of the workshop, the Open Language Archives Community was formally established. In the following weeks, those with archived resources set about mapping their catalogs to DC and developing OAI-compliant metadata repositories.[9]

The first twelve months were a period of active development of the repositories and supporting infrastructure. The metadata format alone went through a succession of four versions during this time. In the second year, 2002, we froze the format and recruited new archives to join, more than doubling the level of participation. In December 2002, on the second anniversary of OLAC's formation, we revised the format and infrastructure based on the previous year's experience, and in 2003 we are now in a period of refinement and adoption of the core standards upon which OLAC is built.

Taking OAI and DC "off-the-shelf" as proven standards having widespread acceptance in the digital libraries community was decisive, permitting OLAC to unite disparate subcommunities and reach consensus. In particular, DC was simple, applicable to all kinds of resources, and widely used outside our community. Significantly, DC represented neutral territory, since it was not developed by any special interest within the language resources community. Had we come to our first workshop with the proposal that the community needed to invent a metadata standard, all our resolve would have dissipated in factionalism. Thus, not only was DC both simple and mature, it was also a political expedient.

During this period, three standards were developed and adopted: OLAC Metadata, for the metadata format which extended DC; OLAC Repositories, for the functioning of the repositories which extended the OAI-PMH; and OLAC Process, for governing the organization and operation of the OLAC community. The sections that follow will treat each of these standards in detail.

OLAC METADATA: A STANDARD FOR RESOURCE DESCRIPTION

As seen in figure 13-1, language resources can be divided into three broad categories: data, tools, and advice. By "data" we mean any information that documents or describes a language, such as a published monograph, a computer data file, or even a shoebox full of handwritten index cards. The information can range in content from unanalyzed sound recordings to fully transcribed and annotated texts to a complete descriptive grammar. By "tools" we mean computational resources that facilitate creating, viewing, querying, or otherwise using language data. Tools include not only software programs but also the digital resources that the programs depend on, such as fonts, stylesheets, and document type definitions. By "advice" we mean any information about what data sources are reliable, what tools are appropriate in a given situation, what practices to follow when creating new data, and so on.[10] In the context of OLAC, the term "language resource" is broadly construed to include all three of these resource types: data, tools, and advice. The purpose of OLAC metadata is to facilitate the discovery of language resources.

Over the past three years, work on OLAC metadata has centered on two key issues: extensions to the Dublin Core Metadata Element Set to support the description of language resources, and a suitable XML (Extensible Markup Language) representation of this metadata.[11] In the following subsections we will summarize the requirements on OLAC metadata, review our first solution and its problems, and then present our OLAC application profile based on the recent DC XML Schemas.

Principal Requirements for OLAC Metadata

While the OLAC community has complex resource discovery needs, we adopted DC's minimalist philosophy and identified a small set of widely used categories and descriptors that could be used to extend DC for application to language resources. The most important of these are subject language, language codes, and linguistic types, discussed below.

Subject language. This is a language that the content of the resource describes or discusses, as distinct from the language the resource is in. For example, a grammatical description of French written in English would have English as its language and French as its subject language. The same description would apply to a French text with English annotations. The OLAC metadata set needs to distinguish language from subject language.

Language codes. These are a standard set of codes for language identification. The existing ISO 639 vocabulary covers less than 10 percent of the world's languages, however, and does not adequately document what languages the codes refer to.[12] The use of conventional language names in resource description is fraught with problems, leading to low precision and recall.[13] However, SIL's Ethnologue provides identifiers for some 7,000 living and recently extinct languages, while LINGUIST List provides identifiers for some 400 ancient and constructed languages.[14] In order to meet the need for precise identification of the language or subject language in any language resource, OLAC employs the unambiguous International Organization for Standardization codes, augmented with Ethnologue and LINGUIST codes.

Linguistic types. These are a standard set of codes for classifying the content of a language resource according to recognized structural types of linguistic information (e.g., dictionary, grammar, text). This permits members of the community to identify resource types according to the most fundamental linguistic categories.

In addition to these requirements on OLAC metadata, there are three basic requirements on OLAC metadata management: migration, evolution, and extensibility.

Migration. OLAC metadata originates in existing institutional and individual repositories, and there are extant guidelines and examples for exporting this metadata to DC. To facilitate migration to OLAC metadata, we must specify all OLAC refinements and encoding schemes as optional. Thus, a DC record is a valid OLAC record and a repository can enrich its exported records by progressively replacing free text with coded values (e.g., Spanish → es) and selecting suitable refinements (e.g., Subject → Subject.language). A related requirement concerns the ability to "dumb down" to DC for interoperability with the wider digital library community.

Evolution. Once an encoding scheme has been adopted, subsequent changes must be carefully controlled. Redefining a coded value to mean something different would cause problems for users and repositories that employ the existing coded value. In particular, when the interpretation of a coded value is narrowed in scope, the existing code must be expired and a new code adopted.

Extensibility. Subcommunities with specialized resource discovery needs should be able to extend OLAC metadata with their own refinements and encoding schemes and build services based on the enriched metadata.

OLAC 0.4 Metadata: Proliferating Vocabularies

In its first six months of development, OLAC metadata went through versions 0.1–0.4, the last of which was in active use for about eighteen months. Version 0.4 consisted of the fifteen DC elements plus eight community-specific element refinements.[15] Each of the latter was a refinement to an existing DC element and supplied a vocabulary for encoding its values. Two additional community-specific vocabularies were defined, one for specifying role as a refinement of Creator and Contributor, and one for encoding values of Rights. The ten community-specific vocabularies (many of which were never developed) are listed in table 13-1.

The draft OLAC metadata standard provided additional comments on these elements to describe usage, e.g., for Format.markup:[16]

For a resource that is a text file including markup, Format.markup identifies the markup system it uses, such as the SGML DTD, the XML

TABLE 13-1   OLAC qualifiers (version 0.4)

Element	Qualifier	Definition
Creator/Contributor	Role	The role played by the creator or contributor in the creation of the resource (author, editor, translator, . . .)
Format.cpu	CPU Requirement	The CPU required to use a software resource (x86, mips, alpha, ppc, sparc, 680x0)
Format.encoding	Character Encoding	An encoded character set used by a digital resource (vocabulary never defined)
Format.markup	Markup Scheme	A markup scheme used by a digital resource (vocabulary never defined)
Format.os	OS Requirement	An operating system required to use a software resource (Unix/Linux, Unix/Solaris, OS2, MacOS/OSX, MSWindows/win95 . . .)
Format.sourcecode	Source Code Language	A programming language of software distributed in source form (C, Java, Python, Tcl, . . .)
Rights	Rights Management	Information about rights held in and over the resource (vocabulary never defined)
Subject.language	Subject language	A language which the content of the resource describes or discusses (aa, ab, ae, af, am, ar, . . . , x-sil-AAA, x-sil-AAB, . . .)
Type.functionality	Software Functionality	The functionality of a software resource (vocabulary never defined)
Type.linguistic	Linguistic Data Type	The nature or genre of the content of the resource from a linguistic standpoint (transcriptions/phonetic, lexicon/thesaurus, text/dialogue, . . .)

Schema, the set of Standard Format markers, and the like. For a resource that is a stylesheet or a software application, Format.markup names a markup scheme that it can read as input or write as output. Service providers will use this information to match data files with the software tools that can be applied to them. Recommended best practice is to identify the markup scheme by a URI giving an OAI identifier for the markup scheme as a resource in an OLAC archive. Thus, if the DTD, Schema, or markup documentation is not already archived in an OLAC repository, the depositor of a marked-up resource should also deposit the documentation for the markup scheme. A resource identified in Format.markup should not also be listed with the "requires" refinement of Relation.

Several refinements and encoding schemes (cpu, os, sourcecode) were primarily for describing linguistic software. Some were easy to define but none were heavily used, there being only two small software repositories holding less than one percent of the total number of harvested OLAC records. Other vocabularies (for encoding, markup, functionality, rights) were never employed, or else were used in a completely unconstrained manner, providing inadequate data on which to base an encoding scheme. Once a good extension mechanism had been found (in version 1.0) these were all dropped, leaving only the basic refinement (subject language) and encoding schemes (subject language and linguistic type) and a small number of additional encoding schemes and refinements (discourse type, linguistic field, participant role, subject language, language codes, and linguistic type).

Language codes were derived from external authorities and required no particular attention in the context of OLAC. Linguistic type, on the other hand, proved extremely difficult to manage. It mushroomed to a seventy-item vocabulary with two levels of detail separated by a slash (e.g., transcription/phonetic). However, the two-level organization was unstable, and there were three problems: terms that were introduced to improve coverage led to subtle problems of demarcation; the details of the two-level structure could not be finalized; and the terms were found to be of two cross-cutting domains where some describe structure and others describe content. The final resolution, reached in version 1.0, consisted of just three terms.[17]

The OLAC 0.4 metadata set was formalized both as a proposed standard (the human readable document) and as an XML Schema (the machine-readable document).[18] The XML representation expressed refinements using dotted element names (e.g., subject.language), and expressed coded values using a "code" attribute. An XML Schema was used to validate the content of the "code" attribute, according to the name of the host element. Element content was left unconstrained, either for holding free-text descriptions in the case when no coded value was provided, or for holding free-text elaborations in the case when the coded value was insufficient on its own. For example, <subject.language> Spanish</subject.language> expresses a refinement without an encoding scheme and is an intermediate step on the way to an encoded value: <subject.language code="es"/>. A language code is inadequate for identifying dialects, so free-text content can be used to provide the necessary elaboration, e.g.: <subject.language code="es"> Andalusian </subject.language>. A second attribute permitted third parties to represent encoding schemes involving element content: the "scheme" attribute held the name of the scheme, and the content was assumed to be constrained accordingly. A third attribute, "refine," was used for elements having vocabulary of refinements (Contributor, Creator, Date, Relation).

The OLAC 0.4 metadata set satisfied the requirements listed in the preceding section for representing the subject language refinement, language codes, and linguistic types (and a selection of other qualifiers), and it satisfied the migration requirement. However, the evolution and extensibility requirements were not well supported. Vocabulary evolution had unacceptable bureaucratic overheads, as each vocabulary revision entailed a new release of the XML Schema and the metadata standard. Extensibility was not well supported, since the XML Schema language is unable to constrain element content based on the value of the scheme attribute. In sum, the OLAC 0.4 metadata proved too difficult to manage over the long term. Administratively, it encouraged us to seek premature closure on issues of content description that can never be closed. Technically, OLAC 0.4 metadata forced us to do two things: release new versions of the metadata format with each vocabulary revision, and create software infrastructure to support an unwieldy conglomeration of four syntactic extensions of simple DC:

```
<element.EXT1 refine="EXT2" code="EXT3" scheme="EXT4">
```

After a year of using this model, we realized it was untenable and discovered new Dublin Core Metadata Initiative (DCMI) work on the XML representation of DC and DC qualifiers.[19] This provided the missing support for vocabulary evolution and extensibility that OLAC 0.4 was lacking. At this point OLAC metadata was a *semantic* extension of DC metadata, but was syntactically unrelated to DC. With the arrival of a standard XML representation for DC, it was now possible to reconceive OLAC metadata as also being a *syntactic* extension of DC.

OLAC 1.0 Metadata: An Application Profile
for Language Resource Description

An application profile is a type of metadata schema that combines elements and attributes from multiple authorities.[20] We can view OLAC metadata as an application profile for the language resources community, combining DC elements with a small selection of community-specific extensions. With the new XML representation of Dublin Core, it is straightforward to implement this model in XML Schema.[21]

Consider the XML representation for the following DC subject element: <subject>Spanish</subject>. We can specify the language refinement and encoding scheme using the special "xsi:type" attribute, thus: <subject xsi:type="olac:language" code="es"/>. The xsi:type attribute is defined in the XML Schema standard; it directs the schema validator to override the definition of the XML element using the specified type (here, olac:language). The OLAC-defined types add an optional "code" attribute and restrict its range of values. Element content is reserved for unrestricted commentary. Thus, the following are all acceptable OLAC 1.0 elements:

<subject>Spanish</subject>

<subject xsi:type="olac:language">Spanish</subject>

<subject xsi:type="olac:language" code="es"/>

<subject xsi:type="olac:language" code="es">Andalusian</subject>

The preceding example also illustrates the migration path from simple DC to OLAC metadata. Dumbing down to DC is straightforward (though OLAC provides this service centrally to ensure that best practices are followed; see the following section, "OLAC Repositories: A Framework for Interoperation").

In addition to language identification and linguistic type, OLAC 1.0 metadata currently provides two other vocabulary encoding schemes: discourse type and linguistic field; and a refinement, participant role. Each encoding scheme and refinement is accompanied with human-readable documentation that provides the semantics for the vocabulary.[22] Additionally, extensions provide summary documentation using the OLAC Extension schema.[23] This summary documentation provides six pieces of information:

1. The short name by which the extension is accessed (i.e., the name of the complexType that defines the extension)

2. The full name of the extension for use as a title in documentation
3. The date of the latest version of the extension
4. A summary description of what the extension is used for
5. The Dublin Core elements with which the extension may be used
6. The URI for a complete document that defines and exemplifies the extension

This information is extracted and displayed in human-readable form on the OLAC website.[24] A complete OLAC record is shown in figure 13-3. It conforms to the OLAC schema olac.xsd, which imports DCMI schemas.

Evolution. In OLAC 1.0 metadata, the format of the metadata container is identified as a standard, while the metadata extensions have the status of recommendations.[25] The evolution of the metadata format, and the refinements and encoding schemes, are now decoupled. This was an important step in enabling OLAC metadata to reach version 1.0. It liberated vocabulary editors to continue developing the vocabularies that define OLAC as a community, without forcing a premature closure timed with the 1.0 release of the new container format.

```
<olac:olac xmlns:olac="http://www.language-archives.org/OLAC/1.0/"
        xmlns="http://purl.org/dc/elements/1.1/"
        xmlns:dcterms="http://purl.org/dc/terms/"
        xmlns:xsi="http://www.w3.org/2001/XMLSchema-instance"
        xsi:schemaLocation="http://www.language-archives.org/OLAC/1.0/
        http://www.language-archives.org/OLAC/1.0/olac.xsd">

    <title xml:lang="fr">Petit Dictionnaire Yémba-Français</title>
    <dcterms:alternative>Yemba-French Dictionary</dcterms:alternative>
    <date xsi:type="dcterms:W3CDTF">1997</date>
    <identifier
xsi:type="dcterms:URI">http://www.ldc.upenn.edu/sb/home/publications.html#dictionar
y</identifier>

    <!-- Elements with OLAC extensions -->

    <subject xsi:type="olac:linguistic-field" olac:code="morphology"/>
    <creator xsi:type="olac:role" olac:code="editor">Bird, Steven</creator>
    <creator xsi:type="olac:role" olac:code="editor">Tadadjeu, Maurice</creator>
    <language xsi:type="olac:language" olac:code="x-sil-BAN">Dschang</language>
    <type xsi:type="olac:linguistic-type" olac:code="lexicon"/>
    <type xsi:type="olac:linguistic-type" olac:code="language_description"/>
</olac:olac>
```

FIGURE 13-3   Example of an OLAC 1.0 metadata record

Extensibility. An OLAC metadata record may use extensions from other namespaces. This makes it possible for subcommunities within OLAC to develop and share metadata extensions that are specific to a common special interest. By using xsi:type, it is possible to extend the OLAC application profile without modifying the OLAC schema. For instance, suppose that a given domain required greater precision in identifying the roles of contributors than is possible with the OLAC Role vocabulary, and defined additional "role" terms, including "commentator."[26] If the extension were named "example:role," this new term would be used as follows:

<contributor xsi:type="example: role" code="commentator">Sampson, Geoffrey</contributor>

In order to do this, an organization representing that domain (say, example.org) could define a new XML Schema providing the complexType declaration shown in figure 13-4.

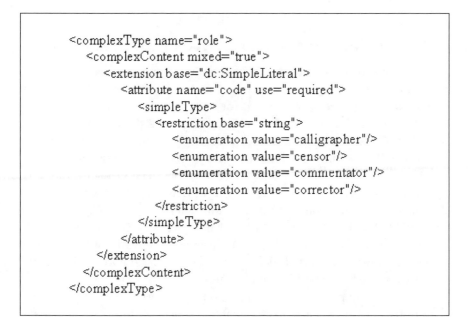

```
<complexType name="role">
    <complexContent mixed="true">
        <extension base="dc:SimpleLiteral">
            <attribute name="code" use="required">
                <simpleType>
                    <restriction base="string">
                        <enumeration value="calligrapher"/>
                        <enumeration value="censor"/>
                        <enumeration value="commentator"/>
                        <enumeration value="corrector"/>
                    </restriction>
                </simpleType>
            </attribute>
        </extension>
    </complexContent>
</complexType>
```

FIGURE 13-4   A complexType declaration for a third-party extension

The extension schema is associated with a target namespace (e.g., http://www.example.org/role/) and stored on the organization's website.[27]
   Remaining shortcomings of this approach. OLAC 1.0 metadata is implemented in XML Schema following DCMI guidelines.[28] This has two unfortunate consequences. First, thanks to the use of the xsi:type attribute, the XML representation of OLAC metadata is now tied to XML Schema, which is just one of many available methods for validating XML. Given the volatility of XML technologies, it seems undesirable to complicate the metadata representation by embedding special directives to be interpreted by the validation technology. At such time as the validation technology is changed, every repository that uses the format will have to modify its XML representation of the metadata. The second shortcoming is that the xsi:type declarations are not constrained as to which DC element they modify. For instance, it would not be a validation error for a metadata record to use the "role" extension on the "title" element, even though this violates the intended semantics. Despite these problems, we believe that the significant benefits of conforming to DCMI guidelines outweigh the disadvantages.

OLAC REPOSITORIES: A FRAMEWORK FOR INTEROPERATION

OLAC Repositories is the second of the three standards that govern the operation of OLAC.[29] In order to put metadata into practice, it is not enough to simply define a standard for expressing metadata descriptions. There must also be an infrastructure that supports the interoperation of metadata across the community in order to meet its resource discovery needs. OLAC has built that infrastructure on the Open Archives Initiative Protocol for Metadata Harvesting (OAI-PMH).[30] The OAI-PMH and its application are well documented on the OAI website. The authors have described its application to OLAC in an issue of *Library Hi-Tech* dedicated to OAI and elsewhere.[31] Rather than repeat a description of the harvesting protocol here, we will focus on practical steps that were taken in developing the OLAC infrastructure to make it easier for would-be participants to interoperate within the community.
   In the OAI approach to interoperation, institutions that want to make their resources known participate as data providers by publishing metadata about their holdings. Other institutions that want to provide value-added

services for the community participate as service providers by harvesting the metadata and incorporating it in the information pool that their service is based on.

The OLAC Repositories standard specifies how a would-be data provider must construct a repository of metadata descriptions so as to make it harvestable by service providers. Two approaches are described: a data provider may construct either a dynamic repository or a static repository. With a dynamic repository, the data provider implements a Common Gateway Interface (CGI) that dynamically queries a database. This is the standard OAI approach and was the only method available when OLAC was launched in December 2000. This is a straightforward task for a programmer who knows how to build dynamic websites; thus there were several repositories interoperating within a matter of weeks. However, the number of participants did not continue to grow, and we soon concluded that programming a dynamic repository went beyond the technical capacity of most potential providers of language resources.

In response we developed Vida, the Virtual Data Provider.[32] This is a service hosted by OLAC that allows would-be data providers to submit the metadata description of their archive and its resources as a static XML document. Vida then provides the CGI interface that allows service providers to harvest the metadata from these XML documents. When this service became available, we experienced a dramatic increase in the number of data providers within a few months. This is because most potential OLAC data providers found it much easier to map their existing metadata catalogs into a static XML document than to implement a dynamic interface to a database. After seeing the success of Vida for OLAC, the OAI generalized the idea by publishing specifications for a "static repository," and implemented a "static repository gateway" that provides the harvesting interface for a set of static repositories.[33] The OLAC Repositories standard now includes the option of submitting OLAC metadata records as a static repository that is registered with OLAC's static repository gateway.

OLAC has taken one more step to make it even easier for metadata to be put into practice by the language resources community. Learning the XML technologies required to create a static repository still poses an obstacle for many small projects and individuals who would like to publish metadata describing their work. To meet the needs of this portion of the community, the Linguistic Data Consortium developed the OLAC Repository Editor (ORE), and it is now hosted on the LINGUIST List website.[34] This is a forms-based metadata editor that any potential contributor may run from a web browser; it creates and registers a static repository.

It is not enough just to publish metadata. To complete the circle of interoperability, it must also be easy for would-be service providers to harvest the information and offer value-added services. While using the OAI protocol to harvest metadata from all OLAC data providers is straightforward for an experienced programmer, it is beyond the reach of many potential OLAC service providers. Thus, OLAC has implemented two services to make this easier. The first of these is the OLAC Aggregator, a derivative of the OAI Aggregator (OLACA).[35] The OLACA service harvests all the metadata records from all registered data providers and republishes them through the OAI protocol. Thus a would-be service provider can harvest all OLAC metadata records from a single source. Even more significant in simplifying the task of being a service provider is Viser, the Virtual Service Provider.[36] It takes advantage of a query facility that is built into OLACA to make it possible for any website to dynamically display a page showing relevant OLAC metadata records by simply creating a link to the Viser URL that contains the appropriate query within its parameters.

OLAC PROCESS: A METHOD FOR DEVELOPING COMMUNITY CONSENSUS

OLAC Process, the third in the trio of OLAC standards, describes the purpose and vision of OLAC and the four core values that guide OLAC's operation: openness, consensus, empowering the players, and peer review.[37] It is through documents that OLAC defines itself and the practices that it promotes; thus a key aspect of the OLAC process is how documents are developed and promulgated. The OLAC Process document sets out an organizational structure consisting of six categories of participants: the coordinators, an advisory board, the council, archives and services, working groups, and participating individuals. The process document specifies three types of documents (standard, recommendation, and note), along with a detailed document process involving six levels: draft, proposed, candidate, adopted, retired, and withdrawn. The process document also defines a process for the working groups that are responsible for creating documents and taking them through their life cycle. Finally, there is a registration process concerning OLAC archives and services.[38]

Versions of the process document prior to December 2002 incorporated community-wide voting as part of advancing standards and recommendations through the document process. After two years of experimentation with the process, it was clear that this aspect was too cumbersome. At the OLAC workshop in December 2002, Diane Hillmann presented the model of the DCMI Usage Board and described its operation.[39] Workshop participants discussed this new model, and agreed that a new OLAC "Council" would be created to replace the voting process, and that this would streamline the document process. At the time of writing, the initial council members have been nominated by the coordinators and approved by the advisory board, and we are moving forward quickly with the promotion of several OLAC documents from proposed to candidate status and from candidate to adopted status.

CONCLUSION: OLAC METADATA IN PRACTICE

The future of language technology and empirical linguistics depends on the ability to create and reuse a rich array of language resources, including data, tools, and advice. Until recently there has been no systematic way for members of the language resources community to describe the resources they have created or to discover the resources they need. Over the past three years, the Open Language Archives Community has built consensus around a community-specific metadata set. Building on the Dublin Core foundation, OLAC has adopted the elements and qualifiers of DC and identified a small set of language-related extensions, including subject language, language identification, and linguistic type. These apply across the whole field, and have now gained widespread adoption.

Over this period OLAC has learned from its own experience in three significant ways. The difficulty in finalizing vocabularies and in supporting extensions led to the adoption of a more flexible and open-ended model based on the recently established DC XML format. The technical challenges of becoming a data provider or a service provider led to the development of services that have made it significantly easier for potential participants to interoperate within the community. The unworkable community voting process led to the establishment of the OLAC Council, modeled on the DC Usage Board. In each of these three areas, OLAC began with a model that was too cumbersome in practice, then found a new formulation that worked in practice.

The decision to build on the DC foundation was critical to the acceptance of OLAC metadata. Dublin Core was simple, well established, and widely accepted. Different factions of the community were not pitted against one another to argue for their own approach. Instead, we united around the external standard and got the basic infrastructure up and running within a matter of weeks. Moreover, DC demonstrated the value of a minimalist approach. Linguists are known for their preoccupation with faithful data modeling and would never have invented a metadata format with a flat structure in which all elements were optional and repeatable. However, this minimalist approach proved to be a key factor in achieving stability, scalability, and acceptability. We hope that other specialist communities contemplating the development of digital archive infrastructures will benefit from the OLAC experience reported here.

NOTES

1. Carl Lagoze and Herbert Van de Sompel, "The Open Archives Initiative: Building a Low-Barrier Interoperability Framework," in *Proceedings of the First ACM/IEEE-CS Joint Conference on Digital Libraries* (New York: ACM, 2001), 54–62, also available at http://www.cs.cornell.edu/lagoze/papers/oai-jcdl.pdf (accessed 3 December 2003).
2. Gary Simons and Steven Bird, "OLAC Metadata," 2003, http://www.language-archives.org/OLAC/metadata.html (accessed 3 December 2003); Gary Simons and Steven Bird, "OLAC Repositories," 2003, http://www.language-archives .org/OLAC/repositories.html (accessed 3 December 2003); Gary Simons and Steven Bird, "OLAC Process," 2003, http://www.language-archives.org/ OLAC/process.html (accessed 3 December 2003).
3. For discussion of the details of the OLAC vocabularies, and on how OLAC builds on the Open Archives Initiative foundation, see Gary Simons and Steven Bird, "Building an Open Language Archives Community on the OAI Foundation," *Library Hi-Tech* 21, no. 2 (2003): 210–18; and Steven Bird and Gary Simons, "Extending Dublin Core Metadata to Support the Description and Discovery of Language Resources," *Computers and the Humanities* 37, no. 4 (2003): 375–88.
4. Linguistic Data Consortium (home page), http://www.ldc.upenn.edu/ (accessed 5 December 2003).
5. SIL International (home page), http://www.sil.org/ (accessed 5 December 2003).
6. LINGUIST List (home page), http://www.linguistlist.org/ (accessed 5 December 2003).
7. Gary Simons and Steven Bird, "Requirements on the Infrastructure for Open Language Archiving," 2000, http://www.language-archives.org/docs/ requirements.html (accessed 3 December 2003); Gary Simons and Steven Bird,

"The Seven Pillars of Open Language Archiving: A Vision Statement," 2000, http://www.language-archives.org/docs/vision.html (accessed 3 December 2003).
8. Steven Bird and Gary Simons, "A Survey of the State of the Art in Digital Language Documentation and Description," 2000, http://www.language-archives.org/docs/survey.html (accessed 3 December 2003); Steven Bird and Gary Simons, "White Paper on Establishing an Infrastructure for Open Language Archiving," 2000, http://www.language-archives.org/docs/white-paper.html (accessed 3 December 2003).
9. The technical infrastructure developed by the authors to support this work is reported in Simons and Bird, "OLAC Metadata."
10. Steven Bird and Gary Simons, "Seven Dimensions of Portability for Language Documentation and Description," *Language* 79 (2003): 557–82.
11. Dublin Core Metadata Initiative, "Dublin Core Metadata Element Set, Version 1.1: Reference Description," 1999, http://dublincore.org/documents/1999/07/02/dces/ (accessed 3 December 2003).
12. International Organization for Standardization, "ISO 639: Codes for the Representation of Names of Languages—Part 2: Alpha-3 Code," 1998, http://lcweb.loc.gov/standards/iso639-2/langhome.html (accessed 3 December 2003).
13. Peter Constable and Gary Simons, "Language Identification and IT: Addressing Problems of Linguistic Diversity on a Global Scale," in *SIL Electronic Working Papers 2000–01* (Dallas: SIL International, 2000), 1–22. This is a revised version of a paper presented at the 17th International Unicode Conference, San Jose, Calif., 5–8 September 2000, available at http://www.sil.org/silewp/2000/001/ (accessed 3 December 2003).
14. Barbara F. Grimes, ed., *Ethnologue: Languages of the World,* 14th ed. (Dallas: SIL International, 2000), also available at http://www.ethnologue.com/ (accessed 3 December 2003); LINGUIST List, "Ancient and Extinct Languages," 2003, http://linguistlist.org/ancientlgs.html; LINGUIST List, "Constructed Languages," 2003, http://linguistlist.org/constructedlgs.html (accessed 10 December 2003).
15. Gary Simons and Steven Bird, "OLAC Metadata Set," 2001, http://www.language-archives.org/OLAC/olacms.html (accessed 3 December 2003).
16. Simons and Bird, "OLAC Metadata Set."
17. Helen Aristar Dry and Heidi Johnson, "OLAC Linguistic Data Type Vocabulary," 2002, http://www.language-archives.org/REC/type-20021212.html (accessed 3 December 2003).
18. Open Language Archives Community, "Schema for the OLAC Metadata Set," version 1.0, 2002, http://www.language-archives.org/OLAC/1.0/olac.xsd (accessed 5 December 2003).
19. Andy Powell and Pete Johnston, "Guidelines for Implementing Dublin Core in XML," 2003, http://dublincore.org/documents/dc-xml-guidelines/ (accessed 3 December 2003); Pete Johnston et al., "Notes on the W3C XML Schemas for Qualified Dublin Core," 2003, http://dublincore.org/schemas/xmls/qdc/2003/04/02/notes/ (accessed 3 December 2003).
20. Rachel Heery and Manjula Patel, "Application Profiles: Mixing and Matching Metadata Schemas," *Ariadne* 25 (2000), http://www.ariadne.ac.uk/issue25/app-profiles/.
21. Open Language Archives Community, "Schema for the OLAC Metadata Set."

22. Heidi Johnson, "OLAC Role Vocabulary," 2003, http://www.language-archives .org/REC/role.html (accessed 3 December 2003); Helen Aristar Dry and Heidi Johnson, "OLAC Linguistic Data Type Vocabulary," 2002, http:// www.language-archives.org/REC/type-20021212.html (accessed 3 December 2003); Heidi Johnson and Helen Aristar Dry, "OLAC Discourse Type Vocabulary," 2002, http://www.language-archives.org/REC/discourse.html (accessed 5 December 2003); Helen Aristar Dry and Michael Appleby, "OLAC Linguistic Subject Vocabulary," 2003, http://www.language-archives.org/REC/field.html (accessed 3 December 2003).
23. Open Language Archives Community, "Summary Documentation for an OLAC Extension," http://www.language-archives.org/OLAC/1.0/olac-extension.xsd (accessed 3 December 2003).
24. Gary Simons and Steven Bird, "OLAC Recommended Metadata Extensions," 2003, http://www.language-archives.org/REC/olac-extensions.html (accessed 3 December 2003).
25. Simons and Bird, "OLAC Metadata"; Simons and Bird, "OLAC Recommended Metadata Extensions."
26. Johnson, "OLAC Role Vocabulary."
27. See Simons and Bird, "OLAC Repositories," for an example of a complete OLAC extension definition.
28. Powell and Johnston, "Implementing Dublin Core in XML"; Johnston et al., "W3C XML Schemas."
29. Simons and Bird, "OLAC Repositories."
30. Carl Lagoze et al., "The Open Archives Initiative Protocol for Metadata Harvesting," 2003, http://www.openarchives.org/OAI/openarchivesprotocol .html (accessed 10 December 2003).
31. Simons and Bird, "Building an Open Language Archives Community"; Gary Simons and Steven Bird, "The Open Language Archives Community: An Infrastructure for Distributed Archiving of Language Resources," *Literary and Linguistic Computing* 18 (2003): 117–28.
32. Open Language Archives Community, "VIDA: OLAC Virtual Data Provider," 2002, http://www.language-archives.org/vida (accessed 10 December 2003).
33. Open Language Archives Community, "OLAC Static Repository Gateway," n.d., http://www.language-archives.org/sr (accessed 10 December 2003).
34. The OLAC Repository Editor is available at http://www.language-archives .org/vida (accessed 3 December 2003). The Repository header is hosted at LINGUIST List, at http://www.linguistlist.org/ore/ (accessed 10 December 2003).
35. Open Language Archives Community, "OLAC Aggregator," 2002, http://www .language-archives.org/cgi-bin/olaca.pl (accessed 3 December 2003).
36. Open Language Archives Community, "Viser: A Virtual Service Provider for Displaying Selected OLAC Metadata," 2003, http://www.language-archives .org/viser/ (accessed 3 December 2003).
37. Simons and Bird, "OLAC Process."
38. Open Language Archives Community, "Viser."
39. Diane I. Hillmann and Stuart A. Sutton, "DCMI Usage Board Administrative Processes," 2003, http://www.dublincore.org/usage/documents/process/ (accessed 3 December 2003).

14 Mixed Content and Mixed Metadata: Information Discovery in a Messy World

Caroline R. Arms and William Y. Arms

AS DIGITAL LIBRARIES grow in scale, heterogeneity becomes a fact of life. Content comes in a bewildering variety of formats. It is organized and managed in innumerable different ways. Similarly, metadata comes in a broad variety, and its quality and completeness vary greatly. Digital libraries must find ways to accept materials from diverse collections, with differing metadata or with none, and provide users with coherent information discovery services.

To understand how this may be possible, it is important to recognize the overall process by which an intelligent person discovers information. If information discovery is considered synonymous with searching, then the problem of heterogeneity is probably insuperable. By considering the complete process, however, most of the difficulties can be tackled.

MIXED CONTENT, MIXED METADATA

Searching: The Legacy of History

Many of the metadata systems in use today were originally developed when the underlying resources described were in physical form. If a reader has to wait hours for a book to be retrieved from library stacks, it is vital to have an accurate description, to be confident of requesting the correct item. When the first computer-based abstracting and indexing services were developed for scientific and professional information, information resources were physical items. These services were aimed primarily at researchers, with an emphasis on comprehensive searching, that is, on high recall. The typical user was a medical researcher or lawyer who would pay good money to be sure of finding everything relevant to a topic. The aim was high recall through a single, carefully formulated search.

Although there are wide differences in the details, the approaches developed for library catalogs and early information services all employed careful rules for human cataloging and indexing, heavily structured metadata, and subject access via controlled subject vocabularies or classification schemes. The underlying assumption was that users would be trained or supported by professional librarians. As recently as the early 1990s, most services had the following characteristics:

> Resources were separated into categories. For example, monographs, journal articles, datasets, and newspaper articles were organized, indexed, and searched separately.
>
> Catalogs and indexes were built on tightly controlled standards, such as MARC, MeSH headings, etc.
>
> Search interfaces used Boolean operators and fielding searching. These techniques are effective in exploiting the precise vocabulary and structure that are inherent in rich metadata records.
>
> Query languages and search interfaces assumed a trained user. The combination of complex metadata standards, fielded indexing, and Boolean operators is powerful, but not intuitive.
>
> Most resources were physical items.

The Demand for Mixed Content

As digital libraries have become larger, they have begun to amalgamate materials that were previously managed separately. Users now expect one-stop access to information, yet different categories of materials must still be handled differently because the mode of expression or nature of distribution demands specialized expertise or different workflow in libraries, whether the content is digital or not. Thus the Library of Congress has separate units, such as Prints and Photographs, Manuscripts, Geography and Maps, each managing a relatively homogeneous collection. The National

Library of Medicine provides a catalog of MARC records for books and Medline as an index to journal articles. To knowledgeable users, these divisions pose few problems. However, to students, the general public, and scholars in areas not aligned with the category boundaries, the divisions can be frustrating and confusing.

Some digital libraries have been established explicitly to bring together materials from various sources and categories. For example, the National Science Foundation's National Science Digital Library (NSDL) collects information about materials of value to scientific education, irrespective of format or provenance.[1] To illustrate the variety, four NSDL collections based at Cornell University respectively offer data sets about volcanoes and earthquakes; digitized versions of kinematics models from the nineteenth century; sound recordings, images, and videos of birds; and mathematical theorems and proofs. Similar diversity arises even with more conventional library materials. American Memory at the Library of Congress includes millions of digital items of many different types: photographs, posters, published books, personal papers of presidents, maps, sound recordings, motion pictures, and much more.[2] Users of the NSDL or the American Memory sites want to explore the digital collections as a whole, without needing to learn different techniques for different categories of material. Yet the conventional, flat approaches to searching and browsing are poorly adapted for mixed content.

Mixed Content Means Mixed Metadata

Given that information discovery systems must reach across many formats and genres, a natural impulse is to seek for a unifying cataloging and indexing standard. The dream would be a single, all-embracing standard that suits every category of material and is adopted by every collection. However, this is an illusion. Mixed metadata appears to be as inevitable as mixed content.

There are good reasons why different metadata formats are used for different categories of resources. Maps are different from photographs and sound recordings from journal articles. A set of photographs of a single subject may be impossible to distinguish usefully through textual metadata; the user is best served by a group of thumbnail images. Digital forms, such as software, datasets, simulations, and websites, each call for different practices. In the NSDL, many of the best-managed collections were not intended for educational use; a taxonomy of animal behavior designed for researchers is of no value to schoolchildren. Many valuable resources in the NSDL have no item-level metadata. In American Memory, the records for 47,000 pieces of sheet music registered for copyright between 1870 and 1885 are brief, with an emphasis on music genre and instrumentation. In contrast, the 3,042 pieces of sheet music in another American Memory collection were selected from collections at Duke University to present a significant perspective on American history and culture; the cataloging includes detailed description of the illustrated covers and advertisements.

Reconciling the variety of formats and genres would be a forbidding task even if it were purely a matter of schemas and guidelines, but there are other forces behind mixed metadata: the social context. History is littered with metadata proposals that were technically excellent but failed to achieve widespread adoption for social and cultural reasons. One social factor is economic. Well-funded research fields, such as medicine, have the resources to abstract and index individual items (e.g., journal articles) and to maintain tools such as controlled vocabularies and subject headings, but the rich disciplines are the exceptions. Even major research libraries cannot afford to catalog every item fully. For example, the Prints and Photographs Division of the Library of Congress often creates catalog records for groups of pictures or uses very brief records for items in large collections. A second social factor is history. Catalogs and indexes represent an investment, which includes the accumulated expertise of users and librarians, and the development of computer systems. For instance, Medline, Inspec, and Chemical Abstracts services index journal articles, but the services developed independently with little cross-fertilization. Unsurprisingly, each has its own conventions for description and indexing appropriate to the discipline. Any attempt to introduce a single unifying scheme would threaten upheaval and meet with resistance.

METADATA CONSISTENCY

While the dream of a single metadata standard is an illusion, attempts to enhance consistency through the promotion of guidelines within communities and coordination across communities can be extremely valuable. The last decade provides many examples where benefits from metadata consistency have been recognized and steps have been taken to harmonize usage in specific areas.

Developments in the Library Community

Two structural developments for MARC records have enhanced consistency. During the period from 1988 to 1995, *format integration* brought the variants of USMARC used for monographs, serials, music, visual materials, etc., into a single bibliographic format. In the late 1990s, the Library of Congress, the National Library of Canada, and the British Library agreed to pursue *MARC harmonization* to reduce the costs of cataloging, by making a larger pool of catalog records available to be shared among libraries. One outcome was the MARC 21 format, which superseded USMARC and CAN/MARC.[3] The motivation for these efforts was not explicitly to benefit users, but users have certainly benefited because systems are simpler when metadata elements are used consistently.

Other valuable modifications to the MARC standard have been made for compatibility with other metadata schemas or interoperability efforts. Some changes support mappings between MARC and FGDC, and between MARC and Dublin Core. Others support citations to journal articles in convenient machine-parsable form, to use with the OpenURL standard and to allow detail to be preserved in conversions to MARC from schemas used in citation databases.[4]

Recently, in response to demand from the library community, the Library of Congress has developed an XML-based metadata schema that is compatible with MARC, but simpler. The Metadata Object Description Schema (MODS) includes a subset of MARC elements and inherits MARC semantics for those elements.[5] Inherited aspects that are particularly important for American Memory include the ability to express the role of a creator (photographer, illustrator, etc.) and to specify place names in tagged hierarchical form (e.g., <country><state><city>). In some areas, MODS offers extensions and simplifications of MARC to meet known descriptive needs, including some for American Memory. MODS provides for more explicit categorization of dates, all expressible in machine-readable encodings. Coordinates can be associated with a place name. A valuable simplification is in the treatment of types and genres for resources; a short list of high-level types is allowed in one element, and all other genre terms and material designators in another. American Memory users have frequently requested better capabilities for filtering by resource type, both in specifying queries and in organizing result lists. Based on these features, and building on an internal harmonization effort, a migration to MODS is expected for those American Memory collections for which MARC is not used.

The potential benefits of an XML-based schema are significant. Libraries can take advantage of general-purpose software tools available for XML (Extensible Markup Language). Since in XML, any element can be tagged with the language of its content and the full Unicode character set is allowed, MODS permits the assembly of multilingual records.

Federated Searching versus Union Catalogs

Federated searching is a form of distributed searching. A client system sends a query to several servers. Each server carries out a search on the indexes that apply to its own collections and returns the results to the client system, which combines them for presentation to the user. This is sometimes called metasearch or broadcast searching. Recently, systems have emerged, called *portal applications,* that incorporate a wide variety of resources into a federated search for library patrons. Most federated searching products take advantage of the Z39.50 protocol.[6]

In recent years, standard profiles for Z39.50 index configurations have been developed by the library community in the hope of persuading vendors to build compatible servers for federated searching. These profiles represent a compromise between what users might hope for and what vendors believe can be built at a reasonable cost. The Bath Profile was originally developed in the United Kingdom and is now maintained by the National Library of Canada; a comparable U.S. national standard is in development under the auspices of the National Information Standards Organization.[7] These profiles focus on a few fields (e.g., author, subject, title, standard number, date of publication). In the Bath Profile, the highest level for bibliographic searching also includes type of resource and language. A keyword search on any field covers all other fields.

The effectiveness of federated searching is limited by incompatibilities in the metadata or the index configurations in the remote systems. Client applications have to wait for responses from several servers and usually receive only the first batch of results from each server before presenting results to a user. Busy users are frustrated by having to wait and experienced users are frustrated by the inability to express complex queries. Duplicates are a problem when several sources return records for the same item. While federated searching is useful for small numbers of carefully managed collections, it proves unworkable when the number and variety of collections increase.

American Memory and the NSDL both use a different approach, following the pattern of union catalogs in gathering metadata records from many sources to a single location. Both digital libraries have to address inconsistencies in metadata, but have the advantage of doing so in centrally controlled systems.

Cross-Domain Metadata: The Dublin Core

Dublin Core represents an attempt to build a lingua franca that can be used across domains. To comprehend how rapidly our understanding is changing, it is instructive to go back to the early days of the Web. As recently as 1995, it was recognized that the methods of full-text indexing used by early web search engines, such as Lycos, would run into difficulties as the number of web pages increased. The contemporary wisdom was that "indexes are most useful in small collections within a given domain. As the scope of their coverage expands, indexes succumb to problems of large retrieval sets and problems of cross-disciplinary semantic drift. Richer records, created by content experts, are necessary to improve search and retrieval."[8] With the benefit of hindsight, we now see that the web search engines have developed new techniques and have adapted to a huge scale, while cross-domain metadata schemes have made less progress.

For the first phase of the NSDL development, collection contributors were encouraged to provide Dublin Core metadata for each item and to make these records available for harvesting via the Open Archives Initiative Protocol for Metadata Harvesting (OAI-PMH).[9] While this strategy enabled the first phase of the science library to be implemented rapidly, it showed up some fundamental weaknesses of the Dublin Core approach.[10] Although each component (Dublin Core and OAI-PMH) is intended to be simple, expertise is needed to understand the specifications and to implement them consistently, which places a burden on small, lightly staffed collections. The granularities and the types of objects characterized by metadata vary greatly and the metadata quality is highly variable. When contributors have invested the effort to create fuller metadata (e.g., to one of the standards that are designed for learning objects), valuable information is lost when it is mapped into Dublin Core. The overall result has been disappointing for information discovery. Search engines work by matching a query against the information in the records being searched. Many Dublin Core records contain very little information that can be used for information discovery.

INFORMATION DISCOVERY IN A MESSY WORLD

Fortunately, the power of modern computing, which makes large-scale digital libraries possible, also supports new capabilities for information discovery. Two themes are particularly significant:

Brute force computation can be used to analyze the content of resources, e.g., to index every word from textual materials, or to extract links and citations. Computing power can combine information from various sources (e.g., a dictionary or thesaurus), process huge amounts of data, or provide flexible user interface services (e.g., visualizations). The potential for mapping among subject vocabularies or for recognizing concepts even when the terms used are different is a significant area, but beyond the scope of this chapter.

Powerful user interfaces and networks bring human expertise into the information discovery loop. They enable users to apply their insight through a continual process of exploring results, revising search strategies, and experimenting with varieties of queries.

Advances in Information Retrieval

When materials are in digital formats, it is possible to extract information from the content by computer programs. Automated full-text indexing is an approach to information retrieval that uses no metadata.[11] The actual words used by the author are taken as the descriptors of the content. The basic technique measures the similarity between the terms in each document and the terms in the query. Full-text search engines provide ranked lists of how similar the terms in the documents are to those in the query. As early as 1967, Cleverdon recognized that, in some circumstances, automated indexes could be as effective as those generated by skilled human indexers.[12] This counterintuitive result is possible because an automated index, containing every word in a textual document, has more information than a catalog or index record created by hand. It may lack the quality control and structure of fields that are found in a catalog record, but statistically the much greater volume of information provided by the author's words may be more useful than a shorter surrogate record.

By the early 1990s, there were two well-established methods for indexing and searching textual materials: fielded searching of metadata records and full-text indexing. Both built on the implicit expectation that information resources were divided into relatively homogeneous categories of material; search systems were tuned separately for each category. Until the development of the Web, almost all information retrieval experiments studied homogeneous collections. For example, the classic Cranfield experiments studied papers in aeronautics. When the Text Retrieval Conferences (TREC) in the 1990s carried out systematic studies of the performance of search engines, the test corpora came from homogeneous sources, such as the Associated Press newswire, thus encouraging the development of algorithms that perform well on homogeneous collections of documents.[13]

Web search services combine a web crawler with a full-text indexing system. For example, the first version of Lycos used the Pursuit search engine developed by Mauldin at Carnegie Mellon University.[14] This was a conventional full-text system, which had done well in the TREC evaluations. There were two repeated complaints about these early systems: simple searches resulted in thousands of hits, and many of the highly ranked hits were junk. Numerous developments have enabled the search services to improve their results, even as the Web has grown spectacularly. Four developments, in particular, have general applicability:

1. Better understanding of how and why users seek for information
2. Relationships and context information
3. Multimodal information discovery
4. User interfaces for exploring information

Understanding How and Why Users Seek for Information

The conventional measures of effectiveness, such as precision and recall, are based on a binary interpretation of *relevance*. A document is either relevant or not, and all relevant documents are considered equally important.

With such criteria, the goal of a search system is to find all documents relevant to a query, even though a user's information need may be satisfied by a single hit.

In their original Google paper, Brin and Page introduced a new criterion.[15] They recognized that, with mixed content, some documents are likely to be much more useful than others. In a typical web search, the underlying term vector model finds every document that matches the terms in the query, often hundreds of thousands of them. However, the user looks at only the most highly ranked batches of hits, rarely more than a hundred in total. Google's focus is on those first batches of hits. The traditional objective of finding all relevant documents is not the goal.

With homogeneous content all documents were assumed to be equally important. Therefore they could be ranked by how similar they were to the query. With mixed content, many documents may be relevant, but not all of them are equally useful to the user. Brin and Page give the example of a web page that contains three words, "Bill Clinton sucks." This page is undoubtedly similar to the query "Bill Clinton." However, the page is unlikely to be of much use. Therefore, Google estimates the importance of each page, using criteria that are totally independent of how well the page matches a query. The order in which pages are returned to the user is a combination of these two rankings: similarity to the query and importance of the document.

Relationship and Context

Information resources always exist in a context and are often related to others. A monograph is one of a series; an article cites other articles; customers who buy a certain book often buy related ones; reviews describe how people judge resources. In formal catalogs and bibliographies, some relationships are made explicit; automated indexing of online content permits the inference of other relationships from context. Google's image search is an intriguing example of a system that relies entirely on context to search for images on the Web. The content of images cannot be indexed reliably, and the only metadata for an image on a web page is the name of the file, but such images have considerable context. This context includes text in anchors that refer to the image, captions, terms in nearby paragraphs, etc. By indexing the terms in this contextual information, Google's image search is often able to find useful images.

On the Web, hyperlinks provide relationships between pages that are analogous to citations between papers.[16] Google's well-known PageRank algorithm estimates the importance of a web page by the number of other web pages that link to it, weighted by the importance of the linking pages and the number of links from each page. The Teoma search engine uses hyperlinks in a different way. After carrying out a text search, it analyzes a set of several thousand of the highest-ranking results and identifies pages that many other pages link to.

Citations and hyperlinks are examples of contextual information embedded within documents. Reviews and annotations are examples of external information. Amazon.com has been a leader in encouraging the general public to provide such information. The value of information contributed by outsiders depends on the reputation of the contributor.

These techniques for exploiting context require powerful computation.

Multimodal Information Discovery

With mixed content and mixed metadata, the amount of information about the various resources varies greatly. Many useful features can be extracted from some documents but not all. For example, a <title> field in a web page provides useful information, but not all pages have <title> fields. Citations and hyperlinks are valuable when present, but not all documents have them. Such features can be considered clues. Multimodal information discovery methods combine information about various features of the collections, using all the information that is available about each item. The clues may be extracted from the content, may be in the form of metadata, or may be contextual.

The term "multimodal information discovery" was coined by Carnegie Mellon's Informedia project. Informedia has a homogeneous collection—segments of video from television news programs—but because it is based on purely automated extraction from the content, the topic-related metadata varies greatly.[17] The search and retrieval process combines clues derived automatically in many ways. The concept behind the multimodal approach is that "the integration of . . . technologies, all of which are imperfect and incomplete, would overcome the limitations of each, and improve the overall performance in the information retrieval task."[18]

Web search services also use a multimodal approach to ranking. While the technical details of each service are trade secrets, the underlying approaches combine conventional full-text indexing with contextual ranking (such as PageRank), using every clue that they can find, including anchor text, terms in titles, words that are emphasized or in larger font, and the proximity of terms to each other.

User Interfaces for Exploring Results

Good user interfaces for exploring the results of a search can compensate for many weaknesses in the search service, including indifferent or missing metadata. It is no coincidence that Informedia, where the quality of metadata is inevitably poor, has been one of the key research projects in the development of user interfaces for browsing.

Perhaps the most profound change in information discovery in the past decade is that the full content of many resources is now online. When the time to retrieve a resource has gone from minutes, hours, or even days to a few seconds, browsing and searching are interwoven. The web search services provide a supreme example of this. Though weak by many of the traditional measures, they nevertheless provide quick and direct access to information sources that the user can then explore independently. A common pattern is for a user to type a few words into a web search service, glance through the list of hits, examine a few, try a different combination of search terms, and examine a new set of hits. This rapid interplay between the user's expertise and the computing tools is totally outside the formal analysis of single searches that is still the basis of most information retrieval research.

The user interface to RLG's Cultural Materials resource provides a different example.[19] It consists of a simple search system, supported by elegant tools for exploring the results. The search system acts as a filter that reduces the number of records that the user is offered to explore. In the past, a similar system would almost certainly have provided a search interface with advanced features that a skilled user could use to specify a very precise search. Instead RLG has chosen a simple search interface and an easily understood interface for exploring the results. Neither requires a skilled user. The objective is flexible exploration rather than precise retrieval.

Yet another area where Google has advanced the state of the art in information discovery lies in the short records that are returned for each hit. These are sometimes called "snippets." Each is a short extract from the web page, which summarizes it so that the user can decide whether to view it. Most services generate the snippets when the pages are indexed.

For a given page, the user always receives the same snippet, whatever the query. Google generates snippets dynamically, to include the words on the page that were matched against the query.

Case Study: The NSDL

The National Science Digital Library provides an example of many of the approaches already discussed. The library has been explicitly designed on the assumption of heterogeneity.[20] The centerpiece of the architecture is an NSDL repository, which is intended to hold everything that is known about every item of interest. As of 2003, the repository holds metadata in only a limited range of formats; considerable emphasis has been placed on Dublin Core records, both item-level and collection-level. The first search service combines fielded searching of these records with a full-text index of those textual documents that are openly accessible for indexing. Three improvements are planned for the near term: expansion of the range of metadata formats that are accepted, improved ranking, and dynamic generation of snippets. In the medium term, the major development will be the addition of contextual information, particularly annotations and relationships. For an educational digital library, recommendations based on practical experience in using the resources are extremely valuable. Finally, various experiments are under way to enhance the exploration of the collections; visualization tools are particularly promising.

The target audiences are so broad that several portals or views into the same digital library are planned. Moreover, the NSDL team hopes and expects that users will discover NSDL resources not only by using the tools that the NSDL provides, but by other ways such as web search services. An example is a browser extension tool that enables users to see whether resources found in other ways are in the NSDL; e.g., when a page of results is returned from Google, the user clicks the tool, and each URL on a page that references an NSDL resource has a hyperlinked logo appended to it.

IMPLICATIONS FOR THE FUTURE

In summary, as digital libraries grow larger, information discovery systems must increasingly assume the following characteristics:

Users expect to have access to mixed content. Resources with highly diverse content, of many formats and genres, are grouped together. Many different metadata standards coexist. Many resources have no item-level metadata; for some the available metadata is limited, and for others it is excellent.

Most searching and browsing is done by the end users themselves. Information discovery services can no longer assume that users are trained in the nuances of cataloging standards and complex search syntaxes.

Information discovery tasks have changed, with high recall rarely the dominant requirement. The criteria by which information discovery is judged must recognize the full process of searching and browsing with the human in the loop.

Multimodal methods of searching and browsing are becoming the norm. More information about resources—whether metadata or full content—provides more opportunities for information discovery, but services must be designed to use everything that is available.

Perhaps the most important conclusion is that successful information discovery depends on the interrelationship between three areas: the underlying information (content and metadata); computing tools to exploit both the information and its context; and the human-computer interfaces that are provided. Most of this book is about the first of these three, the relationship between content and metadata, but none of them can be studied in isolation.

Acknowledgments

This paper synthesizes ideas that we have gained in working on American Memory and the National Science Digital Library and from many other colleagues. This work was supported in part by the National Science Foundation, under NSF grant 0127308.

NOTES

1. National Science Digital Library (home page), http://nsdl.org/ (accessed 12 December 2003).
2. Library of Congress, American Memory (home page), http://memory.loc.gov/ (accessed 12 December 2003).

3. Library of Congress, "MARC 21 Formats," http://www.loc.gov/marc/marcdocz.html (accessed 12 December 2003).
4. Herbert Van de Sompel, Patrick Hochstenbach, and Oren Beit-Arie, "OpenURL Syntax Description," 2002, http://www.sfxit.com/openurl/openurl.html (accessed 12 December 2003).
5. Metadata Object Description Schema (home page), http://www.loc.gov/standards/mods/ (accessed 12 December 2003).
6. International Standard Maintenance Agency, Z39.50 (home page), http://www.loc.gov/z3950/agency/ (accessed 12 December 2003).
7. Bath Profile Maintenance Agency, "The Bath Profile: An International Z39.50 Specification for Library Applications and Resource Discovery," release 2.0, March 2003, http://www.nlc-bnc.ca/bath/tp-bath2-e.htm (accessed 12 December 2003).
8. Stuart Weibel, "Metadata: The Foundations of Resource Description," *D-Lib Magazine,* July 1995, http://www.dlib.org/dlib/July95/07contents.html (accessed 12 December 2003).
9. Carl Lagoze et al., "The Open Archives Initiative Protocol for Metadata Harvesting," http://www.openarchives.org/OAI/openarchivesprotocol.html (accessed 12 December 2003).
10. William Y. Arms et al., "A Case Study in Metadata Harvesting: The NSDL," *Library Hi-Tech* 21, no. 2 (2003), 228–37.
11. Gerald Salton and Michael J. McGill, *Introduction to Modern Information Retrieval* (New York: McGraw-Hill, 1983).
12. Cyril William Cleverdon, "The Cranfield Tests on Index Language Devices," *ASLIB Proceedings* 19, no. 6 (June 1967): 173–94.
13. E. Voorhees and D. Harman, "Overview of the Eighth Text Retrieval Conference," 1999, http://trec.nist.gov/pubs/trec8/papers/overview_8.ps.
14. Michael L. Mauldin, "Lycos: Design Choices in an Internet Search Service," *IEEE Expert* 12, no. 1 (1997): 8–11.
15. Sergey Brin and Lawrence Page, "The Anatomy of a Large-Scale Hypertextual Web Search Engine," paper given at the Seventh International World Wide Web Conference, Brisbane, Australia, 1998, http://www7.scu.edu.au/programme/fullpapers/1921/com1921.htm.
16. Eugene Garfield, *Citation Indexing: Its Theory and Application in Science, Technology, and Humanities* (New York: Wiley, 1979).
17. Informedia (home page), http://www.informedia.cs.cmu.edu/.
18. Howard Wactlar, "Informedia—Search and Summarization in the Video Medium," in *Proceedings of Imagina 2000 Conference,* Monaco, 31 January–2 February 2000, http://www.informedia.cs.cmu.edu/documents/imagina2000.pdf.
19. RLG, "RLG Cultural Materials," http://cmi.rlg.org/.
20. William Y. Arms et al., "A Spectrum of Interoperability: The Site for Science Prototype for the NSDL," *D-Lib Magazine,* January 2002, http://www.dlib.org/dlib/january02/arms/01arms.html.

15

The Continuum of Metadata Quality: Defining, Expressing, Exploiting

Thomas R. Bruce and Diane I. Hillmann

LIKE PORNOGRAPHY, METADATA quality is difficult to define. We know it when we see it, but conveying the full bundle of assumptions and experience that allow us to identify it is a different matter. For this reason, among others, few outside the library community have written about defining metadata quality. Still less has been said about enforcing quality in ways that do not require unacceptable levels of human effort.

Some stage-setting work is in progress. In a 2002 study of element use by eighty-two Open Archives Initiative (OAI) data providers, Jewel Ward reported that the providers used an average of eight Dublin Core (DC) elements per record.[1] Five of the eight elements were used 71 percent of the time. Ward's study indicates that most metadata providers use only a small part of the DC element set, but her study makes no attempt to determine the reliability or usefulness of the information in those few elements. In 2003, another paper published by Naomi Dushay and Diane Hillmann of the Digital Library Research Group at Cornell University described methods for evaluating metadata, and reported in detail some common errors and quality problems found in harvested metadata, as well as a technique for evaluating metadata using a commercially available visual graphical analysis tool.[2] Both these efforts clearly have some definition of quality in mind, but neither states it explicitly.

Other recent papers by Barton, Currier, and Hey and Moen, Stewart, and McClure have focused on the detection of defects in metadata records and the impact of defects on the utility of collections.[3] Barton et al. strongly believe that defect analysis has major implications for metadata-generation practices.[4] In preparing this chapter, we too have found that it is difficult to talk about quality without also talking about things that betray its absence, but we believe that trying to comprehend quality by enumerating defects risks sacrificing an organized view of the forest to an overly specific appreciation of the trees. Instead, we attempt a systematic, domain- and method-independent discussion of quality indicators.

PAST EXPERIENCE

The library community has repeatedly tried to define and enforce quality in its bibliographic and authority records, but until recently these attempts have been fairly inconsequential. The practice of bibliographic record sharing has been generally accepted for over a century, and such sharing has been the basis for most of the processing efficiencies realized by libraries during that time. Nevertheless, cataloging continues to be a labor-intensive and costly function in libraries, requiring special knowledge and training, and the need for efficient cataloging is all the more keenly felt given the ever-increasing quantity of materials requiring cataloging atten-tion. The resulting tension between "efficient" cataloging and "quality" cataloging has given rise to much conflict between cataloging staff and administrators, with record-selection techniques such as "white lists" giv-ing way to criteria better suited to automation.

In the late 1990s, recognizing that these tensions were increasing even as automated selection of cataloging records from the bibliographic utili-ties was becoming the norm, the Program for Cooperative Cataloging (PCC) developed the BIBCO Core Record standards.[5] BIBCO was an attempt to define a MARC record that could be trusted sufficiently to be reused without human intervention. BIBCO took its cue from the success of the Name Authorities Cooperative Program (NACO), which had revi-talized and diversified the production of name, subject, and series author-ity records for reliable reuse. NACO and BIBCO were successful because they emphasized:

acceptance of agreed-upon standards for record quality;

participation in a training program where each institution desig-nated several catalogers as liaisons, training other staff mem-bers and later, other libraries, in a formalized "buddy" system; and individual review of records by experienced catalogers (from the "buddy" institution) during the training period until an acceptable level of quality is reached.

The acceptance of these programs in the library community reinforces two important points: quality is quantifiable and measurable, and to be effective, enforcement of standards of quality must take place at the community level. Most metadata communities outside of libraries are not yet at the point where they have begun to define, much less measure, quality. However, other communities of practice, particularly those building digital library or e-print systems, are beginning to venture into discussions about metadata quality.

CHALLENGES IN APPROACHING QUESTIONS OF QUALITY

New metadata standards are being developed at a rapid pace, and their introduction into new communities has stimulated discussions of quality. This process has been swifter in some communities than in others, as the early adoption of metadata as a panacea for information overload is followed all too quickly by the recognition that investments in quality are necessary for even modest gains. Furthermore, as communities of all kinds attempt to aggregate metadata (and ultimately services) via harvesting protocols—like the Open Archives Initiative Protocol for Metadata Harvesting (OAI-PMH)—quality standards and measures are sorely missed.[6]

Practitioners and implementers in these communities come from a variety of backgrounds and often have limited experience with information technology or library practices. The documentation and examples available to them may seem too "generalized," and research from ongoing projects that might assist them is buried in places foreign to their discipline. Specialist communities, who tend to see their data as unique, frequently resist the notion that there might be general strategies available to them that could inform their work and enable their metadata to interoperate. Isolation and a tendency to manufacture special solutions for what are really general problems create barriers for coordinated thinking about quality.

Resource constraints, particularly those that come into play as projects scale up, also militate against shared notions of quality. Specialists tend to consider only the attributes that matter to them, neglecting those that might make their data more useful to dimly imagined, and hence easily dismissed, groups of outsiders. Often the potential expense of creating interoperability is given as the reason for neglecting outside influences. Budgets for projects rarely contain sufficient funds to effectively plan and implement metadata components, and projects are quick to sacrifice investments that serve any but the most immediate target audiences. Quality that serves outsiders is seen as unaffordable altruism.

Even now, review panels for projects or grant proposals rarely include individuals versed in metadata standards. Planners' assessment of information technology needs is often limited to website or database design and construction, without considering how their information may function when exposed to aggregators or reused in other settings or by other services. To complicate matters, the rate of change in standards and technologies is so rapid that even careful planners and managers find it difficult to determine when they are compliant with current standards. Indeed, to the extent that a painstaking approach implies substantial time spent in consensus building and review, cautious efforts become even more likely to be superseded.

Legacy data presents special problems for many communities, as it rarely makes a clean transition into new metadata formats. Some data were heavily encoded during the days when expensive storage encouraged highly compressed encoding; most were designed specifically for niche rather than general use. Despite these challenges, a few areas of useful discussion are emerging. In 1997 the IFLA Study Group on the Functional Requirements for Bibliographic Records published a final report.[7] As part of that effort, the group identified four generic user tasks to be accomplished using bibliographic records:

1. To *find* entities which correspond to the user's stated search criteria (i.e., to locate either a single entity or a set of entities in a file or database as the result of a search using an attribute or relationship of the entity)
2. To *identify* an entity (i.e., to confirm that the entity described corresponds to the entity sought, or to distinguish between two or more entities with similar characteristics)
3. To *select* an entity that is appropriate to the user's needs (i.e., to choose an entity that meets the user's requirements with respect to content, physical format, etc., or to reject an entity as being inappropriate to the user's needs)

4. To *acquire* or obtain access to the entity described (i.e., to acquire an entity through purchase, loan, etc., or to access an entity electronically through an online connection to a remote computer)

These tasks provide a useful, though not easily quantifiable, basis for testing the effects of metadata quality (or lack thereof) on potential users. In addition, they extend the conversation about metadata quality beyond simple support for resource discovery toward support of broader functionality that is more applicable to an expansive notion of digital libraries. It is important to note that the "user" in question is one who might be searching a website for materials, rather than the aggregator of metadata, who is also a user, though at a "wholesale" rather than "retail" level. Inevitably, quality is passed downstream from creator to aggregator to user. Most of the definitions of quality discussed in this chapter affect the aggregator first, and only then the user at the website, who trusts that someone, somewhere, has been paying attention.

QUALITY MEASUREMENTS AND METRICS

In this section, we attempt to define general characteristics of metadata quality. Because we are interested in qualities that are domain-independent, they are necessarily abstract. One might think of these characteristics as places to look for quality in collection-specific schemas and implementations, rather than as checklists or quantitative systems suitable for direct application. Recognizing that most metadata projects operate under serious resource constraints, our approach is pragmatic and managerial rather than idealistic. Too often, implementers fall into the trap of bipolar thinking, making the perfect the enemy of the good. Realistic approaches balance metadata functionality against applicable constraints to deliver maximum utility from valuable assets: the willingness of data providers, the data itself, and the effort and expense budgeted for metadata creation, organization, and review.

The categorization of quality measures that we use here was suggested in part by the Quality Assurance Framework (QAF) for statistical data developed by Statistics Canada (STC) and subsequently applied to metadata assessment by Paul Johanis.[8] The original STC QAF described six dimensions of information quality: relevance, accuracy, timeliness, accessibility, interpretability, and coherence. We have reconceived these in a way that is better adapted to the growing number of large-scale projects in which metadata from multiple source providers is aggregated into a unified metadata resource. However, the considerations outlined below are relevant in any setting where metadata is shared. We will examine seven of the most commonly recognized characteristics of quality metadata: completeness, accuracy, provenance, conformance to expectations, logical consistency and coherence, timeliness, and accessibility.

Completeness

Metadata should be complete in two senses. First, the element set used should describe the target objects as completely as economically feasible. It is almost always possible to imagine describing things in more detail, but it is not always possible to afford the preparation and maintenance of more detailed information. Second, the element set should be applied to the target object population as completely as possible; it does little good to prescribe a particular element set if most of the elements are never used, or if their use cannot be relied upon across the entire collection.

Accuracy

Metadata should be accurate in the way it describes objects, a uniquely uncontroversial statement that houses platoons of devils. Minimally, the information provided in the values needs to be correct and factual. At the next level, accuracy is simply high-quality editing: the elimination of typographical errors, conforming expression of personal names and place names, use of standard abbreviations, and so on.[9] In large or heterogeneous collections, accuracy may not be directly verifiable; sampling techniques, statistical profiles, or other alternatives to laborious inspection may be needed.[10]

Provenance

The provenance of metadata often provides a useful basis for quality judgments. Sometimes this is a matter of knowing who prepared the metadata, how experienced they might be, how good their judgment is, or of having some sense of their expertise in the relevant domain and with metadata standards generally. We may also rely on well-understood or certified methodologies as proxies that ensure reliability and quality. Scientists and statisticians are quite at home making judgments about the quality of data based on the methods used to create and handle it. This is particularly true in situations where individual items cannot be directly verified. However, the use of creation and handling methodology as a guarantor of quality is not limited to the sciences; all sorts of content standards and best practice guides exist, the Anglo-American Cataloguing Rules (AACR2) not least among them.[11]

Information about creation is just the starting point of provenance. One should also know what transformations have been applied to the data since it was created. Metadata may come second- or third-hand, and beyond knowing who made it, how it was made, and where it has been, it is useful to know whether value has been added or subtracted since its creation.

Conformance to Expectations

Standard metadata element sets and application profiles that use them are promises from the metadata provider to the user. Moreover, they are promises surrounded by the expectations of a particular community about what such promises mean, how realistic they are, and how they are to be carried out.

Element sets and application profiles should, in general, contain those elements that the community would reasonably expect to find. They should not contain false promises, i.e., elements that are not likely to be used because they are superfluous, irrelevant, or impossible to implement. Controlled vocabularies should be chosen with the needs of the intended audience in mind, and explicitly exposed to downstream users. Sometimes problems with conformance to expectations appear in disguise. Moen et al. correctly point out that problems with omitted metadata frequently occur because users see the particular element as irrelevant or unnecessary, so that what appears at first blush to be a completeness problem is in fact a problem with conformance to expectations.[12]

Finally, metadata choices need to reflect community thinking and expectations about necessary compromises in implementation. It is seldom possible for a metadata project to implement everything that anyone would want; most often, the metadata provider cannot afford to make a project unimpeachable by making it comprehensive. It is therefore important that community expectations be solicited, considered, and managed realistically. Better an agreed-upon compromise that is well executed and documented than an approach that aspires to be all things to all people and ends up poorly and unevenly implemented.

Logical Consistency and Coherence

Consistency and coherence are usually seen as problems only for heterogeneous, federated collections, or perhaps for single collections that are presented in successive "releases" over time. But in fact, very few collections exist in isolation, even at their inception. There is almost always a need to ensure that elements are conceived in a way that is consistent with standard definitions and concepts used in the subject or related domains and are presented to the user in consistent ways.

The use of standard mechanisms like application profiles and common crosswalks enhances the ability of downstream users to assess the intended level of coherence. Standard mechanisms create a track record of intent over time, thus enabling metadata implementers to make comparisons between instantiations easier.

The quality of "searchability" nicely illustrates the value of consistency. Users expect to be able to search collections of similar objects using similar criteria, and increasingly they expect search results and indicative indexes to have similar structures and appearance.[13] This common, reliable user experience depends crucially on metadata being coherent and consistently presented across collections.

Barton et al. describe an interesting and dysfunctional variation on a notion we might term "overcoherence" or "false coherence."[14] It is really a problem with accuracy. In this scenario, the same metadata records are applied inappropriately to multiple components of an object or objects, as if by rote. Similarly, the same study cited by Barton found problems with overreliance on software-supplied default values for some elements.

Timeliness

We use two different terms to refer to two different aspects of metadata timeliness: "currency" and "lag." "Currency" problems occur when the target object changes but the metadata does not. "Lag" problems occur when the target object is disseminated before some or all of the metadata is knowable or available.

CURRENCY

Stale Uniform Resource Identifiers (URIs) are poster children for problems with metadata currency, but almost any element or value can, in time, become detached from its original target or purpose. Information objects move around, whether on shelves, websites, or conceptual maps of an intellectual discipline. Metadata loses quality over time if it loses synchronization with those movements. Beyond knowing that the metadata is in synchronization with its target object, it is important that the synchronization itself has been recently reviewed and verified. This underscores a recurring theme in our analysis: high-quality practices are those that not only accurately describe target objects but also enhance user confidence in the description.

LAG

The dissemination of metadata is not necessarily synchronized with the dissemination of the object to which it applies. New objects take time to describe, categorize, and catalog, particularly if human judgment is involved. The problems thus created become particularly acute if the item being described must be disseminated quickly, leaving metadata lagging behind.

The official citation of judicial opinions provides an instructive if horrifying example. In many jurisdictions, official citation is derived from the page numbers of a printed volume, and hence must wait for the appearance of the volume. In the case of the federal appellate courts in the United States, this can take as long as eighteen months from the time the opinion is originally handed down. Many public archives on the Internet never revisit the issue, leaving opinions accessible but without official citation.

TIMELINESS AS AN ARENA FOR CULTURAL DIFFERENCES

The aging of metadata presents obvious problems in the form of potentially broken URIs, drifting controlled vocabularies, and evolving, sometimes divergent, conceptual maps of the underlying corpus. These are problems that are easy to grasp, though not necessarily easy to solve, given cultural differences among collection developers and maintainers. There are subtle difficulties rooted in the deeply embedded and divergent expectations that library and computing communities have about audiences; the permanence or persistence of metadata design decisions; and the stability of technology. The cataloging of printed materials is generally done with the expectation that metadata creation is a one-time proposition. Library catalog records are seldom revisited, and new views of metadata are seldom created unless there is great economic or political incentive to do so. As an example, one need only look at the techniques developed by libraries to avoid costly updates to authority records, e:g., personal name headings, when established authors die. Current practice is to add the death date and source of information to the body of the name authority record, rather than the heading (even when a birth date is already present), so as to avoid the necessity of updating existing catalog records with a new heading with death date.

By contrast, computer technologists come from a world in which techniques are continually changing and often improving. This encourages a more experimental, iterative approach to metadata extraction and other machine-processing efforts. In addition, the more fluid view of metadata offered by searchable and dynamic databases makes audience customization seemingly more attainable. Unfortunately, this group has been slow to recognize and accommodate practical and efficient updating techniques. As an example, the OAI Protocol for Metadata Harvesting originally proposed a definition of a metadata record "update" that would have required harvesters to unnecessarily replace records in their systems for changes that affected only the administrative portions of the metadata record.

Neither the library nor the computer technology approach is necessarily better. The point is that different members of a project team will approach data-aging issues with different biases. Some will be inclined toward a "do it once right and forget about it" approach, dismissing iterative approaches as impractical. On the other hand, there are others who will take an exclusively iterative approach, dismissing front-loaded strategies as unnecessarily expensive and time-consuming. It may then be useful to ask not only what yields the most utility for the user, but what yields the most utility for the user the soonest, and what yields the most robust utility over the long term. Balance between these competing concerns is needed.

Accessibility

Metadata that cannot be read or understood by users has no value. The obstacles may be physical or they may be intellectual. Barriers to physical access come in several forms. Metadata may not be readily associated with the target objects, perhaps because it is physically separated, comes from a different source, or is not properly keyed or linked to the object being described. Or it may be unreadable for a wide variety of technical reasons, including the use of obsolete, unusual, or proprietary file formats that can only be read with special equipment or software. In some cases, metadata is considered as "premium" information that is accessible only at extra cost to the user, or as proprietary information that is not released publicly at all, often because it represents a competitive advantage that the creator or publisher wishes to retain. In other words, the barriers may be economic or trade-related rather than technical or organizational.

It is hard to reduce or eliminate barriers to intellectual access in a world where both objects and metadata are used by multiple audiences and the extent of dissemination is unpredictable. Controlled vocabularies are particularly difficult in this respect. While systems such as the West key-number system for classifying legal materials provide excellent, fine-grained organization for experts, they are of little value to those whose perspective is different—for example, hospital administrators interested in public-benefits law. There is a need to offer different views or arrangements of metadata to meet the expectations and needs of diverse audiences.

Although metadata providers are powerless to force an understanding of any particular element or set of elements on the user, some intellectual barriers can be lowered by the careful consideration of potentially diverse audiences when designing and documenting metadata implementations. Above all, one needs to avoid the notion that concise and formal expressions of metadata structure are sufficient documentation in and of themselves. Extensible Markup Language (XML) schemas do not convey thinking or intentions. For proper intellectual access, there needs to be more, in the form of practice guides and other similarly rich forms of documentation.

It is natural to ask which of the seven dimensions described previously is most important, or which most urgently needs to be present for a particular project. Where and how should we begin to foster quality? We believe that the ways in which one might prioritize these various criteria are far from uniform, and are dictated by the nature of the objects to be described; whether the implementer is a source provider or an aggregator; and perhaps most importantly, by how the metadata is to be constructed or derived. Three familiar scenarios illustrate the diversity of options for metadata creation: a collection using author self-submission as the principal means of collecting both data and metadata; a project relying heavily on human judgment to create classificatory metadata; and a project using automated text-extraction techniques to pull metadata from a text corpus.

Each of these methods will have different ways of achieving high-quality results. Assuming a relatively stable corpus (a sometimes dangerous but reasonable assumption), a computer program that extracts metadata will produce absolutely consistent results over an indefinite period of time, where a churning pool of student employees assigned to a markup project will not. A project where one person classifies information can make some assumptions about coherence and accuracy that a project relying on voluntary submissions cannot. A project that makes use of topical classification only as a means of creating rough boundaries for full-text search or a current-awareness service will not be as concerned about accurate classification as a project that is intended to produce a fine-grained taxonomic survey of a large body of literature.

DEFINING LEVELS OF QUALITY FOR METADATA

Any definition of quality must address attributes of the metadata at several levels: the semantic structure (sometimes called the "format" or "element set"), the syntactic structure (including the administrative wrapper, generally expressed via a "schema"), and the data values themselves. All of these can be validated to some extent by automated means.

For the purposes of this chapter, the term "element set" will be used for metadata semantics instead of "format" or "schema," while "schema" will be used for syntax and syntactic binding. We recognize that "schema" is often used as a more general term referring to both areas, but such use in this context would create unhelpful confusion.

As a practical matter, we begin with the notion that automated metadata validation or evaluation is usually cheaper than human validation. Automated techniques potentially enable humans to use their time to make more sophisticated assessments. Cost-effective machine-based techniques represent "the least we can do" to ensure metadata quality, possibly with more expensive human techniques following on.

We might define a "first tier" of quality indicators as:

the ability to validate the schema—implying that there is some defined schema, whether XML or some other syntax, that can be checked for validation by programmatic means

the use of appropriate namespace declarations—each data element present must be defined within a specified namespace, which may or may not be machine-readable

the presence of an administrative "wrapper" containing basic provenance (metadata identifier, source, and date)—each metadata record so described should carry an identifier that serves to specify it uniquely. In addition, information about the source of the metadata and the date it was created or modified should be present.

Beyond these basics, we might assert that the quality of metadata is improved by the presence of the following (noting that "presence" is something that can often be confirmed by automated means):

> controlled vocabularies, expressed by means of unique tokens linked to publicly available sources of terms, such as Internet Mime Types
>
> elements defined by a specific community as important to discovery of that community's resources, as defined by a publicly available application profile
>
> a full complement of general elements relevant to general discovery, independent of any particular community, and free of assumptions about who will be using the metadata. The five ubiquitous elements identified by Ward probably define an effective minimum for primarily textual objects.[15]
>
> provenance information at a more detailed level, including (in addition to source, date, and identifier) information about the methodology used in the creation of the metadata

Beyond this point, it is less likely that quality determinations can be made by automated means. But the following are nevertheless useful quality indicators:

> an expression of metadata intentions based on an explicit, documented application profile, endorsed by a specialized community, and registered in conformance to a general metadata standard
>
> a source of trusted data with a known history of regularly updating metadata, including controlled vocabularies. This includes explicit conformance with current standards and schemas.
>
> full provenance information, including nested information, as original metadata is harvested, augmented, and reexposed. This may not record changes at the element level, but should reference practice documentation that describes augmentation and upgrade routines of particular aggregators.

Applying this system of tiered quality indicators to the seven criteria explained earlier yields the chart in table 15-1. It is not meant to be a comprehensive procedural checklist or an all-embracing list of indicators. Rather, it is a series of suggested questions that the project manager seeking to create (or assess) quality practices might ask, as well as some indicators he or she might use to answer them. We emphasize approaches and tools that we have found useful, particularly use of "visual view" (graphical analysis software) described in Dushay and Hillmann.[16] We expect that those with different experiences will undoubtedly suggest other approaches.

TABLE 15-1   Quality: What to ask for and where to look

Quality Measure	Quality Criteria	Compliance Indicators
Completeness	Does the element set completely describe the objects?	Application profile; documentation
	Are all relevant elements used for each object?	Visual view;* sample
Provenance	Who is responsible for creating, extracting, or transforming the metadata?	OAI server info,† File info, TEI Header‡
	How was the metadata created or extracted?	OAI Provenance; colophon or file description
	What transformations have been done on the data since its creation?	OAI About
Accuracy	Have accepted methods been used for creation or extraction?	OAI About; documentation
	What has been done to ensure valid values and structure?	OAI About; visual view; sample; knowledge of source provider practices; documentation for creator-provided metadata; known-item search tests
	Are default values appropriate, and have they been appropriately used?	Known-item search tests; visual view

TABLE 15-1   continued

Quality Measure	Quality Criteria	Compliance Indicators
Conformance to expectations	Does metadata describe what it claims to?	Visual view; external documentation; high ratio of populated elements per record
	Are controlled vocabularies aligned with audience characteristics and understanding of the objects?	Visual view, sample, documentation; expert review
	Are compromises documented and in line with community expectations?	Documentation; user assessment studies
Logical consistency and coherence	Is data in elements consistent throughout?	Visual view
	How does it compare with other data within the community?	Research or knowledge of other community data; documentation
Timeliness	Is metadata regularly updated as the resources change?	Sample or date sort of administrative information
	Are controlled vocabularies updated when relevant?	Test against known changes in relevant vocabularies
Accessibility	Is an appropriate element set for audience and community being used?	Research or knowledge of other community data; documentation
	Is it affordable to use and maintain?	Experience of other implementers; evidence of licensing or other costs
	Does it permit further value-adds?	Standard format; extensible schema

* By "visual view" we mean the process of evaluating metadata using visual graphical analysis tools, as described in the Dushay and Hillmann paper cited earlier.

† Open Archives Initiative (home page).

‡ Text Encoding Initiative (home page), http://www.tei-c.org/ (accessed 28 July 2003).

IMPROVING METADATA QUALITY
IN THE SHORT AND LONG TERM

Better documentation at several levels has long been at the top of metadata practitioners' wish list. The first and most general improvement is in the application of standards. Basic standards documents should be accompanied by best practice guidelines and examples. Though such documentation has been prescribed and described many times over, volunteer documentarians remain few. Most projects do not budget documentation for internal purposes, much less donate time for their staff to create such services for the community at large. Furthermore, many do not expose their internal practices and materials for the use of others. Until this support is forthcoming, and is seen as necessary and rewarding (and perhaps remunerated) work, it will never be as readily available as all agree it should be.

Better documentation and exposure of local vocabularies used by specialist communities would greatly enhance the willingness of implementers to use them in metadata. Support should include making a vocabulary available in a number of ways, perhaps as harvestable files or via a web interface. In addition, a community process for updating and maintenance must be supported. Admittedly, the withering away of the market for printed products and the lack of effective business models for web-accessible vocabularies has led to a fear of revenue loss; this in turn has limited the availability of machine-readable vocabulary files for purposes of quality assurance.

Application profiles are just beginning to emerge as the preferred method for specialized communities to interact with the general metadata world. Application profiles, which by their nature are models created by community consensus, demand a level of documentation of practice that is rarely attempted by individual projects or implementers. Because they mix general and specific metadata elements, they also provide an alternative to the proliferation of metadata standards that reuse the same general concepts with definitions different enough to undermine interoperability.

As critical as documentation is to improving overall quality, cultural change may be even more critical. We must encourage the growth of an implementer and aggregator culture that not only supports better documentation practices, but also sees the dissemination of training, tools, methodologies, and research results as essential. In the library world, the Library of Congress has spurred efforts in this area, but there is no single organization that can take on this role for the galaxy of specialist communities that could benefit from such leadership. Like the data itself, leadership in the non-library metadata communities is likely to be distributed. Marshaling these organizations and their members to contribute time, server space, technical expertise, and training materials—for the general good rather than the good of a particular group—is a significant challenge. There are already some recognized ways to channel this sort of effort—the Dublin Core Metadata Initiative, OAI, and other metadata and technical standards communities offer many opportunities for interested and experienced volunteers, as well as the technical infrastructure for the distribution of tools, ideas, and research.

Another essential component to consider is more focused research on practical metadata use and the influence of quality on that use. One current project with a great deal of potential for supplying answers is the National Science Digital Library's MetaTest Project headed by Elizabeth Liddy at the Syracuse University School of Information Studies.[17] This project seeks to determine how and whether metadata can assist users in locating resources and to understand whether automatically generated metadata is as effective as manually generated metadata in assisting users. This research has the potential of moving the digital library community past the untested, sometimes dogmatic assumptions underlying current metadata discussions and toward a more solid understanding of the role of metadata in future implementations.

CONCLUSION

Another way in which metadata quality resembles pornography is that—as Susan Sontag once remarked—pornography is a theater of types, and not of individuals. It is difficult to come up with checklists of specific quality-assurance techniques that will apply across a wide range of domains, media types, and funding levels. This may be why we have not tried to do so here. But a playbill (or in our case, a chart) that describes the types is useful to project managers. It gives aggregators hints about where they might look for trouble in legacy and multiple-source data. It can serve as a point of departure for communities and for implementers as they develop standards and documentation, the two indicators of quality most often missing in action. The ubiquity of quality concerns is one sign that the metadata community is growing up. The ability to use generalized thinking across community boundaries as a touchstone for practical solutions will be the next.

NOTES

1. Jewel Hope Ward, "A Quantitative Analysis of Dublin Core Metadata Element Set Usage in Data Providers Registered with the Open Archives Initiative," paper presented at the Joint Conference on Digital Libraries, Houston, Texas, 27–31 May 2003, http://foar.net/research/mp/Jewel_Ward-MPaper November2002.pdf (accessed 28 July 2003).
2. Naomi Dushay and Diane I. Hillmann, "Analyzing Metadata for Effective Use and Re-Use," paper accepted for the 2003 Dublin Core Conference, Seattle, Wash., 28 September–2 October 2003, http://purl.oclc.org/dc2003/03dushay.pdf (accessed 28 July 2003). Dushay and Hillmann characterize their visual graphical analysis techniques as "being able to view the forest as well as the trees," an important component of effective evaluation of quality. The techniques rely on a combination of automated sorting and display combined with human analysis of graphical and textual output.
3. Jane Barton, Sarah Currier, and Jessie M. N. Hey, "Building Quality Assurance into Metadata Creation: An Analysis Based on the Learning Objects and e-Prints Communities of Practice," paper accepted for the 2003 Dublin Core Conference, Seattle, Wash., 28 September–2 October 2003, http://purl.oclc.org/ dc2003/03barton.pdf; William E. Moen, Erin L. Stewart, and Charles R. McClure, "The Role of Content Analysis in Evaluating Metadata for the U.S. Government Information Locator Service: Results from an Exploratory Study," http://www.unt.edu/ wmoen/publications/GILSMDContentAnalysis.htm (accessed 19 September 2003).
4. "In this paper we seek to challenge four of the assumptions which underlie both the absence of inquiry into how metadata should best be created, and the trend for authors of learning objects and e-Prints to create the metadata for their own resources" (Barton, Currier, and Hey, "Building Quality Assurance"). The authors go on to list those four assumptions, among them the idea "that given a standard metadata structure, metadata content can be generated or resolved by machine."
5. The Program for Cooperative Cataloging developed the BIBCO Core Record standards. Information on the standards is available at http://lcweb.loc.gov/ catdir/pcc/bibco/coreintro.html (accessed 28 July 2003).
6. Open Archives Initiative (home page), http://www.openarchives.org (accessed 28 July 2003).
7. IFLA Study Group on the Functional Requirements for Bibliographic Records, "Functional Requirements for Bibliographic Records," 1997, http://www .ifla.org/VII/s13/frbr/frbr.htm (accessed 28 July 2003).
8. *Statistics Canada's Quality Assurance Framework* (Ottawa: Statistics Canada, 2002), also available at http://www.statcan.ca/english/freepub/12-586-XIE/ 12-586-XIE02001.pdf (accessed 28 July 2003); Paul Johanis, "Assessing the Quality of Metadata: The Next Challenge," presentation for a Work Session on METIS, Luxembourg, 6–8 March 2002, http://www.unece.org/stats/ documents/2002/03/metis/19.add.2.e.pdf (accessed 28 July 2003).
9. Barton, reporting experience at the Higher Level Skills for Industry (HLSI) Repository, collects a rogue's gallery of defects in this category, including

spelling errors, inconsistent use of terminology, and confusion of content with structure (Barton, Currier, and Hey, "Building Quality Assurance").

10. Dushay and Hillmann, "Analyzing Metadata."
11. American Library Association, *Anglo-American Cataloguing Rules,* 2d ed., 1988 revision (Chicago: Canadian Library Association; Chartered Institute of Library and Information Professionals; American Library Association, 1988).
12. Moen, Stewart, and McClure, "Role of Content Analysis."
13. Moen, Stewart, and McClure discuss many of the same criteria we describe here under the heading of "serviceability," though the assessment methods used were very much from an end user perspective. For example, the "serviceability" assessment also comprehended accuracy problems like misspellings insofar as they interfered with users' ability to retrieve information.
14. Barton, at section 4.1, describing the findings of the HLSI project (Barton, Currier, and Hey, "Building Quality Assurance").
15. Ward, "Quantitative Analysis."
16. Dushay and Hillmann, "Analyzing Metadata."
17. Center for Natural Language Processing, "NSDL MetaTest," http://www .cnlp.org/research/project.asp?recid=21 (accessed 28 July 2003).

16

Metadata Futures: Steps toward Semantic Interoperability

Rachel Heery

DESIGNERS OF INFORMATION services face challenging decisions about metadata: they need to choose appropriate metadata formats, evaluate tools for managing metadata, and establish patterns of interworking with collaborating services. Service providers need to evaluate the impact that the evolution of metadata standards will have on their implementation. Is a particular technology or metadata specification ready for deployment? Are there tools available to enable the uptake of technologies, or is there a need to develop new tools? It is important to be aware of innovations on the horizon. Given the rapid change in technologies and service delivery channels, it is vital to try to future-proof investment in systems.

There is a continuous turnover in the range of initiatives exploring new and emerging metadata standards and protocols. Some of these standards and protocols persist, while others fade away or become marginalized. This environment of change means implementers are faced with complex criteria in the decision-making processes surrounding metadata. This applies especially to information services with a commitment to curation—typical within the library and cultural heritage world—where rapid technology change occurs in the context of curating existing collections of legacy data.

Designers of information services need to be aware of the opportunities offered by this environment of change and ensure that flexibility is there to exploit potential gains. Services need to be prepared for change, whether by introducing service enhancements based on extended metadata, incorporating new data structures, or interoperating with heterogeneous metadata formats. At some stage in this fluid metadata environment, services will almost certainly need to migrate to new metadata formats, merge metadata from different sources, or use existing metadata as the basis for new services areas.

This chapter will focus on a particular area of innovation: the Semantic Web, an environment in which software will be able to manipulate data made available over the Web. The ambitions of the Semantic Web resonate with the objectives of digital libraries, in that both are focused on the automated information exchange and build on common identification, compatible data models, and shared vocabularies. Implementers of digital library systems have questions regarding the Semantic Web; they need to judge when to deploy and what to deploy. This chapter will examine how implementers might take steps to future-proof their services by taking advantage of potential developments toward semantic interoperability.

UPTAKE OF NEW TECHNOLOGIES

The first consideration facing implementers is when to deploy emerging technology. Timing is always important in order to gain an advantage from technology. The corporate world is aware of the need to calculate the return on investment in technology. Although the library and education arena is less explicit about calculating technology investments, nevertheless the same kinds of judgments need to be made. These include calculating the cost-benefit of implementing new technologies, deciding whether the risks inherent in being an "early adopter" are acceptable, and balancing such risks against the potential costs of maintaining legacy systems.

As with other key decisions, those about metadata need to be based on organizational strategy. There is a tendency to consider metadata as a freestanding entity, but metadata does not exist in isolation; it is created, stored, and exchanged as the basis for systems and services. Choices about metadata need to be grounded in the wider perspective of the strategic aims of services. Furthermore, decisions about metadata need to take account of underlying business models, seeking a balance between functional requirements and available resources. These are the factors that will influence the level of innovation to which a service aspires. Within the digital library world, as elsewhere, implementers need to distinguish between metadata formats and technologies that are at "research level" and those at "production level." While a service that has ambitions to be innovative and experimental may risk basing its service on immature technology, a production service may well require an industry-strength solution.

Implementers are unlikely to have the luxury of being able to spend much time tracking new technology. In order to make judgments about a technology's "time to market," they will prefer to look to informed sources for information. Such sources can help implementers judge where in the "hype cycle" a particular technology is located. A variety of organizations now provide technology-watch services. Some of these services are aimed at particular communities (UKOLN, CETIS, JISC TechWatch) and some support regional enterprise (Diffuse).[1] Depending on the budget, advice is available from targeted information sources ranging from weblogs (Information Research) to newsletters (XML.com) to specialist technology market analysts (Gartner).[2]

As a first step, implementers face choices between available standards. However, the standards world is becoming ever more complex. Standards are fragmented; they are spread across industry standards and specifications, de facto standards, and traditional national and international standards. Multiple standards exist to fulfill overlapping requirements. For example, there is a choice between using Dublin Core and IEEE Learning Object Metadata (LOM) to describe learning objects, or a choice between using RDF/XML or XML (Extensible Markup Language) models for instance metadata.

In order to illustrate the decisions facing implementers, the focus will be on the deployment of Semantic Web technology, in particular the uptake of RDF/XML as a syntax for instance metadata. We will explore the benefits and disadvantages of implementing innovative technology, and consider the options for a gradual adoption and implementation of those aspects of Semantic Web technologies that would be particularly useful to digital libraries. We will argue that the gradual approach will assist in "future-proofing" implementations by enabling deliberate progress toward a semantically richer web environment.

PROMISE OF THE SEMANTIC WEB

The vision of the Semantic Web, as articulated by Tim Berners-Lee, offers great potential for services to add value through data aggregation and data exchange.[3] However, there has been little deployment of the enabling technology for the Semantic Web: the Resource Description Framework (RDF). As Berners-Lee notes, "To date, the Web has developed most rapidly as a medium of documents for people rather than for data and information that can be processed automatically. The Semantic Web aims to make up for this."[4]

This vision is built on an infrastructure of interoperable metadata, using a common data model and common syntax so that software can exchange and manipulate "unknown metadata." The Resource Description Framework provides the common data model for making statements about resources, and RDF/XML provides a means of expressing those statements in a common syntax.[5] This combination of model and syntax means that software can manipulate metadata without prior knowledge of the particular metadata element set in use.

The Resource Description Framework allows services to reuse existing RDF/XML metadata available on the Web or in accessible RDF-compliant databases. The potential gain is even greater if the service ingesting RDF instance metadata is also able to refer to associated schemas outlining the relationships between the classes and properties as used in the instance metadata. Through "understanding" the relationships between the data elements, schema-aware software can infer additional information about the resources described.

There still needs to be consensus on the use of identifiers to enable large-scale automated aggregation and reuse of metadata. In addition, agreement is needed on good practices for the types of identifiers appropriate for different sorts of digital objects, as well as agreement on the actual identifier used to name a digital object. A common approach to identification is required, ideally for all aspects of metadata. This would include identification of the resources being described (people, images, documents, or learning objects); the metadata elements (RDF properties); and terms in controlled vocabularies (values). A common policy on identification allows metadata referring to the same entities to be aggregated and, if associated schemas are available, allows inferences to be made across aggregated metadata.

Such data aggregation becomes a powerful means to provide enhanced information about resources, enabling the merging and augmentation of independently created metadata about the same resource. Determining whether this innovative technology is right for your own particular implementation is no simple matter. The following scenario illustrates some of the issues.

Scenario: A collaborating federation of Internet catalog services (subject gateways) holds collections of metadata describing high-quality web-based resources. A parallel federation of e-learning services is established to curate repositories of learning objects. The federations have built their services on different metadata formats, i.e., Dublin Core in one case and IEEE LOM in the other. There is an overlap in the collections from each federation in terms of the resources being described, subject matter, target audiences, and creators of the resources. Taking into account the benefits of aggregating metadata from both federations, and mindful of the likelihood of interworking with other services in the future, the federations decide to explore the use of RDF as a means to enhance interoperability. There is a recommended RDF version of Dublin Core available, and work is in progress on an RDF version of the IEEE LOM. However, the federations realize that reaching consensus on naming and identifying resources will require significant organizational commitment and effort. The learning repository federation decides to encourage progress in the provision of an RDF model for IEEE LOM by getting involved in that activity. Meanwhile, both federations meet to decide on common naming policies, initially aiming at a common approach to assigning Uniform Resource Identifiers (URIs) to both resources and people. The federations plan a pilot project based on a particular subject area to provide examples of metadata about related resource types that would be useful to aggregate. The pilot will allow the federations to demonstrate the benefits of a Semantic Web approach, and review these benefits against the investment required.

This scenario illustrates the level of commitment required to implement RDF in a meaningful way. It also suggests that there is value in implementing RDF within a closed group of collaborating institutions, or indeed within a single institution, both to evaluate benefits and to develop expertise in the technology. Such a "closed world" scenario makes reaching consensus on an identification policy feasible. Moreover, implementation within a relatively closed world helps demonstrate the benefits of RDF by ensuring it is used to describe collections with overlapping coverage of people, resources, or subject matter. Implementing complex solutions as "closed world projects" facilitates the evaluation of technology, which provides organizations with a learning opportunity while allowing proper positioning in relation to alternative technologies.

One project that is taking up the challenge of exploring Semantic Web technology, Semantic Interoperability of Metadata and Information in unLike Environments (SIMILE), aims to enhance and extend DSpace, a digital library system supporting institutional repositories.[6] Using RDF and Semantic Web techniques, SIMILE will enhance DSpace to support arbitrary schemas and metadata.[7] SIMILE's focus on using metadata from disparate sources is very much in parallel with the aims of most digital library initiatives.

As Tim Berners-Lee has commented, it is people who must make the additional effort to deliver semantic interoperability: "The concept of machine-understandable documents does not imply some magical artificial intelligence which allows machines to comprehend human mumblings. It only indicates a machine's ability to solve a well-defined problem by performing well-defined operations on existing well-defined data. Instead of asking machines to understand people's language, it involves asking people to make the extra effort."[8]

Certainly RDF offers potential for interoperability, but there are disadvantages to using it. Critics of the recommended RDF/XML syntax argue that it is verbose and difficult for a human to write and interpret. In addition, although RDF/XML uses XML, it does not work easily with XML tools. Such disadvantages mean that many developers find RDF/XML unattractive and difficult to use, leading to resistance to uptake despite the potential advantages.[9]

However, the close alignment of the digital library and Semantic Web agendas is compelling. Semantic interoperability has been a goal of digital library initiatives for the last ten years. Certainly the objectives of RDF are worthy, but is this the right time to deploy it? It is worthwhile considering whether your organization's strategy fits with the role of an early adopter. Some questions that might inform the decision are:

Is innovation central to the strategy of your organization?

Are there tangible benefits that can be demonstrated?

Is there some underlying commonality between datasets that might be aggregated?

Do you have staff enthused by new technology?

Do you have staff with the expertise to build tools based on immature technology?

Does your organization want to contribute to standards-making activity?

Do you have an ambition to take a technology lead in your community?

Can you risk being left behind?

Will your uptake of RDF facilitate interactions with existing and potential partners?

If the answer to at least some of these questions is "yes," then your decision might be to introduce new technologies in a discrete area of work. If the answer is "no," but you still see the advantages of the Semantic Web, and judge that perhaps with some changes to the technology it will reach wide-scale deployment, then how can you future-proof your implementation? One option is to work toward semantic interoperability by following a number of "semantically informed" approaches: using URIs (Uniform Resource Identifiers) to identify resources, sharing and reusing metadata vocabularies, and instituting collaborative models for sharing instance metadata. These are approaches that fit well with both the vision of the Semantic Web and the interests of digital libraries. Such a graduated adoption of semantically informed developments would contribute toward semantic interoperability, enabling exploration without overcommitment.

NAMING RESOURCES WITH URI'S

The identification of resources, metadata elements, and controlled vocabulary terms is fundamental to establishing the infrastructure for the Semantic Web. Librarians too have an interest in "naming" and identification, both as resources being described and as metadata elements used in resource description. In addition, the library world has made large investments in knowledge organization systems, and has an ongoing interest in leveraging these systems within the context of the Semantic Web.

The World Wide Web Consortium recommends that URIs should be assigned to each resource that is intended to be identified, shared, or described by the reference.[10] A URI is defined as "a compact string of characters for identifying an abstract or physical resource."[11] The Semantic Web builds on the use of URIs as identifiers for resources (entities being described), metadata elements, and terms in knowledge organization systems (controlled vocabularies, thesauri, classification schemes). All need to be unambiguously identified using a URI of some kind.

Within the web community, among RDF and XML developers, good practices regarding the allocation of URIs are still evolving. It is still a matter of debate as to what type of URI should be used for various identification purposes. For example, with regard to metadata elements, there is benefit in using "HTTP URIs" (web-addressable resource locators) for identification, since these URLs might be used to access information on the Web about the metadata element. Such information might be a web page or a machine-processable schema. However, others prefer the use of URIs that are not resolvable to information about the metadata element, reasoning that the primary purpose of the URI is identification rather than resolution or retrieval.

Other areas of complexity remain regarding identification. How should identifiers distinguish between web pages as representations of resources, as opposed to web pages as resources in their own right? How might identifiers be best used to distinguish multiple manifestations of one work? These particular issues are considered within IFLA's Functional Requirements for Bibliographic Records, and the distinction of separate entities within that specification for *the work* (a distinct intellectual or artistic creation); *the expression* (the intellectual or artistic realization of a work); *the manifestation* (the physical embodiment of an expression of a work); and *the item* (a single exemplar of a manifestation) might well inform practice regarding the use of URIs.[12] This is an area where detailed analysis within the bibliographic world can inform practice within web technology.

Already some commitment to assigning URIs to metadata elements has been made by a number of standards maintenance agencies. The CORES project brought together several major standardization groups to explore the use of metadata element identifiers and, as a first step, several have signed the CORES Resolution.[13] The signatories of this resolution agree to define URI assignment mechanisms, to assign URIs to data elements, and to formulate policies for the persistence of those URIs.

Standards bodies that have agreed to identify their data elements using URIs include GILS, ONIX, MARC 21, UNIMARC, CERIF, DOI, IEEE LOM, and DCMI (Dublin Core Metadata Initiative).

Achieving widespread deployment of URI identification within instance metadata to the level and scale envisaged by the Semantic Web vision may well prove an arduous task with slow results. In the meantime, the use of URIs can facilitate the representation of metadata element sets and application profiles, whether within human-readable documention or within machine-readable schema registries. Metadata elements to which a URI has been officially assigned can be unambiguously cited by means of that URI. For example, the DCMI Application Profile Guidelines recommend that the metadata element "Audience" should be cited as http://purl .org/dc/terms/audience.[14] The precision of citing metadata elements in this way goes some way to avoid the unnecessary reinvention of properties with the same semantics in different element sets and application profiles.

SHARING APPLICATION PROFILES

There is currently significant and widespread effort spent in formulating metadata schemas for new projects and services. As the number of metadata standards increases, it is becoming more difficult to locate an appropriate standard for one's implementation. Finding information about existing element sets is a time-consuming, intensive activity often involving both computer and information professionals. Increasingly, local extensions and variants to metadata standards are appearing in order to accommodate domain-specific requirements. These locally defined element sets, consisting of subsets of existing standards, sometimes with extensions, can be described as "application profiles." Finding information about such application profiles can be even more difficult. While standard element sets are often documented on the Web, application profiles typically are not.

Methods for facilitating the process of schema selection and creation would be welcome, saving considerable effort, while at the same time encouraging the reuse of existing data elements. Interoperability is supported when existing element sets and application profiles are reused, avoiding the unnecessary proliferation of local "novel" metadata elements. In order to accomplish such reuse there needs to be consensus on the structured expression of application profiles. Machine-readable expression is the long-term goal, but the first step is documentation of application profiles in human-readable form. Recommendations have been drawn up for documenting Dublin Core application profiles, an important first step toward reaching consensus on a machine-readable format in the future. The recommendations are looking toward the future, while acknowledging that at present application profiles "are designed to document metadata usage in a normalized form that will lend itself to translation into common models, such as RDF, that can be processed by machines to automate such interoperability."[15]

Another, more elusive, goal is to reach consensus on a common data model for the various metadata standards that have overlapping semantics and domain areas. Agreement on such a model would make the vision of "mixing and matching" metadata elements more meaningful.[16] The IEEE LOM and DCMI communities are now collaborating under the auspices of the DC Architecture Working Group to define data models for their respective metadata standards, which may go some way toward bridging the gaps to reach a common data model.

Both the declaration of application profiles and agreement on common data models will support the development of metadata schema registries. The vision is of a network of metadata schema registries enabling human and machine navigation across representations of registered element sets and application profiles. Additional "added value services" might be offered by such registries, such as mapping between metadata schemas and providing information about the usage of data elements and versioning history.

Various registry initiatives have emerged in recent years, building on the ISO/IEC 11179 series of standards for registration of data elements.[17] One strand of research has focused on modeling application profiles (DESIRE, SCHEMAS, MEG), and has led to the development of registry software for declaring both element sets and application profiles.[18] The most recent MEG (Metadata for Education Group) demonstrator, an RDF application, offers a web interface for humans to use, enabling navigation by browsing and searching registered schemas.[19] In addition, simple APIs (application program interfaces) are available for machine-to-machine querying of the registry. A schema-creation tool is provided to assist implementers to build their own application profiles by reusing existing registered element sets and application profiles.

Metadata schema registries might take different forms, whether providing:

the management of schemas within a corporate setting

an authoritative source for a particular standard such as the DCMI Registry[20]

a repository of schemas (both element sets and application profiles) relevant to a particular sector or domain, such as the demonstrator MEG registry

a mapping and crosswalk registry, as explored within the DESIRE project

As well as savings in effort, the benefits of such schema registries would be promotion of existing solutions and harmonization between "competing" standards. This in turn would lead to increased interoperability between metadata schemas as more metadata elements are reused.

SHARING METADATA

The reuse of existing metadata assists in the convergence of semantics and identification, due to an expected decrease in localized variant metadata. Little attention has been given to ensuring that the creation of metadata records (instance metadata) is carried out in an efficient and cost-effective manner. The creation of metadata records is undertaken by specialist staff, often subject experts, or information professionals. Collaborative cataloging based on metadata sharing is one approach to the more effective creation of metadata.

In the past, libraries have established collaborative cataloging networks supported by the MARC standard and cataloging rules. Cooperative library cataloging systems, whether regional or product-based, have been the dominant business model for the supply of traditional catalog records, achieving considerable cost savings and efficiencies for libraries. As many digital library services move from project status to production service, it is worthwhile to compare the workflow for metadata creation with the established supply chain for traditional catalog records.

Implementation of the Open Archives Initiative Protocol for Metadata Harvesting (OAI-PMH) has led to the setting-up of large-scale metadata repositories, not unlike traditional union catalogs. The existence of such repositories adds further impetus to some form of cooperation regarding the creation of metadata records. The traditional supply model for cataloging records among libraries has demonstrated that this can become a cyclical process. Bibliographic utilities enhance records with additional metadata (by adding additional fields, by applying authority control, by adding further classification or subject-rich description). Enhancement might be achieved by algorithms that enable a "rich record" to be built up from a simpler one. Processing can also strip records of redundant or low-quality data. The challenge facing new service providers is to do this in an automated way. One can envisage metadata supply utilities automatically enhancing metadata and, in their turn, making this improved metadata available to information service providers.

As the management of metadata workflow matures, metadata sharing may occur at various stages in the "metadata life cycle." Points of reuse might be the supply of records from large-scale metadata repositories, offering enhanced metadata or conversion services to a different metadata format; or smaller-scale metadata exchange between like-minded cooperating services. More challenging, but of significant interest, is the exploitation of current peer-to-peer technologies such as Edutella to automatically link different metadata instances associated with the same resource.[21]

Simple reuse of unenhanced instance metadata requires the least technological input, and is straightforward organizationally. Capturing the added value of metadata enhancement is more challenging but potentially important, as it offers the possibility of passing on the added value of effort expended on metadata creation to third parties. However, adding enhancements to a metadata record using added-value services would require a "hospitable" metadata format that facilitates building up a record from a simple to a "richer" record. It is questionable whether the Dublin Core Metadata Element Set is sufficiently structured to allow this, and it might be that metadata formats such as the Metadata Encoding and Transmission Standard, which are based on "wrapping" different metadata descriptions together, offer a better solution. And yet perhaps the RDF model would provide the means for serving up on request either a "simple" or "rich" record depending on the requirement, using merged properties and resource identifiers, without the need to store duplicate records.

The enhancement of metadata by means of added-value services does raise issues regarding intellectual property rights, provenance, and licensing. An incremental approach toward collaborative business models might lead to growth in complex administrative metadata to track the ownership of particular data elements and values within the record. This would not only be a cumbersome approach but would also be difficult to police. More complex organizational agreements might be required to recognize multiple assignments of ownership in the metadata. This is an area where it might well be possible to build on the experience of collaborative business models within the library world.

CONCLUSION

For any major technological innovation there is clearly a range of related developments that can be viewed as enabling technologies. The primary focus of Semantic Web deployment (or lack thereof) has been on RDF syntax within instance metadata. However, the other "semantically aware" options explored in this chapter can be viewed as contributing to progress toward a Semantic Web. There are a number of steps that services and projects can consider now which, though falling short of the use of RDF in instance metadata, will enable services to exploit innovations of the Semantic Web: steps such as allocating URIs for identification, declaring and sharing element sets and application profiles, and establishing methods of collaborative metadata creation. These steps will benefit interoperability, while enabling implementations to familiarize themselves with some of the issues related to the use of RDF.

A similar story might be constructed for the relationship between digital libraries and other new technologies, such as the web services architecture. Digital libraries might well consider the wide-scale uptake of web services architecture as unrealistic. However, there are a number of projects now evaluating the use of particular distributed infrastructural services as part of their metadata workflow. For example, the ePrints UK project is collaborating with OCLC Research whereby remote OCLC services would apply authority file control and automated classification to a collection of metadata harvested from British institutional repositories.[22]

The Semantic Web activity concentrates on building interoperability into a technical infrastructure. The library world has an interest in technology too, but also draws on a tradition of collaboration, exchange, and consensus. As we have seen, the deployment of technology to support the Semantic Web is challenging and may be beyond the immediate ambition of digital library implementers. However, by bringing the strength of organizational collaboration and consensus building to technology, we would argue that the digital library world can combine use of the Semantic Web approaches with collaborative and cooperative working agreements. Where "high-tech" solutions are too difficult, libraries are in a good position to provide "low-tech" alternatives supported by interworking at the organizational level.

The various approaches to "partial implementation" of the Semantic Web as outlined in this chapter show how digital libraries can position themselves to exploit potential gains from this emerging technology. Strategic exploitation of key features of the Semantic Web provides a means to future-proof one's system, so as not to be left behind by advances toward a semantically informed Web.

What is perhaps the most striking aspect of the Semantic Web for the library community is the commonality between traditional information management and library interests (constructing vocabularies, describing properties of resources, identifying resources, exchanging and aggregating metadata) and the concerns that are driving the development of Semantic Web technologies.

NOTES

1. UKOLN (home page), http://www.ukoln.ac.uk/ (accessed 16 December 2003); CETIS (home page), http://www.cetis.ac.uk/ (accessed 16 December 2003); Techwatch: Technology and Standards Watch (home page), http://www.jisc.ac.uk/index.cfm?name=techwatch_home (accessed 16 December 2003); Diffuse, "About Diffuse," http://www.diffuse.org/diffuse.html (accessed 16 December 2003).
2. Information Research weblog, http://www.free-conversant.com/irweblog/209 (accessed 16 December 2003); O'Reilly XML.com (home page), http://xml.com/ (accessed 16 December 2003); Gartner (home page), http://www.gartner.com/ (accessed 16 December 2003).
3. Tim Berners-Lee, "The Semantic Web," *Scientific American* (May 2001), 34–43, also available at http://www.sciam.com/article.cfm?articleID=00048144-10D2-1C70-84A9809EC588EF21&pageNumber=2&catID=2 (accessed 16 December 2003).
4. Berners-Lee, "Semantic Web."
5. Dave Beckett, ed., "RDF/XML Syntax Specification (Revised)," World Wide Web Consortium (W3C), October 2003, http://www.w3.org/TR/rdf-syntax-grammar/ (accessed 3 December 2003).
6. Semantic Interoperability of Metadata and Information in unLike Environments (home page), http://web.mit.edu/simile/www/ (accessed 15 December 2003); DSpace Federation (home page), http://www.dspace.org/ (accessed 15 December 2003).

7. Mick Bass and Mark H. Butler, "Introduction to SIMILE," http://web.mit.edu/simile/www/documents/introduction/introduction.html (accessed 16 December 2003).

8. Tim Berners-Lee, "What the Semantic Web Can Represent," September 1998, http://www.w3.org/DesignIssues/RDFnot.html (accessed 16 December 2003).

9. T. Bray, "The RDF.net Challenge," in Ongoing weblog, 2003, http://www.tbray.org/ongoing/When/200x/2003/05/21/RDFNet (accessed 16 December 2003).

10. Ian Jacobs, ed., "Architecture of the World Wide Web, First Edition," World Wide Web Consortium (W3C), October 2003, http://www.w3.org/TR/webarch/ (accessed 3 December 2003).

11. Tim Berners-Lee, Roy Fielding, and Larry Masinter, "Uniform Resource Identifiers: Generic Syntax," August 1998, http://www.ietf.org/rfc/rfc2396.txt (accessed 16 December 2003).

12. IFLA Study Group on the Functional Requirements for Bibliographic Records, "Functional Requirements for Bibliographic Records," http://www.ifla.org/VII/s13/frbr/frbr.pdf (accessed 16 December 2003).

13. Thomas Baker and Makx Dekkers, "Identifying Metadata Elements with URIs: The CORES Resolution," *D-Lib Magazine*, July/August 2003, www.dlib.org/dlib/july03/baker/07baker.html (accessed 16 December 2003).

14. Thomas Baker et al., "Dublin Core Application Profile Guidelines," *CEN*, September 2003, ftp://ftp.cenorm.be/public/ws-mmi-dc/mmidc076.zip (accessed 16 December 2003).

15. Ibid., 19.

16. Rachel Heery and Manjula Patel, "Application Profiles: Mixing and Matching Metadata Schemas," *Ariadne* 25 (September 2000), http://www.ariadne.ac.uk/issue25/app-profiles/ (accessed 16 December 2003).

17. ISO/IEC 11179-3:2003, "Information Technology—Metadata Registries—Part 3: Registry Metamodel and Basic Attributes."

18. DESIRE Registry (index page), http://desire.ukoln.ac.uk/registry/index.php3 (accessed 16 December 2003); SCHEMAS (home page), http://www.schemas-forum.org/ (accessed 16 December 2003); MEG (home page), http://www.ukoln.ac.uk/metadata/education/ (accessed 16 December 2003).

19. Rachel Heery et al., "The MEG Registry and SCART: Complementary Tools for Creation, Discovery and Reuse of Metadata Schemas," in *Proceedings of the International Conference on Dublin Core and Metadata for e-Communities, 2002* (Florence: Florence University Press, 2002), 125–32, also available at http://www.bncf.net/dc2002/program/ft/paper14.pdf (accessed 16 December 2003).

20. Dublin Core Metadata Initiative, "Dublin Core Metadata Registry," http://www.dublincore.org/ (accessed 16 December 2003).

21. Project Edutella (home page), http://edutella.jxta.org/ (accessed 3 December 2003).

22. Ruth Martin, "ePrints UK: Developing a National e-Prints Archive," *Ariadne* 35 (March/April 2003), http://www.ariadne.ac.uk/issue35/martin/intro.html (accessed 16 December 2003).

CONTRIBUTORS

Edward Almasy is codirector of the Internet Scout Project at the University of Wisconsin-Madison. He has more than twenty years of industry software engineering and design experience, including fifteen years spent developing technology and applications for the Internet. His primary focus is on creating turnkey web-based software solutions for the digital library and research communities, with a recent emphasis on recommender systems and highly accessible user interface design.

Caroline Arms is a project manager in the Office of Strategic Initiatives at the Library of Congress. She previously acted as a technical coordinator for the Library of Congress/Ameritech National Digital Library Competition, integrating twenty-seven collections from other institutions into the American Memory project. Earlier in her career, she ran the Microcomputer and Media Center at the Falk Library of the Health Sciences at the University of Pittsburgh and was the first director of computing at the Amos Tuck School of Business Administration at Dartmouth College. In the late 1980s, she edited *Campus Networking Strategies* and *Campus Strategies for Libraries and Electronic Information.*

William Arms is professor of computer science and director of the information science program at Cornell University. His career has included a faculty position at the British Open University and head of computing at Dartmouth College and Carnegie Mellon University, where he was closely involved in the development of networked computing and the transition to personal computing. His current research interests are digital libraries and electronic publishing. He is the Cornell principal investigator for the core integration team of the NSF's National Science Digital Library.

Steven Bird is associate professor of computer science and software engineering at the University of Melbourne, Australia, and senior research associate at the Linguistic Data Consortium, University of Pennsylvania. After completing his doctoral research in computational linguistics at the University of Edinburgh, he conducted linguistic fieldwork on the languages of western Cameroon, published a dictionary, and helped develop several new writing systems. Later, at the University of Pennsylvania, he led a research and development team working on open-source software for linguistic annotation. Bird's current research interests include linguistic databases, human language technologies, and computational methods in linguistic fieldwork.

Liz Bishoff is vice president of digital collections and preservation services at OCLC and the owner of the Bishoff Group. She was previously the executive director of the Colorado Digitization Program (CDP). Bishoff has been the project manager on three major Institute for Museum and Library Services grants and three Colorado Library Services and Technology Act grants, as well as a series of smaller grants that support the CDP initiatives. She chaired the Western States Dublin Core Best Practices Metadata Working Groups, which were responsible for development of the Western States Dublin Core Best Practices document. Bishoff has served as project consultant on many statewide digitization initiatives and has published many articles and made numerous presentations related to her areas of interest, most recently on creating digital libraries, standards, and museum-library collaboration. She holds a master's degree in library science from Rosary College.

Rachael Bower is codirector of the Internet Scout Project, a research and development center in the Department of Computer Sciences at the University of Wisconsin-Madison. Her primary research interests involve projects that ultimately deliver high-quality web-based software and services to users. In her role as director, Bower also has a strong interest in issues related to sustainability, evaluation, and accessibility. She has worked in academic research centers, academic libraries, and in the private sector and received an M.L.S. from the University of Pittsburgh's School of Information Sciences.

Thomas R. Bruce is the co-founder and director of the Legal Information Institute at Cornell Law School, where he developed one of the first web browsers (Cello). He has consulted on Internet matters for Lexis-Nexis, West Group, IBM, and the Harvard Law School Library. He is a director of the Center for Computer-Assisted Legal Instruction, a fellow of the University of Massachusetts Center for Information Technology and Dispute Resolution, and a senior international fellow of the University of Melbourne Law School. He teaches and writes about public policy affecting legal information.

Timothy W. Cole is mathematics librarian and professor of library administration at the University of Illinois at Urbana-Champaign. He has held prior appointments at Illinois as assistant engineering librarian for information services and as systems librarian for digital projects. Cole was principal investigator for the Illinois OAI Metadata Harvesting Project, funded by the Andrew W. Mellon Foundation, and is currently principal investigator for the IMLS Digital Collections and Content Project, funded by the Institute of Museum and Library Services. He was a member of the Open Archives Initiative Technical Committee and is current cochair of the National Science Digital Library's Technology Standing Committee.

Karen Coyle is a librarian with over twenty years' experience in digital libraries. She worked on the University of California's MELVYL catalog from its inception in the early 1980s through its re-creation in 2003. After conquering the university's MARC data, the MELVYL team went on to load data from vendors of abstracting and indexing databases. Coyle has served multiple times on the MARC Standards Advisory Committee and has contributed her metadata expertise to the NISO OpenURL standard. She is currently active in the development of the MODS metadata standard. Her writings on issues relating to libraries and the Internet are on her website at http://www.kcoyle.net.

Norm Friesen has worked in the area of instructional web development and information management at the University of Alberta and Athabasca University since 1997. Since 2000 he has held a position with the CAREO Project (Campus of Alberta Repository of Educational Objects). As part of this work, he has participated in several international e-learning standardization forums and has collaborated in the development of CanCore, a generic application profile for the Learning Object Metadata standard. Friesen previously worked as a librarian and teacher and holds a master's degree in library and information studies from the University of Alberta, a master's in German literature from Johns Hopkins University, and a Ph.D. in education from the University of Alberta.

Rachel Heery works for UKOLN as assistant director leading the research and development team. She has wide experience in the implementation and development of information management systems in the commercial and library sectors. She has undertaken research over recent years in the fields of metadata, resource discovery and information architectures, and has a particular interest in schema registries and application profiles. Heery has been active in the development of the Dublin Core and has published in the area of metadata management. She cochairs the DCMI Registry Working Group and is a member of the Dublin Core Advisory Board.

Harriette Hemmasi is executive associate dean of the Indiana University Libraries, Bloomington. She was previously associate university librarian for technical and automated services at Rutgers University, a music librarian and adjunct faculty member at the Rutgers University School of Library and Information Science, a cataloger at the University of California at Berkeley and Humboldt State University, and a music educator. Hemmasi earned a master's degree in music from Indiana University and an M.L.I.S. from the University of California at Berkeley. She is an active member of the Music Library Association as director of the Music Thesaurus Project. Hemmasi also serves on the research team of Variations2, the Indiana University Digital Music Library project, with her primary focus being on the development of metadata specifications, the data model, and improved searching capabilities for web-based resources.

Linda L. Hill is a faculty research specialist with the Alexandria Digital Library Project at the University of California at Santa Barbara. She is currently focusing on metadata design, the design and implementation of gazetteers and gazetteer services, thesaurus creation, and the design of gazetteer and thesaurus protocols for the searching of distributed knowledge organization resources. Hill has a Ph.D. degree in library science from the University of Pittsburgh and an M.L.S. from the University of Michigan.

Diane I. Hillmann is currently a co-principal investigator for the Core Infrastructure portion of the National Science Digital Library (NSDL) located at Cornell University. Prior to joining the NSDL in 2000, she worked for the Cornell University Library as a cataloger and technical services manager. She was a liaison to and member of the MARBI standards group from the late 1980s to 2000, specializing in the Holdings and Authorities formats. Hillmann was an early participant in the Dublin Core Metadata Initiative and is currently editor of the Using Dublin Core guidelines and administrator of the AskDCMI service, as well as a member of the DCMI Usage and Advisory boards.

Greg Janée is technical leader of the Alexandria Digital Library (ADL) Project, principal developer of the ADL software, and developer of the ADL gazetteer and thesaurus protocols. He is currently working on federated digital library architectures supporting scientists and scientific data. His experience prior to the ADL Project was in the private sector in the areas of object-oriented class libraries; rule-based expert systems; compilers and query languages; and embedded database systems. Janée has an M.S. in computer science and a B.S. in mathematics, both from the University of California at Santa Barbara.

Elizabeth S. Meagher is assistant professor and head of original cataloging and special materials at the University of Denver's Penrose Library. She coordinates and implements the digital initiative and metadata projects at Penrose Library. Meagher has been a member of the Colorado Digitization Program's Metadata Task Force since 1998. She has conducted CDP Metadata Workshops for the metadata practitioners, archivists, catalogers, and museum registrars. Meagher is also a member of the Western States Digital Standards Group's Metadata Working Group and assisted in the writing of the Western States Dublin Core Metadata Best Practices. She has presented at conferences on such topics as using Dublin Core to describe digital objects, the mystery of metadata, and preparing three-dimensional objects for digitizing, as well as on integrating library and museum collections at the University of Denver.

Sarah L. Shreeves is visiting assistant professor of library administration and visiting project coordinator for the Institute of Museum and Library Services' Digital Collections and Content grant project at the University of Illinois at Urbana-Champaign (UIUC). She previously served as a graduate assistant and then as visiting project coordinator for the Mellon-funded Illinois OAI Metadata Harvesting Project. Before coming to UIUC to earn her M.S. in library and information science, Shreeves worked for nine years in public services at the Massachusetts Institute of Technology

Libraries. She has a B.A. in medieval studies from Bryn Mawr and an M.A. in children's literature from Simmons College.

Gary Simons is associate vice president for academic affairs at SIL International in Dallas, Texas. He previously directed SIL's Academic Computing Department and did linguistic fieldwork with SIL in Papua New Guinea and the Solomon Islands. Simons is active in the areas of text markup, standards for language identification, and digital documentation and description of languages. He received a Ph.D. in general linguistics from Cornell University in 1979.

David Sleasman is the metadata and cataloging coordinator for the Internet Scout Project at the University of Wisconsin-Madison. He oversees the Scout Archives, provides project management duties, and leads quality-assurance testing for the Internet Scout's software development projects. Sleasman has worked in academic, special collections, and public libraries as a reference librarian and cataloger, and received an M.L.S. from the University of Pittsburgh's School of Information Sciences.

Angela Spinazzè assists museums, government agencies, and other heritage institutions with projects that employ new technologies to document, interpret, and present our creative past. Her experience includes feasibility studies and strategic planning for new technologies, the design of metadata schemas and associated standards, professional development workshops and seminars, and project management. She holds academic credentials in art history, theory, and criticism, and is an invited expert to international working groups on issues such as interoperability, digital museums and libraries, and visual literacy. For more information about her consulting services, visit www.atspin.com.

Stuart A. Sutton is associate professor at the Information School of the University of Washington, Seattle. He received his M.L.I.S. and Ph.D. degrees from the University of California at Berkeley's School of Library and Information Studies. He is the director of Education Digital Library Initiatives in the Information Institute of Syracuse University and leads research and development for the U.S. Department of Education's Gateway to Educational Materials project. He also serves on the Usage and Advisory Boards of the Dublin Core Metadata Initiative and as co-chair of the Initiatives' Education Working Group. Sutton also earned a J.D. from the Golden Gate University School of Law and an L.L.M. in copyright from the University of California at Berkeley's Boalt Hall School of Law.

Charles F. Thomas earned his M.L.S. degree from the University of North Carolina-Chapel Hill in 1996, with a concentration in archival administration. Since then he has worked in archives and digital library positions at Louisiana State University, the University of Minnesota, and recently assumed a digital library position at Florida State University. He is certified by the Academy of Certified Archivists. In 2003 he was named a Fulbright foundation "senior specialist" and awarded a fellowship to travel to Chile and advise the national government on establishing a national digitization program. Thomas contributes regularly to professional literature, including the 2002 publication *Libraries, the Internet and Scholarship: Tools and Trends Converge.*

Robin Wendler, the metadata analyst in the Harvard University Library's Office for Information Systems, participates in infrastructure development to support the acquisition, management, delivery, and preservation of digital materials. She advises on metadata design and monitors and participates in the development of various international metadata standards. An alumna of MARBI (the MARC standards body), Wendler is currently a member of the METS Editorial Board, the OCLC/RLG Preservation Metadata: Implementation Strategies Working Group, and the Digital Library Federation's Digital Registry Working Group. She has been closely involved with projects in support of the visual resources community, both at Harvard and beyond.

Elaine L. Westbrooks is a metadata librarian at Cornell University's Albert R. Mann Library, where she is responsible for analyzing developments concerning metadata standards and access to electronic publications, as well as creating and maintaining repositories of non-MARC metadata. Most of her projects have involved the implementation and maintenance of Dublin Core, MODS, and MARC metadata for the Open Archives Initiative, as well as geospatial metadata for the Cornell University Geospatial Information Repository. She has presented her research at numerous conferences, including Dublin Core, the Digital Library Federation, and the Association for Literary and Linguistic Computing, and has also authored several articles about metadata.

INDEX